WAKING *from the* DREAM

Waking from the
DREAM

A Wealth of Practical Information Relating to
the Buddhist Path to Enlightenment

DETONG CHOYIN

CHARLES E. TUTTLE CO., INC.
Boston • Rutland, Vermont • Tokyo

Published in 1996 by
CHARLES E. TUTTLE COMPANY, INC.
of Rutland, Vermont and Tokyo, Japan,
with editorial offices at 153 Milk Street, Boston, Massachusetts 02109

Library of Congress Cataloging-in-Publication Data

Choyin, Detong, 1950–
    Waking from the dream : a wealth of practical information
relating to the Buddhist path to enlightenment   /   Detong Choyin.
                           p. cm.
    ISBN 0–8048–3084–3
    1. Spiritual life—Buddhism. 2. Buddhism—Doctrines. I. Title.
BQ4302.C56 1996
294.3'4—dc20   96–46041
                                                           CIP

First edition

1 3 5 7 9 10 8 6 4 2
00 99 98 97 96

Cover and book design by Kathryn Sky-Peck
Printed in the United States of America

Dedication

To perfect peace

Contents

Acknowledgments

I WOULD LIKE TO THANK my sister, Susan Wild, for her generosity, enthusiasm, and many kindnesses after I returned to the United States from a very long stay in Asia and wrote this book. I would also like to thank Therese Bollerup for taking time from her busy schedule to read through the rough manuscript for me.

It has been a pleasure to work with the professionals at Charles E. Tuttle Co., Inc. I'd particularly like to thank Michael Kerber for the care he took with this manuscript, Kathryn Sky-Peck for her thoughtful copyediting, and Isabelle Bleecker for overseeing its publication.

I would also like to thank a few of my former students and friends who contributed so much to this book in so many ways, including Julia Gibbs, Cynthia Verzi, Marianne Whitehurst and Judy Mathari, Peggy Santana, and Rosalynd Friedman.

I would like to thank the Dalai Lama, Tenzin Gyatso, Lama Thubten Zopa Rinpoche, the late Geshe Ngawang Dhargyey, Kirti Tsenshab Rinpoche, and Geshe Pal Tsering for their examples of patience and generosity and for their excellent teachings over many years. Finally, I want to thank the members of the Foundation for the Preservation of the Mahayana Tradition, all of whom helped me to practice. In particular, I would like to thank the members of Instituto Lama Tzong Khapa in Pomaia, Italy; those at O.Sel.Ling outside Granada, Spain; and Sally Walter and Roy Fraser of the Mahamudra Centre in Colville, New Zealand, for their many kindnesses.

May their actions on my behalf be the cause of their enlightenment.

Preface

THIS IS A BOOK ABOUT the Buddhist path to enlightenment. Just reading its words without practicing what it teaches will in no way move you along the path. With practice, however, you will notice a shift in your baseline perceptions—you will begin to think differently about things. Change comes when there is a need for change, a wish for change, a sustained effort to change, and courage to change. A most important ingredient for enlightenment is the heartfelt wish to be of benefit to others.

Progress along the path is not, as so many expect, a tranquil and peaceful journey. It is one of discovery and revelation. And it can be quite disturbing. Don't be afraid, though; insights come as the mind gains the requisite skill to generate them and deal with them. That skill is grown from practice.

Be committed to the path, strong and steady. By placing one foot in front of the other and following in the footsteps of the teacher leading the way, it is hard to fall down or stumble. As you progress, use your joy of discovery as the prod to keep you moving, to not slow down, to never sit down or take a break.

The more you practice, the more exciting the practice becomes. Give up attachments. Like a noble warrior, do it for others. Do it happily.

As you practice, you will find that even when you sleep, your dreams are filled with meditations and your mind is reviewing and puzzling over the teachings. If you're lucky enough to have found your teacher, whether awake or asleep, that person will fill your mind's eye. You just need to look and the teacher is there: watching, smiling, enjoying your struggles and accomplishments, encouraging you to practice with their presence, a vigilant conscience.

The people around you—especially the stinkers—become the best friends of practitioners. Their presence leads to situations that give you opportunities to meditate on the emptiness of the "I" and "objects/others."

In the end, it will be for them that you will give up attachment to self and become enlightened.

When you want to be enlightened more than anything else in order to be of benefit to others, when you have access to perfect teachings and practice according to those teachings, then you will be enlightened in that lifetime. Not until. Commitment to the path doesn't necessarily happen suddenly. However, with whatever level of commitment you begin this quest, through practice and discovery, the feeling grows until it is so compelling, it overwhelms every other inclination.

Renunciation of this suffering state of cyclic existence, the wish to be of benefit to others more than to the self, and the wisdom that understands how things truly exist—in full measure, they become the cause for enlightenment. Practice well. Practice now.

INTRODUCTION

*R*ight now, as you begin to read this book, imagine that you are watching yourself reading from a short distance away. Observe the scene. Try to watch without emotion. Just watch yourself reading these simple words that describe and define a passionless, unattached, and abstract level of knowing. Remember this and discipline your mind to maintain the role of knowing observer. Each time you become aware your mind has stopped observing the scene before it and reasserted its more natural point of view as center of the universe, take a minute to reestablish its role as observer.

In this way you will be able to follow the words in this book—which describe the workings of your mind—as a pathway into your own mind. Having found your way inside, you can then remain to look around and think intensely about what you're reading. Finally, having identified the tools that make up your mind and having begun to understand how they work, you can begin to do some work. That work is what is referred to as the practice of generating the path.

Right now you are viewing the appearance of your mind's creation, although it seems you are observing something that "exists" completely separate from its workings. As is the case with every appearance your mind registers, this one comes as a complete sensation-filled package. The mind is not aware that how things appear is a result of its own action. Instead, it accepts each package without question, first, as having always existed completely separate from its own action and, second, as having qualities that cause it to be inherently good, bad, or unimportant as it relates to the self your mind feels inseparable from.

In this book, we will investigate how [what appears to the mind is nothing more than the mind's creation and how, therefore, there is nothing to be attached to, nothing to be worried about, no one to do the worrying, nothing to long for or to fear.]

What would happen if you, the detached/objective observer, were to get so involved with the objects of your attention that you forgot that they were just the appearance of your own mind? A chain reaction of unavoidable events would occur, all caused by ignorance[1] of how things really exist. Suffering[2] would be the result. While the mind is lost in its own creation, the "self" of that scenario grasps at its own existence, believing it to be substantial and separate from the mind of the perceiver.[3] The self also grasps at the inherent existence[4] of the objects/others of the illusion in its effort to acquire what it believes to be "happiness and freedom from suffering."[5]

The unfortunate chain of events would unfold something like this: (1) You want to be happy, but (2) mistakenly believing that whatever appears to the mind possesses inherent qualities that will affect that happiness, (3) you grasp for what appears to be the cause of happiness, push away what appears to be the cause of suffering, and, for the most part, ignore everything else because those things do not seem to have the power to affect your longed-for happiness.

This chain of events is built on the faulty assumption that what appears to your mind exists separate from the mind's workings and that objects have power to influence your well-being. However, this will not

---

1. *Ignorance.* A level of mind that is unaware, or "ignorant," of the truth that all things are created by and dependent upon its own action for their existence. Ignorance causes the dualistically-oriented self and objects/others to be established and maintained as separate from the mind's action. The result of ignorance is suffering because the self, unaware of the true nature of its existence, grasps at those mere appearances as the cause of happiness, thereby creating the cause for suffering. Ignorance in this context in no way refers to a lack of education or an "unsophisticated" way of dealing with the world.

2. *Suffering.* The mind that believes there is a self and objects/others existing separately experiences suffering when the criteria for happiness are not met in an appearance mistakenly believed to exist separate from the mind's creation.

3. *The mind of the perceiver.* The mind of the one "seeing" or "knowing."

4. *Inherent existence.* To the ignorant, it appears that both self and all objects/others exist separate from their minds, or inherently. Another way of referring to the inherent existence of self and objects/others is to say that self and objects/others have existence established "from the side of the object," and separate from one's mind.

5. *Evil.* In a world where qualities such as good and evil are believed to exist inherently in others and in objects, the reader might at this point wonder if ignorance, because of the suffering

lead to the desired result—a state of lasting happiness freed from suffering. The reasons why are probably not obvious. What happens is that after you acquire what you believe will cause you lasting happiness, the mind begins to grow accustomed to it. Consequently, the cause of your happiness begins to lose its "specialness." What before appeared to be like a precious treasure begins to acquire the look of an everyday object. With time, the object appears ever more common; the mind begins to see faults and shortcomings where before it had seen only perfection. Often, what at one time seemed to be the cause for happiness is now transformed by the action of your own mind into the cause of suffering.

The mind is constantly being reconditioned through its own action. If asked, you might initially equate the concept of "mind" with "brain"; however, upon closer investigation, "mind" will be seen to be a processing machine and "brain," a nervous system—the environment for the process. "Mind" is the (1) coming together of the senses with their objects, which (2) almost simultaneously stimulates, or triggers, a conditioned response from previous similar experience to that particular configuration of sensed objects, which then (3) generates an appearance to the mind that is believed to be either good, bad, or indifferent as it relates to the "self" of that perceiver. As the mind is ignorant of its own action by which each and every appearance is created, it believes its creation exists separate from its action and is inherently either good, bad, or indifferent. Having mistakenly established a separate object, the mind compounds that problem by establishing "self" as separate but in relation to the object. The "self" exists only as a foil for "objects/others" that the mind grasps at as separate. It is through the

---

it causes, is therefore evil. To those who believe in the inherent existence of "power greater than the self," it would be "natural" to assume that ignorance is evil and related to "the devil," or to non-virtuous meddling influences of a "nether-world." However, the path to enlightenment is about coming to know firsthand, as a result of your own practice, that there is no dualistically-oriented self to be affected by any object/other, as both are empowered by the conditioned response of your own mind to sensory stimuli. To equate ignorance with evil is to perpetuate the problem by believing a mere concept, itself based in ignorance, to be "the truth." The truth is that suffering is dependent on the ignorant mind for its existence and will be eliminated when the possessor of such a mind takes the necessary action to eliminate it.

Generally, "evil" is considered to be those things that one or more individuals believe to be "bad" or potentially harmful to the self, either the singular or collective self. In fact, any action done by a mind unaware of its own true nature is the cause for suffering and should be considered harmful. Practitioners of the Buddhist path to enlightenment will be attempting to become aware of the action of their own minds. The practice should include analysis of such concepts based in ignorance and a reconditioning of the habitual patterns of action that cultivate similar superstitious habits.

giving up of attachment to the "objects/others," by gaining insight into the true nature of their existence, that an individual gradually gives up attachment to the conceptual support of "self." Having done so, the individual "goes beyond" this level of existence based in ignorance and wakens from the dream.⌐

This "wisdom" mind of enlightenment that is liberated from belief in an inherently existent self is the unconditioned state of the "mind of enlightenment." Such a mind is no longer fooled by its own creation and, since it no longer grasps at self or objects/others as separate, practices the perfect selfless virtue of an equanimity generated by ⌐the perfection of morality, the wish, based in wisdom, not to give harm to any living being. Until the wisdom understanding how things truly exist is generated, however, the acceptance of the dualistically-oriented relationship of self to object keeps living beings trapped in an unsatisfactory state within which happiness freed from suffering is constantly being sought from objects that appear separate but are not.⌐

The mind trapped by ignorance of the action of its own working is like a leaf in a raging wind, buffeted here and there, one moment experiencing a lessening of the causes of suffering and calling that happiness, the next slammed against a wall, breathless and bruised. To the observer, the scene is inseparable from suffering. To the person seeking happiness for self/me/mine, it is what is called "life." In "life," all things appear to be "real" and substantially and inherently good, bad, or indifferent as they relate to the self. Terrifying thought, don't you think, when what passes as "real life" is nothing more than fabricated images like those in a dream? This dream, however, is of the nature of a nightmare filled with powerful phantoms that, without exception, affect the well-being experienced by the self of the dream, to a greater or lesser degree.

Step back into your role of dispassionate observer again. You are now viewing the appearance of the mind[6] of one who has forgotten how things

---

6. *Appearance of the mind.* The mind is like an instantaneous processing machine that never slows down or stops. The mechanisms that make up the machine include the senses that apprehend their objects. This apprehension stimulates, or triggers, a label previously imprinted on the consciousness due to similar causes and conditions to again be applied to the object of the senses. As a result, the "packaged" appearance includes a value judgment of good, bad, or indifferent as it relates to furthering the well-being of self. When you grasp for the cause of happiness in the object that appears to be separate, the duality of self and object are once again confirmed and another label is imprinted on the consciousness to ripen when similar causes and conditions once again come together and trigger its empowering effect.

(self and objects/others) truly exist. This appearance is the suffering state of cyclic existence.[7] It is within this state that the level of consciousness based in ignorance of how things truly exist cycles.[8]

The appearance of the mind of the one who is thus unaware, or ignorant, is its own prison. The central object of its attention, the self, is its prisoner. It is a complete illusion. It is the level of mind trapped by its ignorance of the nature of the appearances it apprehends. Stuck in a completely unsatisfactory state, all the while unable to admit it is less than satisfactory, believing there is happiness when even that is an illusion, not knowing what else to do, the ignorant mind cultivates all the causes to remain trapped within the prison of its making, and none for liberation.

Having lost the "big view" of how the mere appearances of the mind's creation truly exist, the mind is shrouded from that big view by the heavy mantle of ignorance that grasps at self and objects/others as "real," as existing inherently from the side of the object.[9]

As you are watching yourself read this book, the level of existence you are observing yourself within is the conceptual network developed by your mind as a conditioned response to sensory stimuli. There are two basic levels of existence: (1) the unenlightened level of existence, which is based in ignorance of the truth and is synonymous with suffering, and (2) the enlightened level of existence, where one is liberated from belief in an inherently existent self, having given up attachment to the delusions upon which self is based. The enlightened mind, freed from the conceptual barriers of the dualistically-oriented self and objects/others, is freed from the suffering caused by ignorance. This conceptual network is nothing other

7. *This state* is a level of mind and does not exist, in any way, separate from that level of mind. Such a mind is ignorant of how things truly exist and grasps at the dualistically-oriented self and objects/others of its own creation as "real." Because a permanent happiness freed from suffering is sought within the mind-based and, therefore, constantly changing illusion, the self of that illusion feels suffering.

8. *Reincarnation*. Simply, the changing of the appearance of the base upon which the mind attaches the label "self." It is the process by which the imprinted consciousness is implanted on a new configuration of sensory stimuli, forming a new appearance for the label "self" to be attached to.

9. *From the side of the object*. When we are trapped in the appearances of our own minds by ignorance of the true nature of things, we believe that the objects/others (as well as the self) appearing to our minds exist separate from, and independent of, our minds. It seems that all "things" have inherent existence—or exist "from the side of the object"—as opposed to existing inseparably and dependent upon our own minds. This dualistic orientation is what the Buddhist path to enlightenment seeks to eliminate through analysis of the faulty assumptions generated by a lack of awareness of how the mind works.

than the appearance generated by one's senses (the causes) coming in contact with their objects (the conditions), i.e., eye/form, nose/smell, etc. This coming together of causes and conditions has triggered a quality-filled imprint left on the consciousness from some previous experience with similar causes and conditions to ripen and come into play. A "quality-filled imprint" is the impression of the object as it was believed to relate to the happiness of self on a previous occasion. It is stored on the stream of the consciousness.

Although the consciousness is formless, for easier understanding it can be visualized as a seed tape that is sometimes used in the garden. The seed tape is a nondescript ribbon of material upon which seeds have been attached every inch or so. It is meant to help the gardener very easily lay down even rows of perfectly spaced seeds when planting. You should visualize the "consciousness" like such a seed tape. Each seed indicates an imprint left from previous conditioning. When the causes and conditions come together—the senses with their objects—like the sun and the rain, the imprint (or seed) ripens quickly and takes the form of what was previously sowed. We grasp at the "fruit" with pleasure, dissatisfaction, or even indifference, believing that those qualities exist inherently in the object/other that we are perceiving. When we grasp at appearances, a similar imprint is deposited along the tape, like a seed that will ripen later when the necessary causes and conditions come together again.

The object/other thus appearing is mistakenly believed to be inherently either good, bad, or indifferent. The self then, believing there is a substantial cause for happiness, ignorantly grasps at the mind's mere appearance, thereby positing a new quality-filled imprint on the consciousness that will ripen later. It is this quality-filled consciousness that travels from death to rebirth in a seemingly beginningless and endless cycle. These empowering imprints are based in ignorance of how every appearance truly exists. They constitute the conceptual network within which the ignorant are trapped. These imprints—or seeds—are implanted upon the fertilized egg at the moment of conception. As the form develops, the form's ability to sense objects (mind) and its predisposition for various actions (likes and dislikes) become more assertive. From the moment of birth, the "self" of that being responds to sensory stimulation according to its previous conditioning, ignorant of how all appearances are created by, and are dependent upon, the mind for their existence. This level of existence is based in ignorance and grasps at self and objects/others as inherently existent. It is called the suffering state of cyclic existence. It is the level of existence, the level of mind, that you are observing yourself within at this time. It is a dream world that is believed to be real. It is built on the untenable mistake of believing that *what you yourself have merely conceptualized* exists separate from your own mind's creation.

By becoming familiar with the workings of the mind, you will eventually become master over your mind and go beyond its conditioned response based in ignorance, to the truth of the enlightened state. The mind can be compared to a computer. Computers are programmed to process information in certain ways. When incorrect data appears, the computer operator will look for the fault on the level of the program and would never try to manipulate the data to eliminate the error. This is why a dog cannot be enlightened. The level of mind of a creature is not of a type suitable to understand this profound level of existence. That is because the basic instincts of animals are geared for "self" preservation and not for the consideration of abstract thoughts such as virtue and morality. It is only in the human form that enlightenment can be reached. It is because of the need for generating a complex and profound level of understanding that the mere recitation of mantras or the words of practices written in languages you do not understand cannot cause you to be enlightened, just as the dog sitting at the teaching of an enlightened being will not thereby be able to create any cause for its enlightenment.

The mind of enlightenment has to be generated through the action of the ignorant mind in combination with and inseparable from the cultivation of wisdom teachings transmitted by an enlightened teacher.

Every living being[10] believes that the objects of the senses—sights,

---

10. *A living, or sentient, being* is one possessing sense ability who is also trapped within the suffering state of cyclic existence, which is a cycle of death and rebirth. To be sentient indicates an ignorant level of apprehension of self and objects/others that will cause one to reincarnate. A sentient being ultimately is one possessing a mind with the ability to know "things" through the senses; it must, therefore, possess a nervous system. Obviously, humans are sentient beings, as are all creatures possessing nervous systems, such as fish, amphibians, reptiles, mammals, birds, insects. Plants are not sentient beings and do not possess consciousness.

Cyclic existence is not experienced by beings freed from the delusions that bind minds to the cycle. Such enlightened beings have a level of existence freed from death. For them, the final death was the one practiced for and finally, just before the individual's enlightenment, entered into as the result of the highest level meditation which causes the death absorptions to begin and, thereby, the consciousness to split free from the physical support (delusion-based appearance of the ignorant mind) of the body.

sounds, smells, tastes, tactile sensations, thoughts[11]—exist separate from the mind. When we see a sight that pleases us, the object viewed is believed to be "good." When sounds of a city are heard and liked, the sounds of the city are believed to be "good," and the city associated with those sounds, by association, is "good" as well. When we smell a "good" smell, we believe the object of that smell to be really "good" and wish to keep it near. When something tastes "good," then that thing is believed to be "good," and we wish to consume it because it will make us happy. When something feels "good," then we think that thing is "good" and want to keep it close in order to secure another cause of happiness for self/me/mine.

If it were true that any object/other existed separate from the mind of the one perceiving it, then every living being of similar intelligence and sense ability would know it in a similar way. However, if one hundred people with similar intelligence and sensibility were asked to describe any object put before them, they would give one hundred widely differing descriptions, or impressions, of the object. One's good sight, good sound, good smell, good taste, good feeling, good thought, might appear to be horrible to another. This is because the object is believed to be the cause of happiness or suffering dependent on the individual's conditioned response to sensory stimuli.

If a smooth, gray, irregularly shaped rock is held up for study, one person may like it very much while another may think it boring, and still

---

11. *There is a sixth sense power listed here: the sense power of mind.* In addition to the five sense powers that are commonly purported to exist, there is a sixth sense power: that of the mind itself. Within the mind, there is a secondary processing unit that creates appearances from remembered instances of sensory contact by the five physically based senses. When asked to visualize your beloved, for instance, your senses will be immediately stimulated. The power of the mind to formulate quality-filled appearances is based on its ability to trigger imprints on the consciousness. This is what is referred to as "the sixth sense power." This sense power goes beyond what appears to be merely "physically"-oriented. It uses information left previously by the physically-oriented senses to formulate abstract thoughts relating those appearances to the self on levels other than the most obvious, the physical level.

To say that thoughts, because they are generated by the "mind," are, therefore, not stimulated by the five physically oriented senses is incorrect. The mind is nothing other than the sum total of the senses coming in contact with their objects, triggering an imprint that generates an appearance, which is then grasped at as "real." Although the level of involvement of each of the senses may appear to vary according to the type of object under scrutiny (for instance, music will appear to involve the ear sense power more than the eye; a painting, the eye sense power more than the ear, and so on), unless the ability of the individual to sense objects is impaired, each sense is equally involved in the apprehension of every object. It is only the conceptual barriers of the ignorant mind, trapped within the body, that ascribe specific sensory functions to particular organs.

another may hate it. When asked, the person who liked the rock might say it reminded him or her of a lovely island off Hong Kong, and in his or her mind, the sight of the rock would stimulate the memory of a picture of an island he or she had seen romantically silhouetted in the moonlight when flying into Hong Kong the first time. The person who found the rock boring would be reminded of the millions of rocks lining the dry river beds of some town in which he or she had worked. The person who hated the rock would see that gray stone color and be reminded of death, of tombstones, of the cold, and of lonely, dark, and wintry things.

[For the individuals who find the rock either very pleasing or very awful, the object is empowered, by their own minds, to be the cause of their happiness or suffering according to previous conditioning to similar objects of their senses (whether remembered in this lifetime or not). Both individuals have strong enough attachment to the memories or conditioned responses stimulated, or triggered, by the sight of the rock to affect his or her present sense of well-being.] Those memories (imprints on the consciousness), and how the previous objects of the individual's experience related to the well-being of self/me/mine, were triggered when the senses came in contact with objects of a similar configuration. For the individual who finds the object to be boring, no preconditioning has occurred that will cause his or her mind to sufficiently empower the object to be the cause of either happiness or suffering.

All of these concepts—good, bad, or indifferent—are based in ignorance of how things truly exist. To grasp at any mere appearance of your mind as either good or bad or indifferent leaves an imprint (the cause similar to the effect) that will ripen later when similar causes and conditions arise. To believe that an interest or a lack of interest in any thing is either a positive or negative response is as ridiculous as believing that something is inherently good, bad, or indifferent.[12]

The mental sense power is a cumulative one. It gathers and sifts through the appearances of the mind to formulate some order to those appearances as they might relate to the self, both the singular self and the collective. It is not possible to have any thought that is independent of, or separate from, prompting by the five physically-oriented senses. What is "thought" except the product of the mind? What is the product of the mind except the cumulative effect of the mind's response to sensory stimulation due to its conditioning?

12. *In the vernacular of cyclic existence*, it can be said that any action of the mind based in ignorance—thus creating another cause to continue in cyclic existence—is negative. Conversely, it could be said that any non-attachment, or the giving up of attachment to an object, by one who has generated insight into the true nature of the appearance of that object is a positive action. It is only through the giving up of attachment to the mere appearances of one's mind by generating some insight into the nature of that appearance, that one burns the delusion associated with

The mind, ignorant of its own conditioned action, having thus empowered those objects to be "good," "bad," or "indifferent," generates the quality-filled appearance that is then believed to exist separate from its action (or inherently). The problem is compounded by an endless cycle of grasping for the cause of happiness, and grasping to be freed from the cause of suffering. The self thus grasping is as illusory as the objects/others believed to be a source of either happiness or suffering.[13] The self exists only in its role of sounding board, or foil, to the appearance of objects/others mistakenly believed to be separate from the action of the mind.

What difference does it make whether an individual thinks the rock is lovable, boring, or awful? The person who loves the rock will want, or feel a need, to possess that object in order to capture a cause of happiness. The one who finds the rock to be boring will choose to ignore it, since it does not have the power to affect happiness. The one who hates the rock will make an effort to get away from it, since it appears to have the power to cause suffering. When we tire of being pawns[14] to the appearances of our minds, we will begin to question the illusion and seek a way out.

This lack of awareness, or ignorance, of the illusion can lead only to suffering—never to happiness. First, it sets up the conditions for conflict with others who perceive others/objects differently. Second, it causes you to seek a lasting happiness from among the mere appearances of objects/others, which are merely fabricated by and dependent upon your constantly changing mind. The mistaken premise that there is an inherently existent self and objects/others is extremely gross. One might assume that, because something is "gross," it should be easy to see. Yet, it is because the quality of the ignorance is so gross and all-encompassing that,

that quality-filled appearance of the consciousness. It is through this difficult action of giving up attachment to the illusions (of those things that cause the self to suffer or be happy) that one eventually gives up attachment to the basis supporting the umbrella delusion of an inherently existent self, and becomes enlightened.

The concepts of positive and negative emotions are completely "self" centered and based in the ignorance that believes there is an inherently existent self as well as objects/others.

13. *Emotions* are like bridges by which we establish links between our selves and objects/others in order to differentiate objects/others and cultivate the happiness and security of self/me/mine separated from suffering. Although the sincere practitioner will definitely feel emotions, it is the practice to investigate the nature of the self and the objects/others that appear to be separate, in order to generate a loving-kindness, freed from limited concepts of good and bad, by cultivating insight into the nature of every aspect of those attachments.

14. *Pawn*. Like a brutal master, the individual's own ignorance of the true nature of every appearance controls every single action of that ignorant individual's body, speech, and mind.

like the black of night that completely obscures the day, the ignorant mind cannot know the truth.

In reality, the self is simply the umbrella concept over the delusions of good, bad, and indifferent. Generally believed to exist substantially, in some concrete form, upon investigation, no self can be found. Yet, "I" am here. How does the "I" or the "self" one calls one's own truly exist? The mind, having mistakenly grasped at objects as separate from its making, relates all those good, bad, and indifferent objects/others to the similarly illusory "self." The self exists in no other way. Created by the mind, it is the foil for objects/others and is dependent on ignorance that grasps at objects/others as inherently existent for its continued existence.

Ultimately, this means that the level of existence that is based in ignorance is inseparable from suffering. Beings who are ignorant of the illusory nature of all within their perception seek happiness freed from suffering in the objects/others that are mistakenly believed to exist separate from their own minds.

All living beings seek a happiness for self/me/mine that is freed from suffering. What exactly does that entail? Each individual, due to his or her conditioning, will have his or her own unique criteria for happiness as well as for suffering. For one person a sunny day is the cause for happiness, a rainy day the cause for suffering. For another person living homeless on the street, a good and solid cardboard box to sleep in is the cause of happiness. Yet another person will suffer if he or she does not own a palatial home, an apartment in France, and a chalet in Switzerland. For one individual, classical music is the cause of happiness; to another, rap. One individual loves the sounds of birds early in the morning. Another tries to drive the birds away in the morning because their "noise" is so disturbing.

What is happiness? What is suffering? Neither exists. There is no such thing coming from the side of any object. How each exists is dependent on your mind due to your own conditioning. It is the nature of the ignorant mind, however, to believe that happiness exists separate from the mind's creation. What is happiness, actually, except the lessening of the causes of suffering? When the causes of suffering have subsided sufficiently to meet one's criteria for happiness, then one says, "I am happy now." When the appearance of the causes of happiness similarly subsides, causing the appearance of suffering to grow stronger, one suffers; "I am unhappy now." Up, down, up, down, like a yo-yo, responding to the mere appearances of the mind as though those objects/others existed separately.

Grasping for happiness. Grasping to be freed from suffering. Grasping with indifference.

How can living beings suffer by grasping at mere illusions if the illusion has no substance or inherent ability to affect the being? Remember the last time you said to yourself, "This makes me happy; I must have it to be happy," "This makes me unhappy; I must get away from it to be happy," or "I don't care about this, so I'll ignore it—it doesn't affect my happiness"?

Can you see that all living beings believe objects have the power or ability to make them feel happy, unhappy, or indifferent? No? How about the people you grasp at with love? Don't you believe having them in your life is a cause of your happiness? On the flip side of that particular coin, what about the people who believe in things contrary to your existing belief system? If they exert enough "presence" in your life, won't they become the cause of your suffering? Don't you choose to stay away from them in order to secure your happiness freed from suffering? Although probably not aware of it on a conscious level, all individuals trapped in cyclic existence do in fact believe there is power coming from the side of objects/others (as opposed to their own minds) that has the ability to affect their "selves." Most objects/others we come in contact with have not been empowered sufficiently to affect the self, because we are not yet sufficiently conditioned to know those objects as the cause of our happiness freed from suffering. In fact, nearly all objects/others we come in contact with are ignored, or not dealt with, as a cause of our happiness or suffering.

The Buddhist path to enlightenment is about nothing other than understanding that how things truly exist is completely dependent on the mind of the one doing the looking. Until you realize this directly, however, the self of the dream grasps at the objects/others of the dream in its endless search for happiness freed from suffering. Because objects/others are dependent on the mind of the perceiver for their existence, and because the mind is constantly changing by reconditioning itself to the new appearances being generated by its action, what was once the cause of your happiness will eventually become the cause of your suffering, and vice versa.

Consider the music you disliked so much until forced to listen to it, or the person who yesterday seemed to be a friend but today seems to be an enemy. Forced to listen to the music that was the cause of your suffering, the mind got to the point where it could handle no more suffering, gave up attachment to that particular appearance (the music) as a cause of suffering, and, thereby relaxed and then receptive, began to perceive qualities in the music. As qualities were perceived, the mind, having renounced attachment to the previous cause of its suffering, began to look for the cause of happiness. The mind, reconditioned to "know" the qualities of happiness, begins to generate the appearance of music that then makes the self happy.

Like a cascading avalanche that gathers momentum and material with its action, the mind similarly seeks the cause of happiness in ever more vivid "self"-fulfilling appearances as your senses come in contact with their respective objects. In the case of music, sound is the primary object, although all the objects apprehended by all the senses will be similarly affected to some degree by the general "uplift" to the mind that is "feeling happy." The music was empty of inherent existence. Whether or not it was the cause of happiness or suffering was completely dependent on your own mind due to your conditioning.

Although it may seem impossible, upon investigation you will find that suffering results only when one of the eight worldly desires is not met. Sometimes referred to as the "eight worldly dharmas," the eight desires that cause living beings to remain attached to the mistakenly apprehended appearances of their own minds are the desire for (1,2) gain and not loss; (3,4) praise and not criticism; (5,6) kind words and not unkind words; (7,8) happiness and not suffering. These are the eight motivating factors behind every living being's search for happiness freed from suffering for self. If you wish to be freed from the cause of your suffering, simply give up attachment to the mere appearance of the mind. Abandon the desire that caused the attachment in the first place. By giving up attachment to the desire you are attached to, you can end your suffering.

Absolutely nothing exists from the side of any object. Neither the object that seems to be the cause of your happiness or suffering nor the self, which is nothing more than the sounding board of all the mind's mistaken appearances. Nothing exists separate from, or independent of, the mind of the perceiver. If you are conscious of why you are doing it and give up attachment to the appearance that is causing the self to suffer as well as the desire you wish fulfilled, you will actually remove that ignorant imprint from the consciousness. This is the practice by which all attachment to all delusions, one after another, is given up. This is the practice that causes the mind to eventually attain the wisdom level of knowing, called enlightenment, and freedom from the suffering state of cyclic existence. This is the Buddhist path to enlightenment.

In the first two chapters of this book, the groundwork for the ensuing chapters is laid out and you may find it necessary to read more slowly, stopping occasionally to reorder your thoughts. By so doing, you will find the text to be not only easy to follow but logical and practical as well. The Buddhist path to enlightenment is a way of life, not a religion or philosophy. It is very important to keep an open heart and a receptive mind to this teaching. Whether the information presented here is read in the year 2000, or 4000, the path out of cyclic existence will remain the same. Only the mere appearances of the circumstances of life will change. The ignorance that imprisons us in the conceptual prison called the suffering state of cyclic existence will not change. The path to the generation of the wisdom mind of enlightenment, freed from the delusions upon which self is based, will not change, either. The Buddhist path to enlightenment has to do with generating the wisdom understanding the true nature of every appearance of the mind's creation. So—no matter what form the appearance may take due to the era in question—each appearance is generated by the same level of mind: the mind of ignorance.

As a practitioner, it is also important to consider that until you are enlightened, you are going to suffer from your desire for happiness and freedom from suffering. The path to enlightenment is long and difficult. I'm not saying this to put you off. I'm saying it at the beginning so that you will know you're all right if you're doing the very best you can by practicing morality and eliminating the delusions as you become aware of them. Still, the path to enlightenment is not a place to dawdle or drag your feet. It is the time to focus every ounce of your being on the goal in order to be of benefit to others.[15]

The path to enlightenment is about overcoming the obstructions that are created by, and completely dependent upon, the delusions based in desire. There is no obstruction to your enlightenment except your own mind. Most readers will find something of benefit in this book. The highest level practitioner will find a skeletal guideline to follow that will be filled in by his or her highest level practice. For the beginner, the insight gained from information presented in this book will be entirely different from that gained by the highest level practitioner. The beginner will gain a primary intellectual involvement with the information that is still very far from the path. The practitioner is actually generating the path that is the practice.

---

15. To be discussed in chapter two.

Whatever the level of mind, every student will generate a level of insight into the path to enlightenment followed by an enlightened being, according to the level of his or her interest and/or practice. The information shared here is born from the practice and is, therefore, not mere speculation. If and when the sincere practitioner finds a fault in the teaching, he or she should immediately look within his or her mind for the source of the mistake. Through just such devotion to the teaching/teacher, the sincere practitioner will attain enlightenment in this lifetime. Needless to say, if the practitioner does not always look for the fault within his or her existing conceptual network, then that practitioner will not eliminate the associated delusion, will reassert the superiority of his or her self in relation to the perceived teacher/teaching, and will continue to create the cause to remain within the suffering state of cyclic existence until the practice is corrected.

The teaching of an enlightened being is perfect. It is only by generating some faith in that being's perfection through your own practice that you will get beyond the problem by analyzing the nature of the obstruction in your own mind. This is how the path to enlightenment works. There is no such thing as blind faith here. Faith is generated only from practice. The more you practice, the more faith you will generate with every fiber of your being. The more faith thus generated, the more inspiration you will feel. The more inspired you feel, the more you will practice. The more you practice, the less attached to the mere appearances of this world you will be. With the lessening of the number of attachments to the delusions that bind you to the suffering state of cyclic existence, the more insight into the true nature of things you will generate. With more insight comes increased clarity of mind, a lessening of distractions to your practice, and an increased focus to your concentration. With increased focus, one enters the path and begins the way out.

Never look over your shoulder to admire the ground covered. Instead, become like a noble warrior whose only thought is to save others. By practicing like this—only for others—you will create the cause for your own enlightenment. Only then will you be of ultimate and lasting benefit to others, by teaching them the correct path to follow out of the suffering state of cyclic existence. Through this practice, all worthwhile things are accomplished.

Chapter One

LIFE IS JUST A DREAM

Life is just a dream, but in this dream
the dreamers have forgotten they are sleeping.
Silent, steady, slow, sure they slipped—
like stones released beneath the darkened surface of the sea—
far beyond awareness of the truth of their enchanting fantasy.
When will they even think to free themselves?

*L*ife is just a dream. It is not *like* a dream; it *is* a dream and nothing other than a dream.⌉

Have you ever had a dream that you became so involved in, you completely forgot that you were dreaming? Because you dreamed, ignorant of the truth of the dreaming, the "self" in the dream seemed as completely real as the objects/space/time of the dream continuum. In fact, the self of the dream space was so far removed from awareness of the dream that if, in the dream, someone had told you that you were just dreaming, you would never have believed it: both the world of the dream and the self posited in the dream felt real and concrete and appeared to exist absolutely separate from the creation of your mind. It wasn't until you actually awoke from the dream that, shocked, you realized it was just a dream.

During the time an individual is one with the dream, the individual is "ignorant" of the truth that it is indeed just a dream. During the time that one is ignorant of the truth of the dream, or the truth of "reality," one is "deluded."⌈The suffering that is experienced as a result of grasping at the mere appearances of the dream is caused by ignorance of the true nature of that dream⌉

During the time the dreamer's mind is trapped in such a web of delusion far removed from the truth, the individual can be said to be "hallucinating." Within such a mental environment, the individual mistakenly believes that the mere appearances of his or her mind truly exist. An individual deluded in this way mistakenly believes that the objects[16] of the dream exist inherently separate from the action, or karma,[17] of the mind.

The hallucination suffered by individuals trapped in the illusory cycle of existence of the dream can be compared to the level of mind of an individual under the influence of LSD.[18] The drug-affected mind becomes completely removed from the "truth" or true nature of the illusion appearing to the mind due to the drug. In the same way, a person becomes trapped within the dream because he or she is ignorant of its cause. For example, if the blades of grass under the hallucinating person's feet suddenly appear to be worms, that person cannot separate from the belief in

16. *Objects/others.* For ease in reading, when just the word "object" is written, "objects/others" is implied. The reason for the doubly qualified name is to indicate the appearances of objects and of others—the one generally believed to be inanimate and different from the second generally believed to be animate—are, in this discussion at least, not different at all but indicate that appearances, whether considered to be of an inanimate or animate nature, are equally empty of inherent existence.

17. *Karma.* Karma is the action of the mind synonymous with ignorance and delusions that causes objects to appear to be good, bad, or unimportant as they are believed to relate to self. Through the elimination of the delusions upon which self is based, the genuine practitioner will be freed from the suffering state of cyclic existence and no longer reincarnate within that level of mind. To the worldly, "good" karma is incorrectly believed to be when "pleasant" things happen to the self and "bad" karma when "difficulties" befall the self. The correct definition based in the wisdom of understanding how things truly exist is far different. Any action of the mind that causes the individual to continue within the suffering state of cyclic existence is what is considered to be "bad" karma, while any action of the mind that causes the individual to eliminate the delusions that bind him or her to cyclic existence, "good" karma.

How individuals perceive objects/others is the result of the conditioned action of their ignorant minds, or karma, in response to the coming together of the causes (the senses) with their conditions (the objects of those senses). This establishes the basis for information imprinted on the consciousness from previous similar causes and conditions to ripen and enter into the equation. The imprinted information empowers the objects/others to appear to have qualities such as good, bad, or indifferent. Ignorant of the action of its own mind—the "persona" of the mind—the self, which is nothing other than the foil for the objects/others created by and dependent upon that mind for its existence, grasps at those objects/others in order to secure happiness freed from suffering. Grasping at the mind's creation, mistakenly believing it to be "real," leaves an imprint on the consciousness that will empower the next similar causes and conditions to again appear to exist in the way they were mistakenly believed to exist before.

There are two ways to consider karma: (1) It is the cause that is exactly similar to the effect that is created by the individual's conditioned response to sensory stimuli, or the predisposition, or volitional force, that causes objects/others to be known in certain ways. (2) It is synonymous with ignorance since the mind, unaware of its own action and the faulty conceptual network it has mistakenly established as "real," is responding to sensory stimuli due to the volitional force of imprints based in the mind's ignorance of its own action. It is a closed system until the understanding of how things truly exist is introduced.

18. *LSD.* Lysergic acid diethylamide—a hallucinogenic drug. LSD is used here as a cause/effect example of an altered state of mind because most readers will have seen or heard many reports on the drug or may have even personally experienced this 20th-century phenomenon and so will be able to relate to the following analogy.

the inherent existence of that appearance. In other words, those worms are real to that individual. This is the effect caused by the drug. Believing the hallucination to be the truth, the mind, conditioned to find worms repulsive and frightening, attaches those qualities of "repulsive" and "frightening" to the objects of its drug-affected senses. Thus labeled—like magic—a quality-filled object appears. Immediately, the hallucinating mind, unaware of its sole role in the creation of the loathsome scene appearing before it, grasps[19] at it as "real" and responds with fear and dread.

Although they appear to be "real," or existing in a way separate from the action of the mind of the perceiver, in actuality every appearance of every object/other is dependent on the mind of the perceiver for its existence. For instance, if the "beloved" is truly a "wonderful" person from the side of the person and separate from the mind of the perceiver, then any human being of similar intelligence and sensibility as the perceiver of the "beloved" will know the one perceived as "beloved." In fact, each person who sees that individual will perceive a range of qualities in the individual, from very positive to very negative. This is due to the preconditioned response of the perceiver's mind to sensory stimulation.

The first step in creating the cause for happiness and freedom from suffering is understanding and accepting that the unenlightened mind is operating under a powerful delusion due to this simple but very subtle shift in perception. The "blissful state of lower nirvana" is attained when attachment to the delusions that bind us to the suffering state of cyclic existence is given up.

There are two elements to every illusion: (1) appearance of an object/other and (2) the "self" of the observer who believes the illusion and reacts to it. The "self" is established only in relation to the objects/others appearing to it, so if it is lost within the illusion, the "self" identifying itself in terms of its relationship to those objects/others—"I like this, not that"; "this is good," "that bad"; "this is mine, that yours"; and so on—is also an illusion. How both elements of the illusion exist is dependent on the mind of the perceiver of the illusion. Because the perceiver is "ignorant"—not aware of the true nature of what is appearing—the "self" of the illusion becomes "stuck" within that ignorant state.

---

19. *Grasps.* It is commonly accepted that "to grasp" means to pull something toward oneself. In fact, the grasping of the mind at its own appearances, whether those appearances are of happiness or suffering, as it is always based in the thought to secure happiness freed from suffering, should be considered to be a form of grasping, or pulling "toward" oneself.

The self that relates to the illusory object does not exist separately from that level of mind. The "self" of the drugged state exists only as it relates to (and is inseparable from) the hallucinations generated by the drugged mind; it does not, in any way, exist inherently or separately from that mind's creation. However, when the drug takes over and the mind forgets that the images appearing are a result of the drug, the images seem to be "real," or inherently existent.

Because the illusion is inseparable from the truth, the truth inseparable from the hallucination cannot be known. Because the lack of awareness of the true nature of what is appearing is so complete, the self of the illusion grasps to secure the causes of happiness and grasps for freedom from the causes of suffering within the mind-generated hallucination. Ignorance of the illusion causes the mind to initiate and maintain an endless series of involvements in the illusion in order to secure a happiness freed from suffering for the self, mistakenly believed to be inherently existing. Because the ignorance of the cause of the appearances of self separate from objects/others is so overwhelming, the drugged mind cannot free itself from its delusions simply by its own effort.

In the case of the drug-affected person, it is not until the effects of the drug begin to lessen that the mind can know with more and more clarity that the frightening vision of the worms underfoot was "empty" of inherent existence[20] and completely dependent on the drug-affected mind itself for its existence. When completely freed from the drug-induced delusions, the individual clearly sees that both the delusions (what was mistakenly believed to be real and was, therefore, grasped at) and the self that appeared to be similarly real within the limitations of the hallucination were mere illusions.

---

20. *"Empty" of inherent existence.* To those who are unaware of how things truly exist, it appears that objects have "inherent existence," that is to say, that they exist separate from the mind of the perceiver. In truth, however, how anything exists is completely dependent on the mind of the perceiver due to his or her conditioning and is known to be "empty" of inherent existence.

Too often this profound concept is referred to as "the void," and an impression of an empty bucket, for instance, is insinuated—as though there was some "thing" with nothing in it. For this reason, the term "the void" should be avoided. "The void" is actually intended to refer to the source, or the mind of the one "gone beyond," from which, to the wisdom-based mind, all appearances owe their "beginnings." The term "the void" is meant to refer to the process by which the mind creates and maintains every appearance. However, as the term refers to a state, or level of mind beyond the ability of the ignorant mind, that has no experience of that level to comprehend, the term is too easily misinterpreted. "Empty" of inherent existence, on the other hand, for the thoughtful practitioner implies the action of the mind that results in every appearance as the primary level of meaning.

Because the "self" trapped within the delusions believed the illusory appearances were "real," the individual reacted to the objects/others of that level of mind with happiness, sadness, bravado, fear, hope, despair, and so on. The individual's imprisonment within the hallucination was sealed when he or she grasped at the illusion in an effort to secure happiness and freedom from suffering.[21]

Just as the drug overwhelms the drug-affected mind's ability to know the truth of what is appearing before it, ignorance that obscures the mind to the true nature of the dream causes living beings to stay within the level of existence that is of a suffering nature.

From within the dream, it seems that both happiness and suffering are dependent on external circumstances, or "things." The "self" constantly seeks freedom from suffering, and it is only during those times of suffering that the self is sufficiently motivated to go beyond the obvious in search of relief. By thinking about the causes of one's suffering to a degree sufficient to uncover the roots of that suffering, [the practitioner will discover that any and all suffering is generated by his or her attachment to a concept, and nothing more. When the suffering felt by the self in relation to the objects/others is great enough or oppressive enough, then the mind of the practitioner will gladly give up attachment to the concept causing the suffering.]

For instance, take the case of unrequited love. Imagine that someone is in love with another but is not acknowledged by that individual. When the suffering caused by the repeated spurning becomes great enough, the sufferer will give up attachment to the desire for the object, and as attachment is given up, it will no longer "appear" to be a "love object." In fact, due to the degree to which the security of "self" is threatened, the former appearance of the "love object" may even change into that of "enemy." By giving up attachment to the mere appearance of the mind's creation— "love object"—the individual will feel freed from the suffering caused by his or her previous attachment to the delusion.

---

21. *Security*. Just as the self feels insecure, or threatened, when inundated by the "unknowns" encountered during a drug-induced hallucination, so the self feels secure again when the drug's effect subsides and the self's normal milieu, which is the appearance of good, bad, or indifferent objects/others that appear to the self in an organized and understandable way, is restored.

Suffice it to say that when the delusions upon which self is based are finally eliminated, replaced by the wisdom that understands perfectly how things truly exist, as there is no longer a self to be affected, nor a dualistically-oriented object/other to be a cause, the perfect peace of enlightenment reigns.

How can the thoughtful practitioner begin to recondition his or her mind to give up attachment to its mere appearances? Only by hearing teachings of the path to enlightenment wherein the wisdom of how things truly exist is shared. [This practice of reconditioning the consciousness is actually the process by which the practitioner gives up attachment to the delusions that support the umbrella concept "self." When the individual is liberated from belief in an inherently existent self—having given up attachment to the delusions that support it—he or she is enlightened.]

[Individuals caught in cyclic existence are bound to their "karma," or the conditioned response of their ignorant minds to sensory stimulation, just as the drugged individual was bound to the mind's hallucination. Ignorance is the root cause of all suffering. Karma and delusions go hand in hand, as do karma and suffering. When speaking of the two—delusions and suffering—we are speaking of cause and effect. Karma is the law of cause and effect. It is the mind's conditioned response to sensory stimulation that is based in the all-obscuring ignorance of how all effects are the mind's own creation. Ignorance is the cause, cyclic existence its effect.]

Living beings are trapped in a dreamlike level of existence because the level of their minds is based in ignorance of the truth of the dream. That is why when one is enlightened and the mind is freed from suffering caused by ignorance of the true nature of things, there is a different appearance[22] to the mind. As a result of the final meditation at the time of enlightenment, when the imprints of the gross delusions are removed and the consciousness splits free from the physical support of the body, all activity of the mind is stilled and the truth body (Dharmakaya) is attained. This is a state beyond mind; this is what is referred to as the mind "gone beyond." The mind "gone beyond" does not perceive cyclic existence. This is because, at this point, the enlightened mind has transcended the level of mind based in cyclic existence (which is nothing other than the appearance generated by that level of mind). However, having been enlightened in order to be of benefit to others, the individual can and does return one last time to the level of existence within which living beings suffer, in order to

---

22. *Sambhogakaya*. When the now wisdom-based mind (the mind of clear light) begins its very subtle movement, it is in union with its own appearance (the illusory body). The mind inseparable from its own appearance, freed from the ignorant limitations of subject, action, and object, is lovely beyond description, the senses and their objects one and inseparable. This is what is referred to as "the blissful state of lower nirvana."

teach the receptive few the truth and to remove the subtle delusions still remaining. When even these delusions are removed, the mind has attained the omniscient state of the Buddha wherein the true nature of all things is understood perfectly.[23] It is a common misconception of Buddhists and non-Buddhists alike that "omniscience" refers to an encyclopedic type of knowledge. That type of knowledge, while it may be useful on a worldly level for worldly reasons, is not a level of information or motivation of a "holy" being. Omniscience refers to a "perfect" way of knowing that is freed of every delusion based in the ignorance that will grasp at self and objects/others as existing separate from or independent of the action of the mind of the perceiver.

The reason we are trapped within the dream is that the ignorant mind continues to grasp at mere appearances as though they exist separate from the mind's creative process. The mistaken belief, or delusion, that there is something inherently existing to grasp at is, through the grasping, what is then imprinted on the consciousness. This conditioned conscious-ness, imprinted with a myriad of separate delusions, is the storehouse for the volitional forces that make up the individual's conditioned response to sensory stimuli. These object-empowering imprints, and the individual's ignorance of how the mind works to create appearances, cause the indi-vidual to believe those appearances to exist inherently, separate from the mind's creation. The thus conditioned mind is trapped within its mistak-

---

23. *Omniscient state of the Buddha.* The terms *omniscience* and *enlightenment* are often confused and intermingled with worldly levels of insight into the existence of things. One Buddhist practi-tioner went so far as to inform me that if an individual was truly enlightened, then he or she, without any training or experience, would be able to drive an automobile well, for instance. If that was true, then Shakyamuni Buddha would have "naturally" acquired the knowledge and skill to design an build an engine to power such a vehicle, or medical expertise to cure the sick and dying or the lepers who are and were so prominent in India. According to that practition-er's reasoning, Shakyamuni Buddha would have been known for his physically oriented feats of skill, which would have been "like magic" to his "unskilled" students. In fact, Shakyamuni Buddha, as is the case with every enlightened being, is known for and remembered because of the wisdom teachings left behind. In no way is Shakyamuni Buddha remembered for a level of worldly expertise that surpassed the level of the worldly masters of the day. Such a focus was never a concern and was never the point of any practice done by Shakyamuni Buddha or any other similarly enlightened being on the Buddhist path to enlightenment.

That same practitioner informed me that "skill," or "skillful means," on the Buddhist path to enlightenment refers to such a worldly level of involvement. In fact, on the Buddhist path to enlightenment, "skill" refers to the way in which the practitioner who will be enlightened in the current lifetime uses his or her ignorant mind to eliminate the delusions based in ignorance and, thereby, cultivate the insight that leads to enlightenment that is based in wisdom. On the path, "skill" is synonymous with the generation of the mind of enlightenment.

en conceptual network by its own action, or karma. The result can only be unsatisfactory since the nature of such a mind is based in ignorance and so is inseparable from suffering. Ignorance is the cause, the suffering state of cyclic existence is the effect.

Here is an example. Imagine a city plans to widen its main street, and the crew is ready to begin the work. In order to complete the project, a large old maple tree will have to be cut down. The man in charge of the project grew up in an urban setting of concrete and tall buildings. His only personal experience with trees was as a young boy when his weekend chore in the fall was raking up the endless leaves that littered the pavement in front of where he lived. This chore, for which he wasn't even paid, kept him from playing with his friends and was the source of many unhappy scenes with his parents. In the boy's mind, raking leaves was akin to punishment.

On the other hand, the person living in the house in front of which the grand old tree slated for removal stands has had a very different experience with trees. She grew up in a part of the country where the houses were nestled cozily among forests of such trees. When she was a child, her grandfather took her with him every fall to check the trees that would be tapped come spring for their sweet syrup. In the spring, when the weather was warm again and the sap was flowing, the whole family was involved in gathering and processing the syrup. Grandmother made special maple syrup candies for all the children. It was a time of warm renewal that followed the dark cold of winter.

Every time the project manager looks at that tree, he sees trouble, aggravation, and senseless work. He sees the cause of suffering, not the cause of happiness. Every time the woman merely glances at the tree or simply thinks of it standing there, she feels happy. She believes the tree is good and lovely and important. She believes these qualities exist from the side of the object, as opposed to in her own mind. She believes the autumn leaves are vibrant orange in color and the season exhilarating. The man, however, knows the leaves to be dead, dry, brown, and a harbinger of the cold of winter. He believes the tree is a large obstruction to progress and removing it will require carefully thought-out planning; that is his job. He does not feel the tree is anything more than or other than an aggravation or work. He also believes that his perception exists from the side of the object or inherently and has not been created by the conditioned response of his own mind to sensory stimulation.

So what will happen? Each individual believes that what he or she perceives exists inherently in the object. Neither feels mistaken. Each has developed a sense of "self" according to what he or she believes to be the truth. "She" exists in relation to the objects she perceives; if asked to attempt to explain who "she" is, she will, without hesitation, say that "she" is a person who believes trees are good and important and necessary for happiness. She may even go so far as to say, "If there were more trees and less concrete, there would be more peace and harmony in the world today."

"He" also exists in relation to objects mistakenly perceived to be separate from his mind or inherently existing. If asked, "he" might say his idea of a good life would be to live in the penthouse apartment of a tall building in a big city, have a big car, and lots of money. Trees would not be a criterion for his happiness. In fact, until now, he has believed trees to be a cause for suffering. He's had no reason to give up attachment to that view.

When the project manager and the woman finally meet—as they will when the tree in question comes due for removal—what do you suppose will happen? Doesn't it happen all the time? Each individual will be positive the other is wrong, dim-witted, insensitive, and overreactive. What will be the truth? That both are similarly and equally ignorant of the true nature of the mere appearances of his or her mind. It does not matter what form the conflict takes. It will always relate to objects/others as if they are believed to exist inherently (and in relation to an equally mistaken apprehension of self/me/mine).

That is what is called cyclic existence. It is, by its very nature, nothing other than a self-centered level of mind that is based in ignorance and is trapped, by its own conditioning, within a completely unsatisfactory conceptual network. Ignorance of how things truly exist causes individuals to grasp at objects/others. Likewise, the similarly misapprehended "self" attempts to secure the causes of happiness freed from suffering. Life is just a dream.

Everything appearing to the mind is nothing other than another mere appearance, or illusion, that is generated by that mind. Every quality-filled object/other is the appearance of the causes and conditions coming together with the volitional force of the imprint thus stimulated, or triggered. In short, all appearances to the mind are the mirror reflection of that mind. The self only exists dependent on a dualistically-oriented relationship the mind sets up with the objects/others it unwittingly generates.

Living beings who are imprisoned in the conceptual network that is cyclic existence also believe there is something situated in the approximate place of their bodies, which they call "self," "I," "me," etc. Upon closer scrutiny or investigation, however, no such thing can or will ever be found to exist separate from the mind or as more than a mere concept of the mind's own making. It *seems* like there are objects/others and self. It *seems* like there are two things and that the objects/others are *there* and "I" am *here,* each existing completely separately.

The "self" of each individual trapped in cyclic existence is nothing more than the mere label, or umbrella concept, that reflects the complete output of the mind's conditioned response to sensory stimulation. The process goes like this: The senses come into contact with their objects, stimulating an imprint left on the consciousness from similar causes and conditions to ripen. That imprint attaches qualities to the object of good, bad, or indifferent. The mind so labels the object, and thus it is perceived to contain the power to affect the well-being of "self." When the individual grasps at the appearance as good, bad, or indifferent and reacts accordingly—oblivious to the truth—a new imprint is seeded onto the consciousness. That, in turn, will ripen when the appropriate causes and conditions come together. It is a seemingly endless round of mistakes that perpetuate suffering and trap living beings in their cycling.

It's like a jar of red sauce found on a grocery shelf: until you put the label "spaghetti sauce" on it, there is no appearance of spaghetti sauce. Once labeled, however, your senses immediately generate a quality-filled appearance based on previous conditioning to similar causes and conditions. As soon as the object is labeled, the mind will ascertain some basic qualities associated with that label and the red appearance of the concoction in the jar: it is probably made of tomatoes, oregano, mushrooms, and so on. You will have some feeling of "I like spaghetti sauce," "I don't like spaghetti sauce," or of a general indifference to the object "spaghetti sauce" based on past experience with the object. Associated memories of some intimate spaghetti dinner with a loved one may arise that further qualify the objects of the senses and result in more or less attachment to the object as a source of happiness or suffering.

The quality-filled object "spaghetti sauce" did not exist from the side of the object in any way. It was a concept generated by the mind of the perceiver after the senses apprehended their objects, thereby stimulating an imprint left on the consciousness previously. The imprint, thus stimulated, becomes bound to the causes and conditions like a label and so appears as though it has nothing at all to do with the perceiver's mind. That mind, ignorant of the true nature of the appearance, grasped for the object as good, bad, or indifferent as it was believed to exist inherently. The grasping was done for the sole purpose of securing happiness for self and freedom from suffering. Once the mind mistakenly believes its own illusion to be "real," a new empowering imprint is left on the storehouse consciousness that will be stimulated when similar causes and conditions come together.

The "self" of "I like this spaghetti" exists only as the respondent to the quality-filled object. Although those trapped in cyclic existence believe there is a self existing inherently, in truth "self" exists as nothing more than the label that sums up or reflects the totality of an individual's conditioned existence. When that individual renounces attachment to the gross delusions based in ignorance, and renounces attachment to all appearances of suffering, then the basis for the label "self" is eliminated. At that point, the highest level practitioner enters a meditation that, if done perfectly, ends in enlightenment—liberation from belief in an inherently existent self.

Every living being is truly doing the "best" he or she can within the limitation of the conditioned existence that grasps at good/bad, this/that, here/there, or you/me. Every individual asserts "self" as superior and separate from "other." Each individual establishes his or her "self" as ultimately superior to objects/others because of a completely mistaken belief in the correctness of his or her own assessment of the true meaning of the relationship of mere objects/others to the self. Any time "good" is established on an object/other, "bad" is insinuated, or assumed.[24] It is the natural action of the conditioned mind that when positing the position "here," the position "there" is simultaneously assumed, or insinuated; where there is "good," then the criteria for "bad" have been established; where there is "you," then there is "I"; where there is "then," then there is "now," and so on. Belief in the inherent existence of the separateness of these "things," from one another as well as from the "self," which is the

---

24. This is not a dialectic, per se, whereby, (1) through the positing of its opposite the truth is reached or (2) as in Marxist doctrine, the fomenting of change through the establishment of opposing forces, the primary overcoming the secondary, which establishes the basis for a new level of conflict, is attained.

reference point for all concepts, causes living beings to remain locked tightly within the conceptual prison of their own minds, which is the suffering state of cyclic existence.]

By cultivating the criteria for happiness ignorant of how things truly exist, you only create the cause for suffering. When objects/others that meet the mind-generated criteria for "bad" eventually come into a close enough relationship with an individual's self to threaten the security of that self, then that self will rise up as superior, to fight off the perceived threat. This is much like the hallucinating person who scrambles to be freed from the odious worms that to the observer (not affected by drug) are known to be simple blades of grass.

Seeking happiness freed from suffering for self/me/mine is the motivation for every single action taken by beings trapped by their minds within its faulty conceptual network. The cause of all suffering is believing there is something called "happiness" separate from the mind of the perceiver and then grasping for it among the mere appearances of the mind. The complete lack of awareness (or ignorance) of how things truly exist is the root cause for all suffering. This ignorance posits a merely conceptual self separate from similarly illusory objects/others; it believes both to be inherently existent, or "real," and therefore attainable, or graspable. It is the nature of illusion to fool the unaware.

Ignorance of the illusion causes individuals to believe what is merely a dream image to be the truth, and the truth, the dream. "Death" within the dream is nothing other than the changing of appearance or form that can be apprehended by the mind, which subsequently grasps at the conditioned appearances of its own action.

The storehouse that is the consciousness of ignorant beings acts like the sounding board of a piano when the fingers come in contact with the keys. It projects a world filled with quality-filled objects/others that are empowered, by previous conditioning, to affect the well-being of self. This storehouse consciousness is what reincarnates over and over until its cause—ignorance of how things truly exist—is eliminated, and a consciousness, freed from the imprints based in ignorance of the truth that is the fully enlightened state, is attained.

[When is the cycle finally broken? When the self of the dream gives up attachment to the mere appearances of the dream that secure it. This is accomplished only by one who is compelled to be of benefit to others and has vowed to not give harm to any living being by any action of body, speech, or mind. It is only by always putting others' well-being first that the concepts supporting and securing self are replaced with concepts based in the greatest loving-kindness for others. In this way, one generates a beautiful heart of giving, which is the essence of the practice of the Buddhist path to enlightenment. Through the cultivation of the warm feeling generated by the practitioner's thoughts for others, the practitioner can step by simple step give up attachment to the delusions that had previously made the mind feel comfortable and secure in objects mistakenly believed to exist separate from its own creation.)

This is the heart of the highest level practitioner who will be enlightened. This is the heart of the practice that culminates in enlightenment. It is based in morality and the wish to be of ultimate and lasting benefit to others, and it is inseparable from the generation of the perfection of generosity. The cycle is broken when one renounces attachment to all the mere appearances of the mind's creation and, having known in the heart—one's inmost being—that life is, truly, just a dream.[25]

Many individuals trapped within the dream (1) are aware that something isn't "right"; (2) at various points in their lives spend some moments pondering the purpose, or meaning, of life; and (3) generally attempt to be "good," as they are conditioned to believe that concept exists and relates to self and objects/others, while (4) filling their lives with meaningless activities that distract them from thoughts of their imminent death. Those distractions play into, and are inseparable from, the dream. Such individuals don't know for sure, but hope that "something's going to happen someday." It's like the passing over of the magician's wand—voilá! things will be different, things will change: children won't die, no one will get sick, peace will reign, all will be well. That's how it is, too. No one ever fantasizes to be in an inferior or dependent position. Somehow, the fantasy always promotes the self as important, even if it's in its own imagined suffering or even death.

Some of you trapped in the dream, with the good fortune to read these words, might assume that if you wait long enough that just as the effects of a drug eventually subside, so will your attachment to the dream. No individual, trapped within the dream by his or her ignorance of the

---

25. *The three principal aspects of the path.* The path can be completed only when these three principal aspects of the practice are cognized on the highest level. Briefly, they are (1) bodhicitta, (2) renunciation, and (3) emptiness.

empowering imprints of the storehouse consciousness, will *just* arise from that somnolent state without having first created the cause. Like a sleeping person who is dreaming, the cause—a disturbance or feeling to arise—creates the effect: one wakes from the dream. In this example, the sleeper, disturbed, grows more and more "conscious," exits the dream, and arises, aware of the quickly fading dream. The cause was not created to drive a car or read a book. The cause was created similar to its effect: waking from the dream. This cause was created by the action of the mind in conditioned response to sensory stimulation—the disturbance or the feeling—directly similar to the effect generated by the action of the unconscious mind.

What has happened to individuals who are trapped in cyclic existence is more than just a simple one-dimensional misapprehension of objects. The stupor of the ignorance—its totally involving and intoxicating effect—is as profound and inseparable from their minds as is the effect wisdom, its opposite, will have when they finally waken, enlightened.

Truth cannot be known by an ignorant mind. Truth and ignorance cannot exist simultaneously in one mind. To an ignorant mind, what is generally believed to be the truth can only be described as the all-obscuring truth of ignorance. The mistaken way of knowing that is based in ignorance of the true nature of things completely obscures the wisdom that understands how things truly exist, like the thickest cloud cover that hides the brilliant light of the sun beyond. When a person is finally enlightened, having generated the wisdom mind of the enlightened state, that individual will have removed the delusions that obscure the truth of how things truly exist, thereby creating the cause to be inseparable from the unobscured mind that understands, without mistake, the true nature of things.

It is important for you, the practitioner, to understand that you are not creating something new or separate in your mind. The enlightened mind is not a creation. It is an undeluded way of knowing that is itself understood to be empty of inherent existence. Initially, you recognize a problem (suffering) and take responsibility for it. Second, you create the cause to achieve the desired effect. In the case of enlightenment, the practitioner generates a wish (the cause) to achieve the goal (the result). Finally, you do the work of reconditioning your consciousness to the truth by following the wisdom-based teachings of one who went before. That practice will be the cause for the elimination of the delusions based in ignorance and the commensurate generation of the wisdom mind of enlightenment.

Chapter Two

MAKER OF MAGIC, WEAVER OF WEBS

Until now you've been sitting, enchanted, mesmerized, in the audience at the dinner theater of life, happy to be fooled by the endless string of sometimes lovely, sometimes frightening, always enchanting images conjured up by the magician. And so you've spent uncountable lifetimes playing to the magician's tricks, completely duped, over and over again, by your own ignorance of the method behind the magic. Gasping one moment, relieved the next, completely lost in the appearance of your own unknowing, captivated, emotionally tied to the drama. How long will you sit and watch like a small child that is so easily amused? Maybe it's time now to leave your place in front, go behind, and learn the tricks.

"Of course," he smiles, his low voice purring, "it will cost you."

"How much?" you calmly ask, a bit concerned about the price.

Curling the oily black mustachio upward with the well-shaped fingers of his white-gloved right hand, the tall, thin, smooth-skinned tailcoated magician looks down musingly, dark eyes suddenly filled with the lights at his feet and, just loud enough for you alone to hear breathes, "Everything," and vanishes.

Just the slightest hint of his exotic fragrance wafting out on the edges of a swirling breeze lingers to suggest he had ever been there at all.

$\mathcal{F}$or those who have forgotten they are merely dreaming, it is very difficult to give up attachment to the appearances of the dream, because the senses of the dreamer are experiencing the objects of the dream, mistakenly believing them to be "real." The mistake is compounded when the self of the dream relates to those perceived objects and "feels" them. Freeing yourself from the dream—becoming enlightened—is the most difficult practice any human being could do in this life. In no way does the practice perpetuate grasping at any aspect of the illusion. The "practice" involves not only the step-by-step method by which you give up attachment to each appearance of the illusion but also the development of an awareness of the illusions, which awareness is particularly provoked when you experience suffering as a result of your attachment to an object/other.[26] The ignorant mind's lack of awareness of the actual nature of the mere appearances of the mind's creation is complete and total.

To arise from the dream, those mere appearances must be looked at by the mind of the dreamer in a logical and intelligent manner—much as you, the reader, have been observing yourself reading these words. An impartial awareness of the mind's action must be established and maintained. The

---

26. *Others*. Although it is true that the objects/others that appear separate from yourself are just illusions, still, the ignorant mind does indeed believe in the inherent existence of those objects/others as well as self. You must use your present mind to generate the path.

catalyst for the watching must be (1) your wish to be enlightened and, thereby, of ultimate and lasting benefit to others; (2) your practice of renunciation of the mere appearances of your mind; and (3) your understanding their true nature.

Until you renounce attachment to suffering, its cause cannot be eliminated. It is during the "difficult" times when the self experiences some form of suffering, that relief[27] is sought. Through continuous inspection, you, the dreamer, will convince yourself of the illusory nature of that which seems to be so real and will give up your attachment to it as a cause of happiness or suffering.

It is for this reason that dreamers must discipline their minds to pay attention and why, like children struggling to learn multiplication tables, they must go over and over the same information until their minds finally understand the new concepts. Through cultivation of the logic, you will gain objectivity. With objectivity, you can watch your mind create quality-filled appearances. Objectivity also allows you to be removed enough from the self that "seems" to also exist inherently, and to not be frightened by the truth. As is the case with so many of the details of the Buddhist path to enlightenment, the need for objective awareness may be brought to your attention during the first teachings you hear on the path to enlightenment. Then, by a daily practice of discipline and control of your mind, you become a master of the mind. Remember this and do not abandon practices you are introduced to at the beginning as being unimportant in the middle or at the end.

The practitioner is similar to a novice carpenter who will one day build a great house, and has just been given hammer and nails. At first, the work is tenuous, disjointed, and success sporadic. With time, the novice grows proficient with the tools and materials and, by combining with other tools and materials, becomes a master carpenter. Thus qualified to build a great building, the master utilizes every tool toward that end. What were least important, or seemingly most common—the ham-

---

27. *On a worldly level, relief from suffering is sought* (1) through prayer to a power greater than the self, during which the individual seeks intervention of some sort; (2) in drugs; (3) from counseling geared to helping the individual fit back into society comfortably; (4) as a result of various kinds of manic behavior; (5) through various diversions, often physically oriented that allow the individual to temporarily escape the suffering the mind is experiencing; and (6) by cultivating another/a new lover, friend, husband/wife, to name just a few.

The practice that is the Buddhist path to enlightenment is about nothing other than the complete elimination of all suffering through the eradication of its root cause—ignorance.

mer and nail—become an integral part of the building machine when put in the hands of a master. The point is this: the tools must be mastered because skill is achieved on the basics. The beginning must not be thrown away as unimportant. It must be used with mastery born of familiarity from your practice, when you begin the most important work of all.]

The Eight Worldly Desires

[*To end suffering, abandon desire*] ✓

WHAT DOES THIS MEAN? Write down this simple phrase and put it in your pocket. The next time you feel any form of suffering, think about what it means. When living beings are actually suffering, there is always the feeling that something other than your mind is a source of the suffering. When your feelings are hurt, for instance, you believe it is the other person's fault. When the job sought is withdrawn, either the job was wrong or the employer shortsighted. When a personal object of special importance is stolen, the thief is to blame for the suffering that follows. When the car breaks down, it's either the vehicle's fault or the mechanic's. If you run into a low-hanging tree limb, you will blame the tree for the resulting suffering, to the point of kicking back at the tree or hitting the offending limb. People who have been investigating various self-help therapies and have learned "to take responsibility" for their feelings often, in a magnanimous gesture of fairness to the objects/others involved, turn the blame on themselves. The effect of the focus of attention is ridiculous at best and self-centered.

[When suffering occurs, it is because one of the eight worldly desires[28] has not been met. These are (1,2) the desire for gain and not loss; (3,4) for praise and not criticism; (5,6) for happiness and not suffering; and (7,8) for kind words and not unkind words. These four basic groupings of eight worldly desires may, at first glance, appear to be too simplistic. However, if, when you are experiencing suffering, you truly look deep into the foundation of the feeling, you will be surprised to learn, over and over again, that one or more of these grouped desires was behind

---

28. *Worldly.* These desires are only worldly as they are generated by a mind seeking happiness for self that is mistakenly believed to exist separate from objects/others.

the suffering, because the self, which had previously established the criteria for happiness, will suffer when deprived of that "happiness." The reason does not make a difference. Each and every "happiness" is based in the thought of self/me/mine.

Whenever an individual who has renounced attachment to any and all suffering can establish the desire causing the suffering, it is an easy matter to look at the desire and give up the need to have it fulfilled. Truly, those desires are completely conceptual. The basis for their establishment, fulfillment of the criteria for happiness, is completely conceptual. Whether or not an object/other has the power to make a self feel happiness or suffering is completely conceptual. The self that might feel such conceptualized happiness or suffering is itself completely conceptual. To be conceptual means to be created by and dependent upon the mind of the perceiver. Such things can be changed when the individual in question is really, finally, irrevocably sick and tired of being sick and tired.

Only then can the supports of self be removed one by one and replaced with insight into the true nature of how things exist. Through the cultivation of the logic of the true nature of both the object of your suffering and the self that is experiencing that suffering, you can free your mind from the suffering and steadily recondition the consciousness to the truth of having understanding how things truly exist. Through just such a steady practice, the mind, eliminating delusions based in ignorance, comes to generate the wisdom mind of enlightenment.

The Four Noble Truths that make up the complete teaching of the "way out of suffering," or "path to enlightenment," all relate specifically and directly to suffering. Is it any wonder there is nothing else to deal with except the effect—suffering—and its cause—ignorance.

The Four Noble Truths

The truth of suffering, it must be known.
The truth of the origin of suffering, it must be understood.
The truth of the cessation of suffering,
it must be realized directly.
The truth of the path to the cessation of suffering,
it must be meditated on incessantly.[29]

---

29. This is how Shakyamuni Buddha began his first teaching after attaining enlightenment.

ALL THOUGHTS/ACTIONS OF THE ignorant mind are necessarily "self" centered because of the dualistic orientation of self and objects/others. This is
the "reality" of individuals who are lost in the dream and very far from the
truth. An individual trapped in the dream might consider helping someone in distress to be a selfless act—but such actions are not selfless at all.
This is not to say, in any way, that such actions should be discouraged. But
the enlightened individual has come to know that the suffering of those in
need never ends through "worldly" levels of intervention, but only shifts
in meaningless cycles. Ultimate and lasting benefit is given only by sharing the wisdom gained from enlightenment with those few people who are
receptive to such a transcendental, and intangible, goal.

So then to continue our conversation: Why are worldly actions and
forms of service or aid not selfless at all? Because all objects/others exist
only in relationship to self. The mind, ignorant of how things truly exist,
is conditioned to believe objects/others are "real" as they are mistakenly
perceived to relate to self as good/bad, worthy/unworthy, this/that, etc. In
the way of the world, giving aid to another is selfless because it is for
"another" who met the criteria for the label "worthy" and who was
believed to exist separate from the mind of the giver of aid. In the way of
wisdom, perhaps you can begin to see the fault in the logic caused by ignorance of how both the object (other) and self truly exist. The truth is this:

> *Form[30] is emptiness.*
> *Emptiness is form.*
> *Form is not other than emptiness.*
> *Emptiness is not other than form.[31]*

The mind is made up of the six sense-powers. They are (1) eye sense-
power/form; (2) ear sense-power/sound; (3) nose sense-power/smell; (4)

---

30. *Form.* Of the physically based sense powers, the eye sense power is considered to be the
strongest. Its object is form. As a symbol of the complete process by which the mind creates
appearances, the word *form* is used.
31. *Emptiness.* These four lines symbolize the heart of the essence of wisdom. If one wished to have
some phrase to repeat over and over as a focus for concentration and intense contemplation, then
it would be very beneficial to repeat either the very abbreviated version or this slightly longer
one:

> *When there is an appearance, the mind has acted.*
> *When the mind has acted, there is an appearance.*
> *The appearance is not other than the action of the mind.*
> *The action of the mind is not other than the appearance.*

mouth sense-power/taste; (5) body sense-power/tactile sensation; (6) mental sense-power/abstract thought. When the six sense-powers come in contact with their objects/others, an empowering imprint left on the consciousness from previous similar causes and conditions, affixes itself to the cumulative objects of the six senses. This generates a quality-filled appearance that is known to be good, bad, or indifferent as it relates to self, which the mind, unaware of its own action, grasps at in order to secure happiness for self/me/mine.

Every appearance owes its existence to the creative process of the mind of the perceiver and, therefore, does not exist inherently in the object (or with its existence established from the side of the object). That no appearance exists separate from the mind of the perceiver is an indication of the "empty" nature of all things. The nature of each and every appearance of the mind, because each is dependent on the mind for its creation and maintenance, is therefore empty of inherent existence. The process by which the mind creates appearances then is referred to as "emptiness." Every single thing we view, or know, is nothing other than, or more than, the mirror reflection of our own minds. Each appearance is similar in nature to the reflection we see when we stand before a mirror. Each is empty of inherent existence.

With the (1) elimination of the opportunistic delusions based in ignorance of the truth through (2) a constant practice of analyzing the law of cause and effect, combined with (3) a meditation on (a) the true nature of things, (b) renunciation of the mere appearances of the mind, and (c) a most compelling wish to be enlightened in order to be of benefit to those who are still suffering, the practitioner generates insight into the true nature of things that leads to the goal. The goal? Attainment of the wisdom mind of enlightenment, which is freed from all delusions associated with a self that sees all objects/others as either good, bad, or indifferent and/or as friend, enemy, or stranger.

Such a wisdom mind knows that all such appearances owe their creation and continued existence to the mind of the perceiver. With the wisdom that understands correctly and completely the true nature of the dream, and is freed from all imprints based in ignorance of the true nature of the many aspects of its appearances, the flame of desire for the illusory objects/others of the dream is extinguished. Then, when the consciousness splits free from the physical support of the body at the time of death, rather than reincarnating, it enters a wisdom level of existence, freed from the suffering caused by ignorance. This is because there is no longer anything to which the consciousness is attached, because the self and its reflective needs have been eliminated with the delusions. When the ignorance upon which they are based has been replaced by wisdom understanding how things truly exist, no empowering imprints are left on the consciousness of the enlightened being that would cause the mind to grasp at a here or there, this or that, then or now, you or I.

Every time an imprint is burned off the consciousness, like the lessening of the clouds that obscure the brilliance of the sun, the truth is less obscured to the mind, and you will become aware of an ever more subtle level of operant delusion. As each delusion is revealed, it is eliminated through the practice that is the path to enlightenment. As the number of delusions decrease, so your understanding of every level of the teaching, teacher, and practice increases. The further along the path you travel, the more faith you will have in the sanity/goodness of the purpose of the trip. As you see progress along the path, you will have more faith in the perfection of the teachings. As you begin to understand how perfect the teachings have been, you will have more faith in your teacher's ability to give you correct teachings. Ultimately, how do even they, the teachings/teacher, exist? As nothing other than mere reflections of the mind of the perceiver.

As you progress along the path, you will experience the inner joy that arises from the practice, as well as an overwhelming wish to be of benefit to others. [You will become extremely conscious to not give harm to any other living being with any action of your body, speech, or mind. It is this deep inner joy that causes the sincere practitioner to continue progressing along the path without pause and without mistake.] Should you entertain self-centered thoughts, such as the wish to be enlightened for your own gain, or develop pride in your progress, then you will have fallen out of the practice and back into his or her own self-cherishing ignorance. All such attitudes and activities are the cause for remaining in the suffering state of cyclic existence and, therefore, cannot be the cause for enlightenment in this lifetime or any other. Such worldly activities and involvements, wherein the mind is finding fault outside its own ignorant action, becomes the cause to remain in cyclic existence.

How do things really exist? At this point you might draw the conclusion that if every appearance is merely an indication that the mind has acted and that there is no existence "inherently" in objects, then, therefore,

there is no object. It is normal for the mind of the thoughtful practitioner to leap to this extreme conclusion at some point in the practice. This
extreme view is called nihilism. The opposite extreme view is called eternalism. [The extreme view of eternalism is what most ignorant beings
believe in: that there is some essential core of existence that exists inherently in all objects that is of a permanent nature. It is this essence, often
referred to as "soul" or "spirit," of things that is grasped at by the self of
the perceiver as the cause of his or her happiness or suffering.]

Awareness of the tendency of the mind to naturally want to fall into
either of the two extremes creates the cause for the skillful practitioner to
eventually reach the correct middle view free of the two extremes, which
is the truth of how things exist. This is accomplished by analyzing the
mistaken concept called nihilism[32]—that nothing at all exists—and its
opposite, called eternalism—that objects have inherent existence.
Through a correct and complete analysis of objects/others as attachments,
the truth will be reached. Since the "good times" don't generally push us
to want to change things, such an analysis usually begins when suffering
is recognized and a thought to alleviate that suffering arises. Later in this
book we discuss this more completely but, basically (1) a problem arises
that causes you some pain; (2) there is a thought to try to alleviate that
pain; and (3) just like a mantra, you begin to analyze how the elements—
self and object causing the pain—truly exist. Make it simple by saying to
yourself, for instance, "When there is an appearance, the mind has acted.
When the mind has acted, there is an appearance. The appearance is not
other than the action of the mind. The action of the mind is not other than
the appearance." (4) Ask yourself, "How does the self that is suffering
exist?" And then answer with, "Completely dependent on the mind of the
perceiver." Then ask, "How does the object/other that seems to be causing
this pain truly exist?" Then, "Completely dependent on my own mind."
Continue with, "I have no wish to continue this suffering, so I'll give up
attachment to this mere appearance of my mind that is causing my suffering. Since my self exists dependent on my mind, I will also give up attach-

---

32. *Nihilism/eternalism.* One of the two extreme views of how things truly exist. Having been
made aware of the illusory nature of self and objects/others, the practitioner will jump to the
conclusion that, therefore, there is nothing at all existing. That is what is referred to as nihilism
and it is an incorrect view. Its opposite, eternalism, is a similarly mistaken extreme view wherein the individual mistakenly believes that if there is "something" other than the "nothing" of
the nihilist view, then "it" must be of a permanent and unchanging, eternal nature often termed
soul/spirit/essence.

ment to the concept of self that would suffer in reaction to the appearance of my own mind." Then go over it, back and forth, inside and out, until you begin to give up attachment to the object of your suffering and the self that suffers in that situation.

It takes a conscious awareness of your own feelings as they rapidly change with every new appearance. It takes real effort over a long period of time and the ability to work alone—it's much easier to forget about the importance of changing your own mind and go to a movie with a friend, for instance, for rest and relaxation. It takes intelligence and it takes skill. But this is how the goal—enlightenment—will eventually be accomplished. When done correctly, it is an intense process of reconditioning your own mind to develop the wisdom that understands how things truly exist and the wisdom that is free of the extremes of eternalism and nihilism. Only through practices such as the one described above can the correct view of reality be attained.

An analogy of the process would go something like this: Traveling down a walled pathway in the dark, you are not aware of the extremes or outermost boundaries of that path, and so you continually bounce against those walls. To someone who has never traveled such a difficult path, such stumbling might be perceived to be a sign of your inferiority as a traveler. You, however, have a positive mind that helps you get beyond the appearance of obstructions by understanding that any obstruction exists only in your mind. [You meditate on the empty nature of the self that is experiencing the various forms of suffering, and then give up attachment to the mere appearance of the suffering.] Such a traveler becomes more and more compelled to follow the path to its end in order to be of benefit to others. The walls are merely used to define the outermost extremes of the path. Indeed, it is only because of the walls that, in the darkness, you know you are on the path at all. By repeatedly identifying the extremes and repositioning yourself, you learn precisely where the center of the pathway falls between the two, and progress unerringly and without interruptions, comfortably aware of your progress, toward the goal.

Please note that to one kind of traveler—perhaps even the "normal" traveler—collision with the walls would be perceived as an insurmountable obstacle to progress along the path; to another traveler the walls would be perceived as an aid on the unknown path. What is the difference between the two types of traveler? The level of mind determined by the degree to which the traveler is committed to reach the goal, as well as his or her ability to give up attachment to the mere appearance of suffering. Ultimately, the traveler on the path must give up attachment to the eight worldly desires that gear the mind to a need for immediate sense gratification.

The path to enlightenment is about giving up attachment to the conceptual network that is conditioned to know things as permanent, or "inherently" existent. Through analysis of your own existing conceptual network, combined with listening to wisdom teachings from an enlightened being who has the unobscured level of mind that is your goal, you will, step-by-step, give up attachment to the two extremes. The motivation for the practice is to free yourself, and thereby others, from the sweeping suffering caused by ignorance. The suffering is caused when the self seeks to possess what is mistakenly believed to be permanent from among the constantly changing mind-based illusions created within the dream in the hope of securing happiness and freedom from suffering.

If the truth cannot be known by an ignorant mind, but the goal is enlightenment, how then will an ignorant mind become enlightened? By learning about where you are right now, getting some idea of the goal to be obtained, and beginning the step-by-step path back to the source according to the perfect instructions and insights gained by following an enlightened teacher. It is a process. It is a practice. It is not philosophical theory, or speculation, and it is certainly not a religion wherein one believes in and cultivates belief in a power greater than the self.

To be a serious practitioner you must learn to be skillful with your mind; you must learn patience. Every time you suffer, you must identify what it is the self seeks and give up attachment to its mere appearance, which you have been conditioned to grasp at as real. The mind can be changed if it is recognized as the source of the problem and you have renounced attachment to the effect of the problem: suffering.

If you're really serious, then think about these simple words and all that they imply until you truly understand:

Life is just a dream.

To get out of the trap that binds the dreamer within the illusion, you have to have proof that you are, in fact, trapped, right? First, a little more about this dream.

Life is just a dream, and when you waken from that dream, you will be enlightened, liberated from belief in an inherently existent self. On the path to that enlightenment and freedom from cyclic existence, you will actually burn up the gross delusions imprinted on the consciousness with the insight gained from the practice that is the path, through a disciplined practice of meditation on (1) the true nature of each and every instance and object of suffering or feeling of discomfort and (2) the true nature of the self experiencing those feelings.

By renouncing attachment to all suffering and meticulously policing your own mind, you will, step by step, give up attachment to the delusions that cause you to suffer and will thereby gain increasing clarity of mind. When all the gross delusions (upon which the umbrella concept "self" is merely labeled) have been removed, then if you are truly compelled to be enlightened only for others, you will begin a highest level meditation and "go beyond," freed from cyclic existence, and will waken from the dream at last.

If it's just a dream, then why is there suffering? Because the mind, ignorant of the dreaming, grasps at self and objects believing that the causes of happiness and suffering exist inherently in objects/others and are separate from the mind's making. As seen before, there is a sense of self in relation to objects/others, and all appearances are apprehended from a self-centered viewpoint. Feelings assert themselves and cause you to seek to gain an advantage for self over others, or to nurture those you feel to be your own, the family and friends of this life, or groups the self feels to be a part of, at the expense of and in competition with "others." There is jealousy, the wish to compete, and the need to possess. [The cause of all suffering comes down to just one point: the self-cherishing thought that is based in ignorance of how things truly exist.]

Saying life is just a dream probably sounds like a clever riddle spun by a riddle spinner. Although the meaning is profound, those simple words are not a clever riddle meant only for the elitely clever. Those words are actually the truth and very obvious to the enlightened mind of one who has wakened from the dream and, having eliminated even the subtle delusions, is [omniscient, knowing all appearances as they truly are.]

Before continuing, a question: If some night you were aware that you had fallen asleep and so knew that whatever was appearing in your mind was just a dream, you wouldn't, for even one moment, "buy into" that dream, would you? You would just watch it and let everything go by, not grasping or generating needs for the things appearing in the dream. You simply wouldn't be that foolish. Then, because you had not grasped, you wouldn't feel suffering or loss. Even though the appearances of the dream looked completely real and solid, with associated smells and sounds, to grasp at such things that are nothing more than the mind's creation—and so are therefore constantly changing—would be the height of folly. Wouldn't you agree?

The Buddhist path to enlightenment is the practice of individuals who, tired of the suffering of cyclic existence, renounce attachment to that suffering state and eliminate the gross delusions upon which self is merely labeled in order to, ultimately, end the suffering of others. Nothing else.

It begins with morality, the wish not to give harm to any living being. This is followed by the disciplined practice of the giving up of attachment to the mere appearances of the dream by considering how both the self and objects/others are empty of inherent existence and are completely generated by and dependent upon the mind. Developed and interwoven through the whole is the wish to be of lasting benefit to others. This love of others, which is greater than the love of self, is perfected at the time of one's enlightenment. Through this practice, when there is no longer anything appearing to the mind by which one is bound, one wakens. So simple. So difficult.

Since the enlightenment of Siddhartha Gautama, hundreds of thousands of unenlightened scholars, philosophers, and religious leaders have turned this simple practice into riddles beyond practical discussion, into superstitious rituals, and into elaborate forms of god worship or belief in a power greater than the self. *This is all* little more than the stuff of philosophical theory and speculation, or ignorant mumbo-jumbo. What the unenlightened are capable of teaching and qualified to teach is their own ignorant level of mind based on the practice still undone. Such a level of mind has not yet understood correctly or completely any single aspect of the path to enlightenment. Completely obscured to the wisdom born from completion of the practice, unenlightened teachers can only teach from a philosophically oriented viewpoint that is not based in practice, or from a religious orientation of one who has missed the point completely. *That* is not the Buddhist path to enlightenment.

Whether or not the words of an enlightened teaching or teacher cause you to be enlightened is not dependent upon the words. The words are perfect. The teaching is correct. Your enlightenment is totally dependent on your own mind: (1) First, are you receptive? Then, (2) are you or are you not, and to what degree, willing and able to do the hard work of

disciplining the mind—your mind, not someone else's—to give up attachment to its own appearance? (3) To what degree are you willing and committed to give up attachment to the self that is so proud, so sure it is
always right, so ready for combat, so ready for "self"-assertion? The level
of your interest will be reflected in your practice. (4) Is your wish to be
enlightened for others greater than your wish to establish security for self?⌋

This path is by far the most difficult work of all and the most
demanding. It is also the only work that is truly rewarding and of ultimate benefit. It begins at the beginning with the thought wish to stop
the suffering—others' and your own—and ends with enlightenment.
Skillful practice should bear fruit fairly quickly, and you'll begin experiencing moments of joy as you can feel change is occurring and know that
you're on the right path. But how far will you travel before you let your
mind wander from its commitment? Then, tired and discouraged because
you're not enlightened yet, will you allow it to grow weary or discouraged
or angry or distracted, having found interest in something else, or fault
in the teaching/teacher? How long can you last at a solitary endeavor that
yields no physical evidence upon which a friend or family member might
be able to comment, "Good job, well done?" There is no quick and easy
fix here. It is not an easy path. It is not even a peaceful path since, in a
way, you are declaring war on your mind's present state of carefree happiness and entering into some very intense introspective analysis of its
workings. It is, frankly, unsettling to experience in your very core that the
self that is suffering so much, the self you call your own, is nothing more
than an illusion. Yet, it is that very disquieting moment when you first
brush into that particular truth that you can be assured you are headed in
the right direction.

When will you be enlightened? In this lifetime or the next, or the
next, or the next? The answer is, When you are tired of suffering more
than you are attached to it. Only then will you give up its cause, which is
the grasping at the duality established within the dream of self and
objects/others—a most unfortunate mistake that keeps you trapped in the
dream cycle. ⌈You are your own jailer. The key is placed here before you.
When you make it yours, by becoming its possessor, then the door is neither locked nor unlocked.⌋

As you read, it may initially seem like you are simply reading
another's words in this book. What actually is happening, though, is this:
Because of your karma (or the volitional action of your mind due to

cumulative conditioned effects) you are at a time in your life when the causes and conditions have come together—human body/brain, time and opportunity to read these words, interest, qualified teacher/teachings— for these words to be appearing in your dream and for you, now, to be considering their meaning. These words, if considered well and given top priority in your interest, will cause your mind to become aware of its dreaming and thereby to wake up. At the time you awaken, just as you become aware that there was its subject (self) separate from its object (objects/others) other than the mere appearances created by your own mind. You will come to know that the enlightened teaching/teacher appearing to you in this dream does not exist separate from your own mind. Ultimately, you will finally awaken and—more than just having regained consciousness—then eliminate even the subtle delusions and become completely aware. At that very moment, then who is the Buddha? At the very moment of one's enlightenment, who is the teacher and who the taught?

So, when will these teachings attain top priority among your many worldly or dream-bound interests? When you are completely bored by the meaninglessness of the activities of this life; when some tragedy occurs that somehow overloads the boat of tragedy and suffering; when you are thrown squarely up against bigger concerns; when you are no longer enraptured by acquisition of wealth and the property it can buy; when you grow weary of drama and death.

It is difficult for even very strong people in this world to face the reality of this world. Within the dream, every being wants to be happy and not to suffer. Until you are completely freed from delusion, you will feel suffering if deprived of the preconditioned appearances necessary for happiness. It is only when a thoughtful individual has truly renounced attachment to all causes of suffering in order to be of benefit to others that those causes can and will be eliminated. This is exactly the path to enlightenment. It is the first teaching: the truth of suffering. It must be known. And it is the last teaching. It is the reason for the complete awakening of the practitioner into the fully enlightened state.

At any given moment, in any part of the world, you will find human beings ignorant of their dreaming, setting up the criteria for happiness, and thereby establishing the cause for suffering. Such individuals will grasp for conceptually established causes of happiness because they believe them to exist separate from their own minds' making and inherently in the objects/others appearing to their minds. This is the law of cause and effect: the action of one's own mind that creates the effect similar to its cause. Crazy, isn't it? Whether in a war zone or on a tropical isle, on impoverished streets or in penthouse apartments, people everywhere establish a "self" that exists as nothing other than the umbrella concept over ignorant and dualistic delusions such as good/bad, this/that, here/there, you/I. People everywhere set up criteria for happiness according to the mind's conditioned response to sensory stimulation. It is in relation to such judgments that "self" is then posited: "I am this and not that; I believe this is good; therefore, that is bad." This is the illusion. This is what individuals, trapped in cyclic existence, are ignorant of.

What is achieved with the completion of the path to enlightenment? Freedom. Freedom from grasping at dream images, the cause of all suffering. Freedom from the unsatisfactory dream one has always believed to be "reality."

Chapter Three

WHO WILL WAKEN FROM THIS DREAM?

Who will waken from this endless dream of suffering
if the one trapped within its tightly woven web of sense-related
  images
does not exist beyond imaginary boundaries?

What is there to keep the one attached
and looking for the cause of happiness within the dream,
Except the heavy shroud of ignorance that obscures them while they
  sleep?

Cloaked within the misery of their brilliant happiness,
Ignorant of the nature of their shifting fortunes,
What will ever be the cause of their awakening
  when there is still no thought to rise?

When will they ever grow aware of the illusion
and, one straining finger at a time give up their frightened hold,
  and go beyond?
Who will rise from their weary dreaming when you finally waken
  from the dream?

*H*ave you ever dreamt and forgotten you were dreaming? Remember some time when you fell asleep and got lost within the dream? Your mind entered into the "self" of the dream and completely forgot that it was just a dream. Remember how it felt? Remember how your dream self grasped with longing or fear at the mere appearances of your own mind's creation? Remember how, while you were trapped in the dream, it seemed *so* real? Do you remember that? In fact, the self of the dream believed the dream to be "reality." How would the self of the dream have reacted if someone had entered the dream to inform you of the true nature of the appearances before you? What would the self of the dream have thought if told that somehow you had gotten lost within the mere appearances of your own mind? What if the self of the dream knew that simply by giving up attachment to those illusions, you would create the cause to waken from the unsatisfactory conceptual network of the dream that was of the nature of suffering? How would the self of the dream have reacted? Doubtful? Frightened? Afraid of the truth? In the face of truths, what would become of the self of the dream you cherished so deeply?

As you did when you began reading this book, again watch yourself reading. Begin to generate insight into how things truly exist as you mull over the wisdom shared here. Whenever you feel fear, remember that the self does not truly exist from its own side, that there is no one inherently existing to be afraid. Also, there is nothing at all to grasp at, whether it is believed to be the cause of happiness or suffering, except the mere appearance of your own mind, so grasp neither at the loss of an illusion nor at the fear generated at the mere appearance of loss. Be calm and discipline your mind to relax. Don't allow your mind to give in to emotional blackmail at the hands of the threatened "self." Finally, if you have ever felt deep within your heart the suffering of the world around you and the futility of worldly activities to stop it, then perhaps you will remain open enough to get an inkling that this is the way to end all suffering. Because it is.

Returning to the dream analogy: Remember when you were "lost" within the dream by your own ignorance, or lack of awareness of the dreaming? While you were thus trapped, the senses of the dream self were completely involved with their objects. You felt things, smelled them, heard them, and so on. Everything seemed *so* real. The objects/others appeared to exist substantially and inherently from the side of the objects/others, and not from your own mind. Because your ignorance of the dream was so complete, the true nature of the objects/others as well as the self of that dream was completely obscured. When you finally awoke from the dream, you were shocked and probably not just a little relieved to know that it had all been "just a dream." There had been nothing to grasp at after all and no one to do the grasping—there was nothing to feel and no one to experience the sensation.

Because we truly believe there is something good, bad, or indifferent existing from the side of the objects/others or inherently in their appearances, a dualistically-oriented conceptual network is established. Just as we believe in an object separate from the mind's mere creation, we also establish something separate from (and relative to) that object that is then known as "self." We mistakenly believe that objects/others exist inherently because we are unaware of their true nature. And so, too, the self seems also to exist.

What happens when the mind believes its own appearance exists separate from its own action or from the side of the object? (1) The object appears to exist inherently and separate from the self that knows it, and (2) the self appears to exist inherently and separate from the object it knows. Every single quality-filled appearance is fabricated by the mind and, therefore, does not exist inherently from the side of the object. Ignorant of this, the self of the dream is involved in a never-ending, completely futile attempt to create from among those mere appearances a lasting cause for its happiness and freedom from the causes of suffering.

As the mind is constantly being reconditioned due to causes and conditions,[33] (1) the quality-filled appearances of the creations of the mind are constantly changing, (2) value judgments previously grasped must be constantly modified to accommodate the apparent changes in perceived qualities, and (3) what was previously believed to be the cause of one's happiness eventually will be believed to be the cause of one's suffering. Within the ignorant mind, a constant struggle is going on to hold on to mere appearances that are mistakenly believed to exist separate from the mind of the perceiver. This constant grasping for the illusory while believing in and longing for the permanence of self and objects/others is what suffering is about. Life is just a dream, and the reality within the dream is all the dream self is aware of. The mind of the dreamer has lost all awareness of the true nature of either the objects/others or the self appearing in the dream. The mind of the dreamer is conditioned to believe that every mere appearance exists from its own side, or inherently.

The mind, ignorant of the dream—which is the same as saying the consciousness that is conditioned to know the dream as the truth—creates its own illusion. The world of the dream—in which you grasp at self and objects/others—is the effect. That effect is directly similar to its cause—ignorance of the dream. It is because of this ignorance that human beings believe in their own inherent existence, separate from the mind's creation. It is because every object/other is known only as it relates to the well-being of self, and because each self believes there is something real to be gained or lost by grasping, that the "self" exerts its superiority over what appear to be "others" with the thought to gain an advantage for "self/me/mine" over "them." Every action of every living being possessing consciousness is based in ignorance of the true nature of how things really exist. This is the foundation for all that follows. This is the cause exactly similar to the effect—remaining in the suffering state of cyclic existence.

Trapped in the dream, believing that self and objects/others exist inherently, we make choices in our lives that are completely motivated by the desire to possess happiness for self/me/mine and freedom from suffering. We choose to do or come in contact with those things we believe will cause us to be happy. We choose to avoid or push away those things we believe will cause us to suffer, to be unhappy. Mostly though, we ignore

---

33. *Causes and conditions.* Causes—the sense powers, coming in contact with their conditions—the objects of the sense powers.

the vast majority of objects/others appearing in our minds that we believe have no power to affect our well-being at all. In brief, our lives are spent trying to surround our "selves" with those dream images that fit our criteria for lasting happiness and attempting to stay away from those that don't. Unfortunately, everything appearing to our minds is dependent upon our minds for its existence, and our minds are constantly changing due to causes and conditions. The result? It's like putting your hands under a water faucet and trying to hold on to the water spilling through your fingers. Although you may be able to contain some of it for a while, it won't be too long before whatever you were able to hold on to is gone the way of all the other water that passed through your hands. And it won't be very long before what seemed so important to hold on to has been surpassed by a new and, seemingly, even better idea.

How many times have you listened to music because it makes you feel good, or turned music off because it isn't nice to listen to? How many times have you picked foods at the grocery store because they make you happy, and rejected other foods because you don't like them—even the thought of having to eat them makes you unhappy? How many times have you sought out a friend because he or she is "really nice" as a contributing cause to your happiness, and turned away from your enemy because he or she is "not nice" as a contributing cause to your unhappiness? How many times do you judge one thing against another? Every time. Every single time you consider objects/others, you consider them in this way and for this reason: because you lack awareness of their true nature.

In the everyday actions above, the objects of the senses are believed to exist inherently as though those objects had an "inherent" power to affect the self. It seems that some music can make you happy, and other music will make you suffer to some degree; that some foods are tasty, others nasty; that some people are good, others bad. All qualities appear to exist inherently in objects and completely separate from the mind of the perceiver. That is the illusion, and it is the cause of all suffering.

If it is true that some piece of music can *make* you happy, then what you are saying is that the cause of happiness is inherently existing in the music, that there is some essence, soul, or spirit in the music that can affect you. That some harmonic resonance within the particular configuration of notes making up the music has the power, from its own side, to affect the listener. You are saying that *the music* can and does make you happy. By your own definition, however, if it were true that a piece of music could *cause* you to be happy or to feel good, then any individual with a level of intelligence and sensibility similar to your own would feel good and be similarly happy if he or she also heard the music. The truth is, however, that what is believed to be the cause of one person's happiness will be the cause of another's suffering, due to each individual's previous interaction with and conditioning to the objects of the sense powers in question. ⌉

A stereotypical example would go something like this: A person who has grown up with classical music will find an evening at a classical concert a lovely experience. Another person who has grown up with rock-'n'-roll might experience incredible suffering if he or she had to sit in a concert hall listening to classical music. This suffering would be no different from the suffering felt by the classically oriented individual if he or she had to spend an evening listening to rock. Obviously, what one individual believes to be the cause of happiness is another's cause of suffering. Why? Because how anything truly exists is *completely* dependent on the mind of the perceiver. ⌉

Continuing with the music analogy: If it is true that listening to some piece of music is the cause of your happiness or suffering, then it stands to reason that the longer you listen to the cause of your happiness or suffering, then the longer you will be happy or will suffer. In actuality, though, if you listen to what you believe to be the cause of your happiness long enough, it will become the cause of your suffering. Likewise, experience will tell you that the longer you listen to what previously was the cause of your suffering, the more "used" to it you will become, and what before was the cause of your suffering will, eventually, begin to appear to be the cause of your happiness.

Can music be the cause of your happiness, coming from the side of the music? No. How it will appear to exist is completely dependent on your conditioned response to sensory stimulation due to previous similar conditioning. The music is neither good, bad, nor indifferent. It is completely dependent on the mind of the perceiver for its existence. That it is even *perceived* to be music is dependent on the listener's conditioned response to sensory stimuli. Life *is* just a dream. The objects/others of the dream seem to exist inherently but, in truth, do not.

When individuals believe objects exist inherently and separately from their own minds, they believe the objects of their consideration "truly" exist as either good, bad, or indifferent, but not good and bad simultaneously. If the classically oriented individual comes in contact with the rock-oriented individual, each self in this equation angrily and igno-rantly tries to negate the "supremacy" of the other's view in order to shore up the threatened security of self/me/mine. In truth, there is no good or bad music existing inherently or separate from the mind of the perceiver, just as there is no self separate from the object—the good or bad music—to feel threatened when its concept based in ignorance of the truth is challenged.

How does the self exist? If asked to define who you are, you will start by saying, "I am this one, not that one; from here, not there; living now rather than then; relating to you and all others as either friend, enemy, or stranger." Everything you say to define who you are will be in relation to some object perceived to exist separate from the action of your own mind. There is nothing you can say that will not set up a relationship of the self to an object perceived to be separate from that self.

Yet, there is no place where you will find a self existing inherently, or an object/other existing inherently, no matter how long or how well you look. The mistaken belief that the illusory self—as well as the equally illu-sory object/other—is inherently existing is the trap within which ignorant beings are stuck. The mind itself is made up of the senses coming in con-tact with their objects and is bound to those objects due to ignorance. So all of it—the self and objects/others—exists as nothing other than its own action.

When you are thinking, "I am thinking," where is the "I" who is thinking? When you are loving, where is the "I" of "I am loving"? When you are afraid, where is the "I" of "I am afraid"? How will you ever waken from the dream if you don't question whether the mere appearances of the dream really have substance from the sides of the objects?

Where exactly am "I"? It feels like there is an "I" who is thinking, an "I" who is loving, and an "I" who is afraid. It feels like it. You assume there is an "I" really existing from the side of the object, or inherently, to do actions. If the "I" does not exist inherently, though, then there will be no subject "I" to do any action to any object. It follows that if there is no subject to do any action, then there can be no object separate from the sub-ject to be acted upon.

The Four Point Analysis

LET'S INVESTIGATE WHAT IS universally assumed to be the truth but is not. If there were actually an "I" existing to do any action, then upon close investigation, you would be able to find that "I" in one of the following four ways:

1. Inside the body
2. Separate from the body
3. Oneness with the body
4. As the part(s) of the body

If the "I" really exists as anything other than, or more than, the mere appearance of your own mind, the "I" of "I am thinking, loving, afraid," and so on will be found in one of these four ways. There is no other way that the "I" could exist if it exists "inherently." There seems to be an "I" to do things, and it seems to exist in proximity to the body. Agreed? Let's investigate.

1. *Inside the body.* There are four basic areas that can be considered to make up the inside of the body. They are (a) within the skull area, (b) within the chest area, (c) within the abdomen, and (d) within the arms and legs or the parts of the body. There are no other places that lie within the body to look for "I."

• Within the skull area. When you just think, "Where am I," there is a feeling that the "I" is located somewhere in the head area. Keep looking. "Where am I?" As you look, it seems to be within the skull area it seems it must be in the place below the bony exterior of the skull where the gray matter is located, perhaps toward the front of the skull. Looking closer and closer for the "I" of "Where am I?" you get to a more and more specific point, but the "I" is not found. Keep looking. "Where am I"? No matter how long or well you concentrate, you will not find a place or a thing that can be identified as "I."

• Within the chest area. Sometimes it seems like there is an "I" existing in the chest area, for instance, when you're in love, "I am in love with you." There is the feeling of something real and solid called "I" relating to "you," who is separate. To investigate the "I" of such an experience, recall a situation when you felt "I am so in love with you." Visualize the person you were in love with and feel yourself, once again, involved in the

43

experience. "I am so in love with you." As you think those words and visualize the experience, it will feel as though the "I" exists in a way that can be found because it is felt in the approximate center of the chest area. The "I" feels so real that, to those in love, it seems as though there is definitely an "I" loving "you," even to the point where the "I" could almost be seen by an onlooker. Upon investigation, however, the "I" will not be found existing in any place, in any way.

• Within the abdomen. At those times when you've been very afraid, there was probably a sickening feeling in the abdomen associated with "I am so afraid." At that time, the "I" seemed to be in the area of the abdomen. Recall such a time and how you felt when you were afraid. Repeat, "I am so afraid," and look for that "I" that is so afraid. Concentrate. Narrow down the area where the "I" who is so afraid seems to be emanating from. It will not matter how long or well you concentrate on the location of the "I" that is so afraid; it will elude you. Again, you will not be able to find "I" at any point, in any place, in any way within the abdomen.

• Within the parts of the body. The only areas inside the body left where the "I" might be looked for, if it exists inherently within the body, are in the parts of the body—in the arms, legs, fingers, and so on. When you look for the "I" within those parts of the body, however, you won't find it. When one has been aware of a feeling of "I," it usually felt like it could be found within either the skull, chest, or abdominal areas. Investigation within the parts of the body is done just to convince the practitioner that there is no "I" existing inherently anywhere within the parts of the body, either.

2. *Separate from the body.* The second way the "I" could exist, if it exists inherently and separate from the mind's creation, would be as separate from, but in relation to, the body that you associate with your self. However, if the "I" truly existed separate from the body, then your body could conceivably get up and walk out of the room, leaving the "I" behind. Your own mind will tell you this is simply not logical and does not happen.

3. *Oneness with the body.* The third way the "I" might exist is in oneness with, and inseparable from, the body. If that were true, however, you would lose part of the "I" if an arm or leg, or finger or toe, were lost. As this is not the case, this assumption, too, can be discounted as illogical.

4. *As the part(s) of the body*. An individual might say at this point that perhaps the "I," if it exists inherently, is just the parts of the body. If this were true, however, then the parts of the body would be called "I," not "leg," "arm," "foot," etc. As no part of the body is called "I," therefore, one can safely assume that the "I" also does not exist inherently as the part(s) of the body.

Through the practitioner's own investigation, nothing that could be identified as "I" can be found to exist inherently. If you were to decide, therefore, that there must not be an "I" existing at all, you would be making a gross error. When I say, "I am here," there is something called "I" here; it simply does not exist inherently. So then, how *does* the "I" exist? Completely dependent on the mind of the perceiver and only in relation to quality-filled objects/others. It is empty of inherent existence. That it appears to exist substantially from its own side, independent of the mind's creation, is an indication of ignorance of the true nature of the mere appearances of the dream, or ignorance of the action of your own mind.

In fact, to those trapped within the appearances of the mind, the "I" seems so real that even after proof that no "I" exists from its own side separate from the mind's creation, the blanket of ignorance has already begun to close over that insight once again, obscuring the truth from view. At this very moment, could you repeat without major effort, the very simple words of logic of the four point analysis that proved the "I" does not exist inherently and, while so doing, guide your mind through the meditation to its conclusion again? This is what it means to "practice," to begin the practice that is the path to enlightenment.

Chapter Four

NOTHING BUT SUFFERING

When the self of the dream grasps at the objects/others of the dream to secure happiness and freedom from suffering, believing the two to be "real" and separate from the mind's action, there is nothing but suffering.

*T*he one thing no living being wants is to suffer. Even the mere mention of suffering *causes* suffering by calling to mind the one thing all living beings spend their lives attempting to escape. For this reason it takes great courage and a positive mind to explore the true nature of suffering in order to eliminate its cause. This book is for those who are tired of the suffering, their own as well as that of others. It is for those who are able to understand that the answers to difficult questions will probably not be easy. Finally, it is for those who are not caught up in any of the "quick fixes" of worldly paths that, at best, only temporarily change the appearance of suffering.

Buddhism *is* the path to enlightenment. Nothing else. It is a clearly defined step-by-step path to the elimination of the root cause of all suffering[34] through the generation of the wisdom mind of enlightenment.

What is the root cause of all suffering? Ignorance. Ignorance of the true nature of things. Its opposite is the wisdom mind of enlightenment that is freed from the delusions that are based in a mistaken way of knowing "things."

This ignorance is not the worldly concept associated with a lack of schooling, or an unsophisticated way of dealing with the world around

---

34. *The root cause of all suffering.* Ignorance of how things truly exist is the cause for every perception of every living being trapped within the mere appearances of his or her mind. It is like the roots of a mighty tree that nourish and maintain every single leaf of its magnificence.

you. The ignorance that is the cause of *all* suffering referred to here is the mental environment of those trapped in cyclic existence. Based on a faulty premise, all conceptual constructs built within that environment are similarly mistaken. The mind that is unaware of the fault can be said to be "ignorant of the truth," deluded as to the true nature of things.

What is the basic faulty premise that totally obscures the truth and causes us to be trapped in the suffering state of cyclic existence? It is that "things" exist inherently in their own right and are something more than—or other than—the mere appearances of the mind's own making. The umbrella concept "self" is defined by and dependent on its supporting delusions that are constructed within the faulty premise of the mental environment. That an inherently existent self is believed in, and nurtured as the primary concern of individuals, is the telltale indicator of ignorance.

One individual caught in cyclic existence is no less ignorant than any other, although one may be closer to breaking out of the conceptual prison due to his or her practice of the path to enlightenment. It is not until a living being of human form is actually freed from belief in an inherently existent self, however, that he or she will have generated the wisdom understanding the true nature of things and be enlightened.

Why is the human form essential for enlightenment? People mistakenly believe that living beings other than humans can be enlightened. Only in the human form—in its level of awareness—is it possible to consciously practice morality and distinguish between virtuous and non-virtuous conduct. In other forms, such as bird, mammal, fish, reptile, amphibian, and insect, response to sensory stimuli is of a primary conditioned type. Such beings (although one may appear to be basically more peaceful, or less aggressive, or having greater intelligence than another) generally do little more than react to changes in the immediate environment based on the need to ensure the safety and well-being of self and what that self calls "mine." Of course, many humans also operate on this basic level.

A "human" being, however, who has (1) a conscious thought to not harm any living being, (2) a wish to be virtuous rather than non-virtuous, as well as (3) a sweeping thought to be of benefit to others less fortunate has created the cause to do just that by becoming enlightened. On the highest level, to be of ultimate and lasting benefit to others means to develop the wisdom that understands how things truly exist, to give up attachment to the delusions based in self and objects/others, to be enlightened, and then help those receptive few who are still trapped within the appearance of their minds to get out so that they, too, can help those still trapped.

The path to enlightenment is about understanding how the mind is conditioned from countless lifetimes of ignorance to believe, without a doubt, that there is a self separate from "others/objects" and that it can be affected by them. When you are truly sick and tired—*finished*—with suffering, and renounce all attachment to it, then you will begin to do the very difficult work of disciplining your mind to give up attachment to the delusions that cause the suffering. All suffering is caused by grasping at self and objects/others as though they exist separate from your own mind. They don't. By eliminating the delusions step by single step, the most fortunate practitioner generates the wisdom understanding the true nature of things. Through the elimination of the delusions that bind him or her to cyclic existence, combined with a most skillful practice, the practitioner will be enlightened: freed from the gross delusions that bind one to the suffering state of cyclic existence, having become liberated from belief in an inherently existent self.

The remedy for suffering ascribed to by the more thoughtful and strong-minded people in the world today is cultivation of a positive attitude. Unfortunately, this is like a very leaky bandage on a gaping wound. Everything is under control until just a bit too much stress is placed on the wound and it suddenly begins bleeding profusely, or festers quietly, slowly undermining the general sense of health and well-being. The mind is indeed the fabricator of all it sees and knows. For this reason, a skillful individual, rather than merely "masking" the appearance of suffering with a positive attitude, can turn that appearance of suffering into the tool needed to eliminate its root cause.

Two questions come to mind: (1) Why doesn't the one with such sensitivity to the creative nature of his or her own mind use that creative mind, not to create a new and more acceptable drama (be it labeled "good" or "bad") but to get to the root of the real problem and eliminate its cause? (2) How is it possible to observe the gross and rampant suffering of the entire world, through the media as well as in one's more immediate milieu, and pretend it is acceptable?

The level of existence called the suffering state of cyclic existence is dependent on the ignorance of the living beings trapped in it for its continuation. This suffering state is nothing more or less than the level of mind/existence of those trapped therein. Who is trapped? Those ignorant of the true nature of the self who, therefore, grasp at the gross delusions upon which the concept "self" is posited like a label. Cyclic existence is a suffering state of existence because whenever there is belief in "self," then there is "other." Belief in the inherent existence of such duality is the motivating force behind every action of every individual trapped in cyclic existence. The existence of both self and objects/others is dependent on the mind of the perceiver but is mistakenly believed to exist inherently, or from the side of the object. The causes of happiness and suffering are similarly believed to exist from the side of objects. Individuals, due to previous conditioned responses to sensory stimuli, who are ignorant or unaware of how both truly exist posit the cause of happiness and suffering. Believing happiness and suffering also exist separate from their own conceptual network, they grasp to possess the one and grasp to be freed from the other. In actuality, there is nothing at all to grasp at except the mere appearance of mind. Just as quickly as the mind manufactures an appearance, the ignorant machine, like a greedy kitten, laps it up believing it to be the cause of happiness. The ignorant machine grasps to possess happiness and freedom from suffering in order to secure "self," which is mistakenly believed to exist inherently and separate from objects/others. Over and over, over and over, like a locomotive traveling at break-neck speed, just as quickly as the mind manufactures an appearance, it is grasped at as "real."

Why is the duality of self and objects/others so dangerous? Because the self, from its self-centered relationship to objects/others, always presupposes superiority over the object/other of its consideration. Ultimately, the "self" promotes and protects that which it calls its own and does not promote or protect "other." What the self considers its own includes not only particular living beings and personal possessions but also ideas of good and bad, as well as the judgments of right and wrong that those self-centered ideas foment. In order to protect "self," the benefit accrued to self/me/mine will always be at the expense of "others." This leads to a more and more gross form of giving harm to living beings, either through deprivation of materials (of the body, speech, and/or the mind) that would aid the other or through outright aggression. This seeming duality of self and other—the cause of all wars, all problems, all suffering in the world—is nothing other than the illusory appearance of the dream that unenlightened beings are unaware they are trapped within. Ignorance of the nature of the mere appearances of the mind is the cause for beings trapped within that deluded level of mind to believe in the inherent existence of a self and objects/others.

⎣The Buddhist path to enlightenment is the practice toward the self-less state based in wisdom. How does it differ from the worldly concept of selflessness? In the world, when a selfless act is performed by an individual who is ignorant of the true nature of the self, the individual doing the act of charity, for instance, in the very doing establishes the self in relation to its object: "*I* am going to give this to *you*," or "*I* am going to do this for *them*."

In the worldly version of a selfless act, "self" is always posited in relation to "other," thereby reaffirming the dualistic orientation of the ignorant mind. A "self" is believed to be existing inherently to do the act of giving to the other. The activity of the charity, although intended to benefit the other, is, due to the ignorance of the giver, still completely related to self and all that that implies. To the worldly way of thinking, the act of giving is selfless because the intention of the giver is for the profit to accrue to the other.⎦

⎣The enlightened view, however, is that any action done on the mistaken premise of an inherently existent self and other is not "selfless" at all but is still an ignorant and self-centered pursuit that actually establishes "self" as this or that, separate from "other." Whatever one does, if it is not done with the conscious thought that there is no self existing separate from the mind to do any action for objects/others (which also do not exist separate from the mind), then the action is "self"-centered. All objects/others are known as they are mistakenly believed to relate to the well-being of that "self." In this way, the selfless act of one who is ignorant, although based in the thought to be of benefit to "other," becomes another cause for the individual to remain within the cycle of existence. It is nothing other than the level of mind of one trapped within the dream due to lack of awareness of the true nature of every one of its mere appearances.⎦

Let's talk some more about the self and how it really exists. Because it can be proved that there is no self existing from the side of the object—or inherently, or as anything more than the umbrella concept over an extensive series of gross delusions—you might then carelessly assume that there is no self existing at all. As was said before, this is absolutely incorrect and is what is referred to as nihilism. Be very careful about this.

How the self truly exists is dependent on the mind of the perceiver; there is an appearance of "self" within the dream. For instance, as you read this you can say, "I am reading this." If you think that there is no inherently existing "I" to do anything and, therefore, there is no "I" reading this, then you just compound the hallucination. "I am reading this." There is the *feeling* of an "I" who is reading this. It is *this* "I"—empty of inherent existence—that is how the "I" truly exists: dependent on the mind of the perceiver.

The extreme opposite of nihilism is eternalism. This is the other subtle shift in truth whereby the practitioner carelessly assumes that if there is an "I" reading this, then there must also be some "essence" of self, what is often referred to as soul or spirit, that must travel from death to rebirth. This is the common error of beings trapped in cyclic existence. The consciousness is actually conditioned to mistakenly believe that there is a permanent essence or some kind of a static and never-changing entity existing separate from, but in relation to, "objects/others." This mistaken belief is reinforced when the ignorant mind also believes objects/others have a nature that is essentially permanent.

Until enlightenment, when the practitioner has given up attachment to the illusion by generating the wisdom understanding how things truly exist, he or she will bounce back and forth between the two extremes—grasping at the concepts of an inherently existent self (eternalism), and of "nothing" or no-self (nihilism). It is through the elimination of the delusions upon which "self" is merely posited, and cultivation of wisdom understanding how things truly exist, that the distance between the two extremes lessens until finally, when enlightened, the gap has been eliminated and the mind sits firmly in the perfect view freed from attachment to the extremes.[35] Don't be disheartened by your practice and please don't waste any more time denigrating yourself for *the mere appearance* of your failure to find this middle ground yet. This is the path. There is no failure. It is a definition, a searching, a redefining over and over, countless times. It does not *just* happen.

The path is like this: "I" am here now. "I" listen to wisdom teachings and "I" practice. There is some small problem in "my" life. In order

---

35. *Liberation from belief in an inherently existent self.* At enlightenment, the practitioner has a direct realization of emptiness wherein the mind is inseparable from its object, having given up attachment to the delusions upon which self was merely labeled and the dualistic orientation of the mind based in ignorance.

to give up the suffering associated with *the mere* "I," consider well how the "I" that is suffering truly exists, as well as the nature of the existence of the object/other of that suffering. Through such introspection, the desire[36] upon which the self had precipitated its suffering is abandoned. You abandon the object of your desire by cultivating the intellectual understanding that how "it" truly existed was dependent on your mind. Simultaneously, insight into the true nature of the "I" that is suffering is cultivated. Having understood the illusory nature of every element of the suffering, you renounce attachment to the "I" that desired, as well as the "object" of that desire, understanding both to be illusions created by your mind. By giving up attachment to the appearance of that particular delusion, you have actually destroyed the seed imprinted on the consciousness that caused the ignorant mind to empower both the object and the self as it related to that object. This is the practice called the Buddhist path to enlightenment.

By dealing with each and every appearance of suffering or of unsatisfactoriness as it is encountered, you will eventually eliminate the gross delusions, which are the bases for the label "self" and which are the causes for the suffering state of cyclic existence. "The path" is this process of becoming aware of, and then giving up, attachment to the mere appearances of the mind. When the gross delusions that support the umbrella concept "self" are eventually eliminated, then you will give up attachment to the dream.

The more you contemplate intensely exactly who the "I" is of "I am this," or what exactly is "good," or how any thing can "make me happy," the closer you will come to being freed from the dualistic view of self and objects/others. When you are freed from belief in the inherent existence of the objects/others supporting self, then you will give up attachment to self

---

36. *Desire.* Beings trapped in the appearance of their own minds suffer because the mistakenly apprehended "self" desires to possess a happiness freed from suffering. This desire, no matter what the object of one's consideration, will take one or more of four forms: (1) a wish for praise, not criticism; (2) a wish for gain, not loss; (3) a wish for kind words, not unkind words; (4) a wish to be happy, not unhappy. These are the eight overriding concerns of the worldly who seek happiness for self/me/mine. Because of these desires or wishes based in ignorance of how things truly exist, such beings suffer when deprived of the objects of their desire. To end suffering, abandon desire. Anytime you suffer, determine which of these four things is not being fulfilled as you had hoped. Then meditate on the nature of that object/other and the self suffering and give up attachment to the mere appearance of your mind. This will end your suffering and, having given up attachment to a delusion by generating insight into how it really existed, that delusion is removed from the consciousness.

and actually transcend the suffering state of cyclic existence, having eliminated its cause.

What is beyond? Freedom from the suffering caused when the mind mistakenly believes there is a self separate from objects/others that have the power to affect the happiness of self. What difference does it make? Freedom from cyclic existence, having generated the wisdom mind of enlightenment, allows you finally to be of ultimate and lasting benefit to others who seem to be suffering so much within the dream. Not until you have followed the path to its end and eliminated the delusions that bind you to cyclic existence are you qualified to teach others the way out. With the motivation to be of benefit to others, and then doing all actions "for others" in order to accomplish this end, you actually cause yourself to be freed. It happens like this: in order to practice loving-kindness to others, you must give up attachment to self and the objects/others that cause you to give harm to others with actions of your body, speech, and mind. That is the path to the enlightened state.

Why is it important for a healthy person to think deeply about the nature of suffering, thereby causing him- or herself to suffer? Because until you come to feel deep within your heart, inseparable from your very core, the unsatisfactory nature of this life, then you will not be able to generate a wish profound enough to overcome the obstacles to eliminate the root cause of that suffering, ignorance. Only by recognizing and generating an interest in eliminating suffering from life—your own but mostly that of others—will you commit your life to learn that monster's habits and to cultivate the skills necessary to eliminate it completely, once and for all. While it is true your own life would be better as a result of the elimination of the enemy, like a noble warrior you prepare to sacrifice your life for the greater good, thinking it would be a worthwhile use of a precious and otherwise worldly life. With an almost ecstatic disregard for your own suffering, and devotion to saving the "others" from theirs, you live your purposeful life quietly.

Only an individual who has felt the suffering in the world around would look beyond the gross operative level of the world for its ultimate cause. All enlightened teachings of the path to enlightenment must therefore begin with a discussion of suffering, and its cause. The practice that leads to the generation of a mind of enlightenment culminates with the complete elimination of ignorance.

What is suffering? In order to feel happy in the midst of suffering, most people, when asked this question, will conjure up vague images of people dying from starvation, perhaps continents away, flies crawling across their faces, of death camps in other times or other places. The suffering brought to mind by the question is very distant from the happiness one tries so hard to secure in this life.

"...but I don't suffer!"

Everywhere in this world, people set up boundaries of acceptable circumstances for life within which they call themselves happy. Everywhere—from the smiling square-faced porters of the Himalayas to Wall Street brokers, from the black women of the Ivory Coast to the Chinese-conqueror peasants of Tibet, from the affluent families of auto executives in suburban Detroit to the rough-handed wool shearers of New Zealand, *everyone*—in order not to suffer—has established a set of criteria for happiness and, as long as they stay within what is determined to be acceptable, call themselves "happy." When other circumstances intrude, as they do, that were not previously factored into the "happiness plan," then suffering occurs. If the suffering goes on long enough, those individuals will renounce attachment to the previous concept upon which their happiness depended, change the boundary of what is acceptable, and once again, label themselves "happy." The previously unacceptable will be modified to be acceptable through the need of the self to secure happiness and freedom from suffering. It is so obvious that happiness is dependent on the mind of the perceiver, and yet everyone believes "happiness" is real and attainable from objects/others that are believed to be separate from their own minds.

How does the mind actually generate the appearance of happiness? When the self of the dream is pushed to change by its oneness with the causes of suffering and its inability to free itself from those causes, it amends the criteria for happiness to include portions of the previous operative causes of suffering. Having established new parameters for happiness that include the immediate past causes of suffering, the self grasps at the causes of happiness as though they were real and, just like that, the self ignorantly feels "happy" since the criteria for happiness have now been met.

After times of great upheaval and catharsis or change, the self often feels tired but renewed, having come through a great trial. At such times people often say they were forced to change and, almost always, that the change was "for the better." Older but wiser, as the saying goes. This is what living beings do. The fortunate few who experience great trials in their lives that force them to modify their existing criteria for happiness in order to eliminate the perceived cause of their suffering feel better for the experience and more free since they changed the preexisting static conceptual network that supported the self before. As rewarding as the experience seems, how often have you met people who willingly provoked a situation within their own minds for the express purpose of creating the opportunity to change their conceptual network? Just the thought of changing anything, whether the individual is consciously aware of the need for change or not, is enough to cause the individual to begin a mental process of ignoring the problem—or denying it.

For instance, there was an attractive woman in her early forties whose heart's desire was to be ordained.[37] The only thing standing in her way was that she could not stand the thought of having her head shaved and being bald. It was her habit as a laywoman to put henna and other dyes on her hair to enhance its beauty and disguise the signs of aging. In her self-consciousness, which she believed was secured by her outer appearance, she felt she would be "nothing" without her hair or, at the least, "ugly." So, for years she had secretly yearned to take the vows of ordination, but could not.

It was surprising how very self-conscious she was. Even though she only wore inexpensive T-shirts and skirts, it was obvious after listening to her that she took great care to coordinate her daily ensemble in order to put her "in the best light." It was my suggestion to her that, if she truly wanted to be ordained, then she should recondition her mind to get around the first level of obstacles to ordination, which includes the hair. Ways to do that might include wearing unmatched socks one day, or purposely wearing a T-shirt that did not quite fit her concept of "perfect." In those slight ways (which certainly no one would easily notice), she would be forced to confront the self that was suffering so much as a result. *That* would be her opportunity to meditate on the true nature of both the object/other (whether it was the "off" clothing or another person's perceived reaction to that clothing) of the suffering, as well as the self feeling

---

37. *Ordained.* A detailed discussion of the lifestyles and roles of lay and ordained practitioners follows in chapter six.

such discomfort. The obstacle was greater than her wish to be ordained, however, and so she did nothing and did not get ordained. Of course, until she is able give up such attachments (the attachment was not to the clothes but to the eight worldly desires for: gain, not loss; happiness, not unhappiness; praise, not criticism; kind words, not unkind words), she is not qualified to be ordained.

In the world, when things get "too difficult," individuals feel they are "going crazy" and generally seek guidance from one of three avenues: from their friends, from psychologists or psychiatrists or from psychics or mystics. Whether friend, professional, or mystic, these "others" are sought out to help reestablish and reinforce the sense of "self" as it exists in relation to the world. The professional guides the client through a process of "resocialization," by which the self is helped to fit better into the world from which he or she feels alienated. Mystics and psychics, on the other hand, can treat their clients in one of two ways. First, they can guide them through a process meant to either reestablish or to sever a bond with the "powers" greater than the self that are believed to be affecting the client's well-being. Second, they can act as channels, establishing a connection to "those powers." These are the worldly ways in which individuals commonly seek to alleviate the fears associated with the relationship of the self to objects/others. Other methods with similarly temporary benefits include the use of drugs, food, sex, and so on.

It takes the greatest courage to calmly marshal your mind to investigate its own appearance. It is not a dramatic process; there is no audience. It is not exciting, because there is a feeling that there is some reason not to applaud. To begin to create the wish to be freed from your ignorance and to generate wisdom is hard and solitary work, and the end product of that work can be known only to the mind involved in the work. It takes great skill to attain the goal without engaging the superior force of your ignorant mind in battle. It takes a love for others, of the most profoundly kind and generous nature, to keep the angry self of your ignorant mind from rising up to relate to objects/others in self-centered judgment. It takes modesty of spirit and maturity to follow through to the goal without quitting. It takes a really good mind to generate insights into its own workings. The path to enlightenment is not, in any way, how you maintain the status quo of cyclic existence.

For that single reason—*that the path to enlightenment is not, in any way, about maintaining the status quo of cyclic existence*—it is not logical to assume that an enlightened being would tell ignorant beings that everything they're doing is "just fine," or "okay." [The ignorant do not need an enlightened being to help them feel secure in their suffering. They need the enlightened being to shake them from their lethargy and confusion with the brilliant logic that is based in wisdom.]

The very truth of the wisdom teaching regarding the true nature of the self can only frighten someone who is thoroughly conditioned to believe in its inherent existence. However, the *fear* experienced by the novice practitioner upon listening to a teaching on the four point analysis, for instance, is the sure sign that the truth has hit its mark. Of course, to eliminate that fear, the novice must immediately begin the practice that is the path by meditation on the empty nature of the self experiencing the fear.

The fact that an enlightened teacher teaches the way out that he or she followed before indicates there is something to be changed, and some good reason to change it. And, as we all know, change—even just *the thought of the possibility* of change—can throw the mind that needs to change for a loop. It is only by establishing the need for change that change can begin. And it is the role of the enlightened teacher to urge living beings to practice now, not later, since life is short at best.

[Compounding the teacher's problem of motivating students to stop procrastinating and practice *now,* where the focus is on "life is short," the imminency of death has to head up the discussion.]Often, that's all it takes for the "denial buttons" to click in as the heels drag. These are not the kind of thoughts that make for great feelings of eternal security. Whether or not living beings actually practice is then completely dependent on their level of mind. Taking complete responsibility for your own happiness, as well as that of others, is a burden few can accept. Finally, because [it is of utmost importance that a code of behavior based in strictest morality be instituted by the sincere practitioner,]the enlightened teacher will urge the practitioner to practice just as the teacher had done before.

The entire practice, no matter what form it may take, is geared toward giving the practitioner opportunities to better understand the nature of how things exist. At first, it is difficult to get in touch with the notion at all that how things appear before you is not because of any qualities inherent in objects. [Until enlightenment, when all the gross delusions have been put to rest, you, the practitioner, must constantly question the nature of the images—physical, emotional, and mentally fabricated for the purpose of meditation—appearing to your mind.]

Although any appearance of the mind or "object" can be used to illustrate the point that no appearance exists separate from the mind of the perceiver, the following is a very simple one: If a red apple is held up and one hundred people are asked to list its qualities, there will be one hundred different views of the same object. If it is "the truth" that the apple exists inherently, then all individuals with similar sensory abilities and intelligence will "know," or perceive, the same object. But, in fact, some people will find the color lovely; others will find it mediocre. Some will think it sweet to the taste; others, tart. Some will think it smells good; others might find the smell cloying. Some will find the shape pleasing; others, lopsided. Some will want the apple; others will not want it. Because of what they see, some will feel sufficiently empowered to actually purchase some apples of their own in order to be happy by experiencing something believed to be "good," while others will decide definitely not to buy any apples today.

You might now say that the fact that one hundred different people "know" the apple in one hundred different ways is no indication that the object does not exist inherently. You might then say that, besides those "opinions," there is an object existing inherently. In fact, at whatever level the object is investigated, its qualities will be known according to the conditioned response of the mind of the perceiver. For instance, the color, the shape, and the texture all exist only according to the mind of the perceiver, and each perceiver will, therefore, "know" it as an object different from that known by another perceiver. Each perceiver will also believe his or her "view" of the object is the only correct one. Go beyond the appearance of the gross object to even its level of existence on the cellular or atomic level and analyze its nature. Whatever level the individual investigates, whatever the object of investigation, analysis will prove the subject of investigation to be empty of inherent existence—ultimately dependent on the mind of the perceiver for its existence.

How does any simple object like this "apple" truly exist? Dependent on the mind of the perceiver. There is absolutely nothing "good or bad," "this or that," "you or I" about that object. There is nothing at all called "apple" existing inherently, or separate from the mind of the perceiver. What is being perceived is the mere appearance of the mind, which has been previously conditioned by a particular configuration of sensory stimuli. Every single perceived quality of every object exists completely dependent on, and inseparable from, the conditioned response of the mind of the perceiver to sensory stimuli. If there is nothing to grasp at *except* the mere appearance of your own mind, then grasping at such an illusion as "real" would fit into the definition of foolishness, wouldn't it?

The point is this. If you determine that an apple will make you happy, then being deprived of the apple will cause you to suffer. The happiness is dependent on grasping at qualities mistakenly believed to exist inherently in the object. Those qualities, however, were manufactured by and posited on the merely labeled "apple" by your own mind. Having seen "apple"—which, due to causes and conditions, fit your current criteria for happiness—the "I" will suffer when denied what is believed to be the cause of its happiness. The "I" that is suffering is as illusory and dependent on the mind for its existence as the apple or any other appearance. It exists only in relation to, like a foil for, objects/others. Think of it this way. Every image appearing to your mind right now is the mirror reflection of your mind due to conditioning and does not exist on an level separate from the mind's creation. "What?" your mind cries in protest.

Choose an object, any object, and do the four point analysis in order to look for the "essence" or soul or self (or however you are used to referring to it) of that object. An apple, for instance. If there is truly an apple existing from the side of the object, as was the case with our analysis of "self," we should be able to find it in one of four ways:

1. *Inside the object*. If you look within the apple for its "essence," you will find the meat of the apple, not the apple. If you look within the meat of the apple for the apple's "essence," from the cellular level to the atomic and beyond, this thing called "apple" will not be found.

2. *Separate from the object*. If the "apple" exists separate from its appearance somehow, then when the appearance is eaten, "apple" would be left behind, without an appearance.

3. *Oneness with the object*. If the essence of "apple" was oneness with the object, then, if you took a bite of the object, the object would have lost some of its "essence," thereby no longer being "essentially" apple.

4. *As the parts of the object*. If the apple was simply the various parts of the apple—the stem, skin, meat, core, and seeds—then those parts would rightfully be named "apple," rather than "stem," "skin," "meat," "core,"

and "seeds." Since "an apple," however, is not the correct label for the parts, "apple" cannot be found in that way, either.

Yet, there is an apple sitting on the table and soon you'll eat it. How does it truly exist? It is completely created by and dependent on the mind of the perceiver for its existence, in no way existing separate from that mind. Look at the parts of the apple in similar fashion. The same thing will be discovered. For instance, is there "really" a stem coming from the side of the object, or existing inherently? Enter in the four point analysis. You will find that "stem" is not inside the appearance somewhere, nor is it separate from the appearance, nor is it oneness with the appearance, nor is it its parts. Yet, there is a stem from which the apple dangles from the tree. How does it exist, in truth? What is its true nature? Its nature is completely dependent on the mind of the perceiver; it is empty of inherent existence.

No matter what "it" might be, "it" cannot be found in any way separate from your mind. You will find that the more you define what it is you are looking for, the more it will evade detection. You will formulate one new concept after another in your attempt to discover the object's "essence," and the concepts themselves will be nothing other than the appearance of your own mind, ad infinitum. There is nothing except the appearance of your own mind existing. So, investigate the nature of the mind and of the senses that apprehend objects. Continue like this not just once but over and over and over and over until you understand, until you're enlightened, and know from firsthand experience that, having wakened from the dream, life *is* just a dream.

Before going any further with our discussion on the illusory nature of suffering and its cause, ignorance, let's look more deeply into the setup of the conceptual network that individuals trapped in cyclic existence call their world. To those trapped within cyclic existence, the world around seems completely separate from their minds. It seems like "I" am really here and inherently existent. To the ignorant, the "I" is like the hub of a wheel around which all objects/others circle. What one pays attention to are those things that seem more important and either self-securing or threatening, rather than to the far greater number of impressions of objects/others that one has not previously determined to affect one's happiness substantially. Those objects/others, then, are ignored. Just as your own logic led you to understand that how the tree or the music or the apple in previous examples truly existed was completely dependent on the conditioned response of the mind of the one looking at it, so does every object/other exist, including self. Everything perceived exists as a mirror image of the conditioned response of the mind of the one doing the looking.

The mistaken conceptual network, by which ignorant individuals define "self," is belief in the inherent existence of the qualities of objects/others that are completely generated by the mind. If asked, "Who are you?" you would define your "self" by relating it to objects/others believed to exist separate from your own mind. "I am so and so, son/daughter of so and so; I believe this is good and this bad; this is my friend; I am the one who lives in this house," and so on. Beings caught in the prison of their conceptual network, ignorant of the true nature of things, define what is mistakenly believed to be an inherently existing self in relation to what also mistakenly appears to them to be inherently existent quality-filled objects/others. Unaware of the action of their own minds, living beings then grasp at that self and objects/others in order to secure happiness and freedom from suffering. Because of a total lack of awareness, or ignorance, of how things truly exist, we unwittingly continue to create the cause to cycle in the suffering state of existence.

Two things have to happen for you to suffer. (1) You have to believe there is a "self" existing on its own or inherently, which can be made to suffer and, thereby, (2) establish the separateness of objects/others that are mistakenly believed to have the power to affect "self." In this way the dualistic relationship of that self to those mere appearances is sealed. Suffering is inseparable from ignorance, as it exists only in dependence on it, and is synonymous with it. It is the action of the ignorant mind (or karma) that causes suffering.

Objects/others operate as the network or field of experience upon which "self" establishes the boundaries that determine its experience of happiness or suffering. As shown before, what was previously determined to be a cause of suffering, if experienced long enough, will become acceptable through a combination of reconditioning and your wish not to suffer. So how does any object appearing to the mind actually exist—whether it be the table, the sky, the friend, the enemy, suffering, or happiness? Dependent on the mind of the perceiver, due to conditioning from previous similar sensory stimulation.

This sounds simple enough. The truth is most important for those who are sick and tired of suffering, not only their own suffering but that of others as well. The truth is most important to those who are tired of being manipulated by the objects/others of this life. By simply giving up attachment to what is nothing more than the mere appearance of your own mind's creation, you are freed from the suffering associated with the delusion that grasps at the appearance as "real." The suffering state of cyclic existence is other than the intricate conceptual network constructed by the ignorant minds of those caught in the web of their own making. Beings trapped in cyclic existence are inseparable from the illusion and must, therefore, receive wisdom teachings from an enlightened being—whether those teachings are received at the feet of the enlightened being or through the teachings left behind.

A question might arise in the mind of the thoughtful reader that, if in fact this level of existence is dependent on ignorance, then how is it that an enlightened being can teach within it? That is a good question, and the answer necessitates a brief discussion on enlightenment. There are two levels of enlightenment: the first is referred to as the blissful state of lower nirvana; the second is the fully enlightened state referred to as the peace of nirvana.

With attainment of the first, the gross delusions supporting belief in an inherently existent self are eliminated. The state of lower nirvana is reached following the highest level meditation, which leads the meditator to cause the death process to begin and the consciousness to split free from the physical support of the body. The only way to accomplish this in a *healthy* body is through the most intense concentration[38] combined with the highest level practice of the principal aspects of the path: (1) renunciation—of the appearances of the mind—through (2) wisdom—the cultivation of insight into their "true" nature—combined with (3) bodhicitta—the compelling wish to be enlightened only in order to be of benefit to others. Having caused the consciousness to split free from the physical support of the body, the meditator "goes beyond" to a state beyond knowing or knower. When the very subtle mind based in wisdom begins operating again, it is in direct contact with its object and is of a very blissful nature. Due to the meditator's compelling motivation "to be of benefit to others," the mind grows more and more gross until, at the very moment the senses can perceive the level of existence based in ignorance, the consciousness is once again reinstated on the physical support of the body. This enlightened

---

38. This process is explained in detail in the following chapters.

being has transcended the gross delusions that bound him or her to cyclic existence by achieving the blissful state of lower nirvana.[39]

With the wisdom thus generated, the subtle delusions become apparent and are eliminated through the analysis of the enlightened mind that is inseparable from the truth. When the physical body of the enlightened being degenerates in death, the consciousness finally splits free from the physical support of the body—as even the subtle imprints of delusion have been removed from the consciousness—and there is nothing that would empower the consciousness to take a form again. That level of existence which is "completely gone beyond" is what is referred to as the peace of nirvana.]

The enlightened being teaches those who have not yet transcended cyclic existence by sharing the complete and correct path through precise information on the specific points of the practice that must be followed if the practitioner is going to reach the goal.[40] It is only through the correct practice of the path as taught by the enlightened being, and the changes that will be apparent to the mind of the student, that the student will develop faith in the perfection of the teachings and the teacher, and learn,

---

39. *This is the beginning of what is referred to as the "pure grounds,"* which begin with the eighth ground, or *bhumi,* as taught by scholars. Words such as "pure" and "perfect" always refer to a wisdom-based level of mind of one who is enlightened. When the pure grounds—eight through ten—of the bhumis are completed, the omniscient state of the Buddha is attained. The two "extra" levels sometimes alluded to usually symbolize the complete path followed to enlightenment: the first that culminates in achievement of the blissful state of lower nirvana; the second that culminates with the elimination of the subtle delusions.

40. *The teachings of the path to enlightenment are very precise.* Although there is nothing at all "real" about the practice that is the path, the teachings are instructions on how to generate the various levels of mind that are the path and deal with the specific actions you must take in order to put your mind in various situations that cause the "self" to feel insecure. When the conceptual network supporting the self is threatened and you suffer as a result, you then have the opportunity to enter into a meditation of the nature of the self and the object of the suffering that leads to renunciation of attachment to the mind's object and, thereby, the elimination of delusion. Through a methodical practice like this, the myriad delusions supporting self are eliminated.

Ignorant practitioners are caught in the web woven by their own ignorance and so, unfortunately, have a tendency to believe that "they know better" how to follow the path and so reinterpret the teachings according to their very worldly understandings. It is common today to hear practitioners say that the teachings of the enlightened being referred to as Shakyamuni Buddha, who lived more than 2,500 years ago, are not relevant at this time. That is not a reflection on the quality of the teachings of an enlightened being, that is simply a reflection of the level of mind of the practitioner. This "rationale" is often used to explain why today's ordained practitioners are too often found to be working at lay jobs for money, engaging in sexual relationships and chitchat over dinner, and are disrobing in record numbers.

beyond any doubt, the necessity to step precisely in the footsteps of the teacher.

Until the enlightened being enters the peace of nirvana, he or she will teach, or attempt to teach, those still caught within the ignorance of their minds who create sufficient cause to hear the teachings. Why does sufficient cause have to be created? Because if the potential student is not completely ready, having felt a compelling need to hear the teachings of the enlightened being, then the student will only find fault with the enlightened teacher and will be not at all able to follow the path taught. What constitutes sufficient cause? It varies with the individual, his or her sincerity, and other factors. Basically, sufficient cause is created through repeated polite, dignified, and formal requests for teachings by individuals who are humble and modest in their quest. Offerings should be made, the finest offering being that of the supplicant's practice. Following any teaching, with joy at having received what was so earnestly requested, the teacher should be similarly thanked for the information given and the insights shared.

Following the enlightened being's passing into nirvana, the enlightened teachings will be personified by those few genuine practitioners who, by living within the vows of ordination, commit their entire lives to becoming enlightened in that lifetime. Those true practitioners of the highest path to enlightenment will follow the path, step by step, as it was laid out in those teachings by the enlightened teacher who went before. *They* are the true lineage holders of the teachings of the Buddha's path to enlightenment, *not* the ones who have learned the words and merely passed them on through the generations as philosophical theory, devoid of empirical method.

Cyclic existence does not exist separate from the ignorant level of mind. It is the conditioned imprints of the consciousness that empower objects/others appearing in the dream to be believed to be good, bad, or indifferent. It is from this complete illusion that the "self" of the dream grasps to procure happiness and freedom from suffering for self/me/mine. It is because of the ignorant action of their own minds that living beings remain caught within the tangled web of ignorance that only their minds know how to weave.

Chapter Five

IN THE FIELD OF THE PERFECTIONS

Neither a religion nor a philosophy,
it is this practice based in the thought for others
that will free one from the dream.
By transcending worldly concepts of selflessness,
and eliminating the duality of self and object through this practice
of the cultivation of insight into how it all exists,
one disciplines one's own mind
in order to not give harm to any living being.
Having thus established one's practice as genuine,
like a sport one enjoys even more than food or sleep,
one methodically gives up attachment to every cause of suffering,
not stopping until the very end.

The Three Principal Aspects of the Path

*T*he mind of the genuine practition-
er must be engaged in the three principal aspects of the path in order to
begin the practice that is the path to enlightenment. They are (1) *renunciation* of the mere appearances of the mind; (2) *bodhicitta*—the wish to be
enlightened in order to be of benefit only to others; and (3) *emptiness*—at
least a working intellectual understanding of the true nature of things.

It is not until you finally grow weary of the meaningless activities of
this life that you will be able to leave those things behind and achieve the
goal. It is not until you commit your life to become enlightened for others that you will be in a position to begin the practice that will lead to that
goal. It is not until you have gained basic insight, from listening and
thinking, into the true nature of things that you will be able to begin to
turn away from the illusions of this world and enter into the solitary practice that is the path to enlightenment. These three principal aspects
together make up the mind of the fortunate individuals who can actually
begin the practice that, if done correctly and to its end, can lead only to
enlightenment.

Until the practice of the three principal aspects of the path to
enlightenment is actually begun, until that level of practice is *realized*,[41]

---

41. *Realized.* To realize something means to have generated a level of mind or way of knowing
that is inseparable from the mind, having eliminated the delusions that previously kept that
individual from that level of mind. Having generated a new level of mind, with the insight
gained, all appearances will be dealt with according to the new level of insight, rather than the
previous level of delusion.

you will be "practicing to begin the practice"[42] of the path to enlighten-ment. The novice practitioner,[43] while studying the teachings of the path to enlightenment, must cultivate insight into these three aspects. That is the practitioner's main job and until that level of mind is generated, he or she will not begin the actual practice.

What is a novice then? A novice is an individual who is still seeking happiness and freedom from suffering on a worldly level. A novice is one who has not generated sufficient insight into the nature of the illusion, or strength of conviction in the nobility of the path, to begin to give up his or her attachments to the self secured by objects/others. A novice is one who has not yet understood the magnificence of the goal and so has not begun to take action to reach it. Such an individual plays at practice, pick-ing and choosing what is felt to be appropriate for his or her "personality." In that way, the point is missed completely, like a child who picks at din-ner and thereby misses the meal. A novice is often the one with the biggest drum who wants us all to listen. A novice is one who more or less con-sciously deals with his or her practice as a commodity: "If you're not nice to me, I won't be nice to you; if you're nice to me, then, of course, I'll be nice to you; so, be nice to me so that we can be nice to each other." A novice is one who seeks the source of problems in "others." A novice is one who vows to become enlightened in this lifetime in order to be of benefit to others but continues his or her nonstop involvement in cyclic exis-tence—such an individual short-sightedly believes that one can transcend what one is still bound to.

Although students may hear the complete teachings of the Buddhist

---

42. *Practicing to begin the practice.* Until you have entered into some level of practice of each of the three principal aspects of the path to enlightenment, you have not yet begun the practice. Continue to listen to correct teachings on the path to enlightenment and practice virtue to the best of your ability. In this way, the three aspects—renunciation, bodhicitta, and emptiness—will be realized and any work done before will be brought into the path at that point as a refer-ence for the sensitive practitioner. To realize anything does not mean simply to express an inter-est in teachings you have heard. It means to generate a level of mind that affects and substan-tially changes every other aspect of your life. Once a level of mind is realized, an evolutionary process begins that will culminate in the direct realization of emptiness, at which time you are enlightened.

43. *The novice practitioner.* This term has nothing to do with age, gender, or number of years' prac-tice in this particular lifetime. This term refers specifically to a sincere aspirant to the path to enlightenment who has not yet realized the three principal aspects of the path and so therefore has not yet entered the path. What separates such a practitioner from the worldly is that he or she, to some degree for some period of time, has sensed either a need for change or the beauty or the brilliance or the virtue that is the path to enlightenment.

path to enlightenment, until the practice of the three principal aspects of the path to enlightenment is entered into, the practice will not begin. Once the practice is begun, a seriousness of purpose will enter into every activity of the student's life. The three principal aspects of the path will be realized when the individual has taken to heart the truth of suffering, and renounced attachment to it in order to be of benefit to others.

Look to an enlightened being for guidance, not to the unenlightened. Even the lapse of a great period of time following the teachings of an enlightened being does not, in any way, affect the relevance of the teachings. When the Buddhist path to enlightenment is finally completed, the practitioner will find that there is no other path to follow to eliminate the delusions based in ignorance and reach that goal. Ignorance doesn't change with the passage of time, only the superficial appearance of the illusion changes.

What is a vow? A vow is a pledge to perform a specific action in order to achieve some goal over a specified period of time. In the case of the Buddhist path to enlightenment, each vow taken is taken only to create the cause, by generating a level of mind, to become enlightened. *When* one will become enlightened depends on whether one has pledged one's life and practice to keeping the vows that cause one to generate the level of mind freed from delusion, and to what extent the vows are practiced and treasured. At the very least, living beings grow to be the thing they love, the cause similar to the result. The love of virtue that does not give harm to any living being is the heart of the practice of the one who will be enlightened.

In the case of the Buddhist path to enlightenment,[44] various sets of vows can be taken by both laypeople and the ordained. Whatever the level of individual commitment, it is only through a conscious effort to abide within the boundaries of the vows taken that the individual will create the cause to develop the commensurate level of virtue based in wisdom. Highest level commitment and practice is required to enter and remain within the highest level meditation on the empty nature of the self and the objects/others that leads directly to enlightenment and the transcendence of cyclic existence. Vows are not meant to cripple your life or be like a

---

44. *Buddhist path to enlightenment.* The only reason I qualify the path as the "Buddhist" path to enlightenment is that in the world today there are many who claim to be following a path to enlightenment that perpetuates the dualistic illusion of self and a power greater than the self.

prison. They merely act as guidelines for the practice that is based in the kind thought for the "other." The practitioner who consciously practices keeping his or her vows will be led, by his or her mind based in the vow, first to contemplation of the true nature of the self and objects/others, second to elimination of attachment to delusion, and third to the generation of the wisdom mind freed from delusion.

In the world there are few genuine practitioners of the Buddhist path to enlightenment. There are many novices, however, still preparing who have not yet reached the point of "leaving it all behind" in order to begin the process by which they will transcend that level of existence. There are two main obstructions to the novice's entry into the path to enlightenment. The first obstruction is that he or she has not developed sufficient belief in the suffering nature of the world to warrant taking action to institute change; second, the novice has not begun to understand the transcendental meaning of virtue and wisdom sufficiently to "see" the teachings of an enlightened being. If he or she had, then the modesty necessary for a student who would follow the path taught by the teacher would have been simultaneously generated. The novice is still in the "driver's seat," and since that individual only knows what he or she is conditioned to know, the status quo is maintained. When individuals have suffered enough, however, they become more receptive and, being more receptive, they will see more qualities in the enlightened teachings/teacher. They will thereby generate an attitude of listening, and change will begin to take place. What will change? The mind of the listener. Nothing more. Certainly not the world around, as that world is nothing other than the reflection of the levels of mind of the living beings currently trapped within it.

This is an extremely degenerate time in the world as well as in the history of the teachings of Shakyamuni Buddha.[45] It has been a long time, more than 2,500 years, since an enlightened being spoke personally of the path followed. It is no wonder that even individuals who have publicly given up vows taken before in order reclaim wholeheartedly their former

---

45. *Shakyamuni Buddha.* The fourth fully enlightened being of the 1,000 who will appear in what is termed "this fortunate great aeon." How long exactly is "this fortunate great aeon"? It is the number of years it will take for 1,000 fully enlightened beings to appear on this level of existence who will teach those still trapped within the illusion. Shakyamuni Buddha's teacher was the third fully enlightened being, Kasyapa, whose teacher, in turn, was the second, and so on. The fifth fully enlightened being will be known as Maitreya.

worldly lifestyles are teaching the path. Worse, they teach the path as they misunderstood it—with all the mistakes that caused them to renounce their vows, because that is all they know. It is no wonder that "to practice" is often believed to be a physically oriented activity such as chanting or "sitting," separate from the instructions by which the individual might eliminate the delusions that bind him or her to the unsatisfactory level of existence within which he or she cycles. It is no wonder that unenlightened teachers are telling students that they can be enlightened as laypeople while continuing to live their worldly lives. It is no wonder that practitioners often claim all are "really" enlightened already. It is no wonder that so many people want to believe this is true, because to believe otherwise would mean giving up attachment to the self associated with worldly objects/others. It would mean dealing with the mind, which would then suffer. It is no wonder that so many people are making promises to live within vows without any real commitment to keep those vows, because the vows and promises have become things to break, not a lovely treasure to keep well.

Those wishing to follow the Buddhist path to enlightenment correctly and to its end should take their cue from the enlightened being whose teaching they follow. Shakyamuni Buddha lived and taught more than 2,500 years ago in India. What significant actions did he take when he set out on what is known now to be the path to enlightenment? The actions he took are the very same actions taken by every being who will ever be enlightened, by every Buddha. It has to do with mind generation, not with the manipulation of objects in order to create the cause of happiness for self freed from suffering. It is done only for others. Let's look back at the life of Shakyamuni Buddha, who was known as Siddhartha Gautama.

Siddhartha Gautama was the handsome son of the king of a large and wealthy state of ancient India. The king, his father, was the head of the Shakya clan, the region's ruling family. At the time of Siddhartha's birth, a seer predicted that he would either inherit the throne along with the power and the wealth of that position one day and be a great king or that he would be a great holy man. His mother died at the time of his birth, and he was raised by his stepmother.

As a young man Siddhartha was very sensitive to the suffering of those around him. The story is told of how one day the young boy's father took him to the spring planting festival held outside the gates of the palace. During the morning, while Siddhartha watched a poor farmer struggle to turn the soil over in preparation for the seed, he saw a bird swoop down on the newly turned earth and pluck a worm from the dark soil, devouring it while it struggled. Upset by the inevitability of life— the suffering and the death—Siddhartha wandered off to a quiet cool grove of trees nearby, where he was found, hours later, sitting alone, thinking. He was contemplating how every living being—whether a man or a bird or even a worm—wishes only to be happy and free from suffering and yet cannot secure a permanent happiness or freedom from suffering; that no living being wants to die and yet, every living being will die; that death is truly the only reality of life.

Siddhartha was usually not allowed to leave the palace. His father left orders for the boy to be amused, to distract him from his tendency to "worry" over life's bigger questions when left alone. Locked within the palace grounds, Siddhartha took his school lessons as well as training as a Ksatriya, the Hindu caste for nobles and warriors, and played removed from the suffering of the world outside. When he was nineteen, the king arranged Siddhartha's marriage to Princess Yashodhara. For another ten years while he pursued palace activities, Siddhartha could not shake the feeling that all his good fortune—his family, the people's great love for him, his looks, his health and wealth—were nothing more than transitory illusions. He knew that everyone sought these "things" and based their happiness upon securing such things, but happiness could never be secured by such activities. Ultimately, he knew, everything of the world was inseparable from suffering.

When he was twenty-nine, his only child, Rahula, was born. He named the boy Rahula, which means "eclipse of the sun," as a poignant reminder to him of how his own attachment to the lovely child could distract him and cause him to remain in the suffering state without finding a way out. His concern was really never for his own welfare, it was something else. Siddhartha wondered if he might find a way to lead all living beings from the suffering caused when individuals grasp at illusions for happiness. He was troubled by the suffering he saw in the living beings who, he could see, even while they were seeking happiness freed from suffering, were creating its cause. Somehow, he connected with this anomaly and felt that he might uncover the solution to the riddles and thereby help others—truly help others. Their suffering bothered him greatly, more than his own suffering ever could. He therefore made the decision to take responsibility to create the cause of happiness freed from suffering for all "others" by himself alone. And he staked his life on achieving that noble goal.

For these reasons, barely a week after the birth of his son, he left his home and family, the throne, and wealth and power. He and his attendant rode out of the palace one midnight and traveled until dawn. In the light of the new day, Siddhartha dismounted, gave the reins to the attendant, exchanged his fine clothes for those sewed from worthless scraps of worn cloth, and shaved his head. He set out alone, no longer resembling the prince everyone had known and loved so well. The physical transformation had denied the external appearance of the "I" of "I am Siddhartha," as well as the innermost transformation through which he gave up attachment to those objects/others that also defined the "self" of "I am Siddhartha." Looking for answers, he sought out various practitioners, hermits and ascetics,[46] of whom he had heard while in the palace, to see if their practices might hold a key to higher understanding. Siddhartha listened to their ideas and followed their practices, but soon came to know that the goals thus attainable were not the answers of the scope he was seeking.

Finally, he went to a forest near Bodh Gaya in the Bihar state of India with five others, where for six years he practiced the most intense level of asceticism the human body could withstand. Siddhartha believed that only by such intense practice would he either achieve the goal he sought or prove to himself that that practice, as the others he had tried before, would also not create the necessary cause similar to the effect sought. After nearly six years, he realized that even the most ardent practice of asceticism could not cause one to give up the delusions upon which self is labeled, and so he ended his fast by eating some yogurt offered him by a young girl of the region.

---

46. *Hermits and ascetics.* Individuals seeking an "other-worldly" life often decide to live the solitary lifestyle of a hermit as a way of removing his or her bond, or attachment, to the world. The extreme practices of self-discipline of the ascetic are similarly intended to sever worldly ties, through deprivation and sometimes self-inflicted physical punishment, and are mistakenly believed to create the cause for that individual to bond with some "divinity" or "divine" power separate from his or her mind. Siddhartha Gautama practiced asceticism long enough and well enough to know that was not a correct practice of the path to enlightenment. The solitary retreats practiced by some practitioners on the path to enlightenment are not intended to sever the worldly bond through distance, but rather to eliminate the duality of the subject (the mind) with its object (the appearance of that mind) through the generation of insight and elimination of delusion. You should take note of the need to constantly reestablish the correct motivation and skillful means during practice.

In disgust at the weakness they felt he had succumbed to, his five companions left him. Alone and extremely weakened from his ordeal, Siddhartha sat down on an armful of grass[47] given him by a young boy of the area, vowing not to rise again until he had found the way to enlightenment.

And so he sat under a tree[48] in Bodh Gaya investigating the illusory nature of every thought that he found himself attached to, that frightened him, or that might lure him from his practice.[49] The suffering he felt from the rigors of the meditation and all the other creations of his own mind were eliminated one by one with a meditation on the true nature of their existence, and of the self feeling the suffering. Always, deep within his heart, he kept the thought to be of lasting benefit to others. At the age of thirty-five, after six years of rigorous practice in that lifetime, Siddhartha Gautama eliminated the gross delusions upon which self is merely labeled and was enlightened. With the wisdom generated at attainment of the blissful state of lower nirvana, he eventually became aware of the subtle delusions and eliminated them as well. Having eliminated even the most subtle delusions associated with ignorance, understanding perfectly the true nature of all things, he attained the highest

---

47. *Kusha grass.* This is why to this very day Buddhists wishing to enter into uninterrupted and intense concentration will think to put a blade or two of this long-stemmed grass under their seats or meditation cushions. The grass is a symbol of the goal sought, the level of mind of Siddhartha that caused him to purify all the delusions that might distract him from enlightenment, by giving up attachment to the mere appearances of self and objects/others (the delusions) because of his profound love of others, which was greater than his empty self.

48. *The bodhi tree.* The famous tree with heart-shaped leaves under which Siddhartha Gautama is believed to have sat at the time of his enlightenment. A magnificent stupa, in this case a four-sided monument that is symbolic of the path to enlightenment and the various grounds or bhumis generated by the practitioner on the path, stands just behind the tree. The stupa is a place of pilgrimage for Buddhists from around the world.

49. *Mara.* The demonic beings often pictured flying among the leaves of the bodhi tree under which Siddhartha Gautama is sitting before he is enlightened. The mara are usually pictured with various kinds of arrows being hurled toward Siddhartha. Just beyond the tip of each arrow is a flower representing the faith of one who will be enlightened by following a path to its end even though this path goes against all that is generally considered to be the truth. The mara represent the final delusions upon which self is based that have the power to cause harm to the meditator by distracting him or her from the goal. It is only by meditating on the empty nature of the appearance of his or her final attachments and associated suffering felt that the meditator who will be enlightened in that lifetime gives up attachment to the final gross delusions associated with self and objects/others and transcends the suffering state of cyclic existence, enlightened.

level of mind, freed of all delusion, and was omniscient.[50] He taught for another fifty years before passing away and, to those with a level of mind[51] that could hear the quality of his teachings, is now known as Shakyamuni Buddha, the fourth fully enlightened being recognized to have existed in this world system.

If it is true that ignorance cannot exist simultaneously in the same mind with wisdom and that the wisdom of an enlightened teacher or his or her teachings is therefore necessary to do the practice, then who was Siddhartha's teacher? Siddhartha's teacher was Kasyapa, the third fully enlightened being. Somehow, Siddhartha had the good fortune to come in contact with whatever remained of Kasyapa's teachings, and based on the practice he had done in not just that but previous lifetimes, Siddhartha was able to sort through the degenerate teachings of his day, and formulate a correct practice.

Siddhartha's path, although its cause was in his ability to take to heart the suffering of the world around with more than just worldly tears of anguish, did not actually begin until he made the decision to leave the illusory appearances of the world behind him in order to be of ultimate benefit to all others whom he loved more dearly even than his own life.

It is good to consider what the people who knew Siddhartha—who loved him and counted on him—must have thought and said when he left them behind for what must have appeared to them to be a completely ridiculous, perhaps even "crazed," lifestyle. He left his home, father, family, wife, brand-new child, the kingdom, and all the people there who loved their handsome and kind future ruler. He gave up his identity and every single thing that formed it, his clothes, his hair, the horse he loved so much, his friends. According to the rules of our current world, Siddhartha was a horrible child, a terrible husband, selfish and incredibly insensitive to leave the new baby; if he was not a monster among men, then surely he had gone crazy. This must have certainly been said of him by those he left behind. In retrospect, of course, it is easy to see how very short-sighted they were because of their own ignorance and self-centered thoughts.

---

50. *Omniscient*. Having eliminated even the subtle delusions, the level of mind that has understood perfectly the true nature of all things without any mistake.

51. *Level of mind*. Although all unenlightened minds can be said to be ignorant of the true nature of appearances, through the elimination of delusions and commensurate generation of insight into the true nature of things, new "levels of mind," or of understanding, are generated.

Let's complete the story of Siddhartha's enlightenment. Even though Siddhartha was enlightened, he looked no different; he didn't have a "glow" or a halo or wings or any of those things so often equated with "holiness." He didn't wear magnificent robes; he didn't have a beautiful temple; he even had very few followers in his life. He walked the dusty roads teaching, not riding horseback or in a cart, and whether he was welcomed to teach was completely dependent on the level of mind of those he met. In fact, although he taught approximately fifty years following his enlightenment, at the time of his death serious practitioners probably numbered fewer than four to five hundred. Since he appeared so like themselves physically, and because the quality of his mind could not be "known" firsthand by the ignorant, it was only through the students' practice that faith in the enlightened quality of his teachings began to be generated. Through the practice of the serious students, however, the word began to spread that Siddhartha's teachings were those of an enlightened being. Ultimately, the enlightened teachings were so logical that the teachings— as well as the teacher—simply could not be ignored. When listeners became receptive to really listen to the teachings of the enlightened Siddhartha, qualities were perceived and the fame of those qualities grew.

Although at first his family was very aloof with him, eventually his father and then his stepmother and wife and finally even his son took the vows of ordination from him. They then devoted their lives, to the best of their abilities, to listening, contemplating, and meditating on the correct path to enlightenment he laid out for them to follow, with the thought to be of ultimate and lasting benefit to others, as he had been before them.

The serious practitioner must remember that the practice, from beginning to end, is difficult at best. It is those difficulties then, and no others, that become the practice that is the path to enlightenment. Having generated a transcendental wish,[52] you set yourself apart from the rest of the world, even perhaps from those believed to be the most serious practitioners of the day. Alone, whether in a crowd or as a single person, you must then investigate the nature of the various forms of suffering of the self when it comes in contact with not only its own imaginings but also with the appearance of an extremely hostile world around. That is the practice.

---

52. *Transcendental wish.* Having begun the generation of the three principal aspects of the path, a wish to be enlightened for the benefit of others that becomes more and more compelling as the delusions based in ignorance are eliminated.

That is how you get rid of the delusions that are the support for self. [There is no self existing except as a concept that relates to a dualistically-oriented appearance of objects/others mistakenly believed to be separate. To get beyond such delusions, you must eliminate every cause of suffering apprehended by the mind as it appears and, in this way, eliminate the support for self. Having done so, one is enlightened.]

[So simple. So difficult. The path is precise. There are no shortcuts, there are no alternate paths, there are no ways around the obstacles, *except straight through every appearance of your mind by the generation of insight into its true nature.*]

Think of it like this. Imagine it is a cold, dark, and stormy night. The wind is howling through the tall trees in the forest outside, and just to think of going out in that storm puts your mind on edge. You're inside a stone hut, and a group of people huddle near the blazing fire wondering how help will ever reach them if no one even knows they are there. Somehow, this group has become isolated at this place. There is no food; there is no more wood for the fire; one of those deadly storms is approaching that goes on and on. You sit there listening to the storm and to the endless complaints and silly chatter of the others in the hut, tired and worried like the others, your cane over your arm. Weary, lame, and no longer enchanted by the vagaries of life, you have been thinking a lot lately about how unhappy people are and how hard everyone tries to secure happiness for self/me/mine. While you've been listening, you've been thinking about how it doesn't matter if so-and-so makes a fortune from his business dealings or the other seduces the "perfect lover." Ultimately, you know every one of the people in the hut is going to die, and at that time, all the fortunes, all the loves, every one of the never-ending stream of things humans desire, will mean absolutely nothing. If they haven't suffered enough grasping for those illusory "things" in this life, they will surely suffer at the thought, at death, of leaving whatever objects/others they have acquired and believe to be the cause of their happiness.

Since you obviously don't participate in the world they find so completely enthralling, the others think you're a bit odd, probably maybe even a little self-centered. When you don't respond with sufficient angst upon hearing of someone's broken heart from the loss of their latest love, you appear selfish to them.

Actually, for the first time, your thoughts have turned from your own happiness to contemplate the illusion of happiness that is grasped at by the ones struggling around you that always seems to end in suffering. Certainly, because you are not considered to be "one of them," you will be seen as inferior. Nevertheless, here you all are together. Stuck in the hut at the end of a very long and treacherous pathway many miles from help, storm raging in the blackest night, someone has to go for help or all will certainly perish. So you stand up, adjust your cap, clear your throat, and say you're going.

You decide to do this seemingly impossible task because you honestly cherish the others far more than yourself and because, in your mind, there is simply nothing else to do. Perhaps, too, you're more than a bit bored with the tedium of the group's interests. For these and other associated reasons, it is necessary for you to leave to get help. No one else offers. The reason none of the others go for help or offer to accompany you on the treacherous journey is that no one else has, as yet, generated the level of mind that consciously cherishes "other" more than "self." You set out in the dark by yourself then, the others doubting there is any chance of success for your "mission" because if they would fail, then how can you possibly succeed?

How does a lame person follow a rough and rutted path on a dark and stormy night? Very carefully but steadily, one single step after the other. Tapping and making your way, for the first hours of the journey you're aware of the "creepy" shadows lurking in the darkness, a chill, like cold fingers, skittering down your back, and the whistle, like a mournful sighing, of the wind through the trees. You calm your mind by repeating, ["There is nothing to fear at all except the mere appearance of my own mind, and there is no 'I' to be afraid except the one dependent on that same mind."]

In this way, with every tenuous step you calm your mind. Eventually, by reconditioning your consciousness to the truth through analysis of the true nature of the cause of your suffering and the concurrent giving up of attachment to the delusions associated with ignorance of the true nature of things, your mind is conditioned to *not* be afraid of those appearances. You are freed from that particular set of delusions, no longer grasping at their appearance as the truth or as "reality," having given up attachment to the subject (self) and its object (objects/others).

As soon as one delusion is put to rest, another rises in the mind. It might have to do with the fact that you are lonely. Feeling lonely triggers uncountable related impressions from previous conditioning. One moment you feel "put upon" to be experiencing this suffering while the others are more comfortable back at the hut, the next you feel a contemptuous superiority wherein you visualize yourself the "able" one and the others as simpering and very silly children. Haughtily you proceed along the path. This impression in turn generates the next, which generates the next, and so on. All the time, however, as each new impression generated by this particular level of delusion presents itself, you give up attachment to those objects/others appearing to your mind with intense contemplation on their true nature and, always, the wish not to give harm to others.

Like a good horse that plods along, step after single step, because that is the job, you deal with each feeling of suffering appearing to your mind. This is done for the sole purpose of attaining the goal in order to be of benefit to the others left behind who are not capable at this time of taking responsibility for their own rescue. Somehow, you alone have enough clarity of mind to know that in order to reach the goal, you will have to overcome the obstructions that exist only in your own mind *with* your own mind.

And so, as you understand that each and every aspect of the objects/others of your investigation is dependent upon your own mind for its creation and continued existence, attachment to the mere illusion causing the suffering is given up, as well as the self-cherishing thoughts supported by that particular attachment. The various levels of delusion that cause you to feel discomfort or some other form of suffering are eliminated one after the other, and you follow the path.

Too far along the path to consider turning back, not sure how much further you must travel, you have generated some confidence in your ability to do the hard work of following the path to its end. You feel strong and victorious over the apparitions of your own mind that bound your self, as they bind others, to suffering. This leads to an unshakable faith in your ability to control your own life, and for the very first time, you begin to welcome the next challenge. When it comes, as you know it will, and you get by that obstacle with the elimination of delusion and cultivation of insight, you will feel like a great athlete in training for "the big event." With that kind of "all-conquering" attitude, the mind does not shrink away from suffering but almost welcomes it as an opportunity to practice.

The elimination of even one single delusion has a far-reaching effect on the storehouse consciousness. Picture a flock of hundreds of large birds filling a waterway or a field. With one stone thrown in their midst, you will cause all the birds in that particular area—hundreds of them—to fly away. This is how it is with the elimination of delusion; an uncountable number of associated delusions are also removed at the same time. It is for this reason that very quickly after actually beginning the Buddhist path to enlightenment, the genuine practitioner will see amazing gains being made along the path.

At times, the path you must follow in order to help the others seems to go on and on and the work, never-ending. With the elimination of each set of delusions, however, and with generation of insight, the traveler steadily generates the path. With the elimination of each delusion, another becomes apparent. The path is difficult and, at times, exhausting. As the traveler, you do not slow down your steady progress or stop, because if you fail, then help will not reach the others. If you were interested in securing some benefit or happiness for yourself, then you would simply quit the difficulties of the path and accept defeat. Because the motivation is truly to be of benefit to the others left behind in the hut who will suffer so much if help does not reach them, you continue. The selflessness of your practice causes you to overcome obstacles that arise with every bit of progress along the path—the fatigue, the loneliness, and the feelings associated with understanding, at long last, the nature of the delusions that previously secured your happiness—all are eliminated. This happens, moment by moment, through the correct and courageous investigation into the true nature of those delusions, as well as investigation into the self experiencing the immediate suffering associated with the delusions and the secondary suffering associated with the giving up of attachment to them, or the loss. This, actually, is the path. The practice is its generation.

Although there is a constant destabilization of the foundation for the security of self, the farther along the path you travel, the more joy is experienced. Because of the nature of its cause, *that* joy is of a transcendental, rather than a worldly, nature. It is a feeling experienced only by practitioners as a result of generation of the path. This type of joy is never experienced as a result of worldly success or the appearance of "happiness." The joy develops in direct proportion to the freedom felt as you eliminate the delusions, one after another, that trap the mind within the ignorant conceptual network that is the cause of all suffering.

The attitude of the traveler progressing on the path is much like that of a fly that has unwittingly fallen into the intricacies of a spider's web. The more the fly struggles within the web, the more entangled it becomes

The more it calmly and methodically gives up attachment to the sticky threads that bind it, the less bound it is. For the very first time, the practitioner knows what "freedom" truly means. This joyous freedom fortifies the practitioner's resolve to reach the goal in order to be of benefit to the others who are suffering so much. The mind, by its own action, is inspired to continue and not give up.

By remembering analogies like this one of the traveler, practitioners of the path to enlightenment, in the midst of their practice, can ground themselves. The practice is one by which you methodically give up the attachment to the illusions that are mistakenly believed to secure "self." Although those delusions (as they are not "real" and yet are believed to be "real") are not inherently existent, still the "self" (believed to exist inherently) "feels" it is secured by those mere illusions. During the time of the practice, therefore, the motivation to achieve the goal *only* in order to be of benefit to others grounds the mind in a thought that, to the virtuous, causes happiness for self. In this way, by reorienting the thrust of worldly actions done for self to transcendental actions done for others, insight into the true nature of the self and the objects/others of its suffering is generated, and the goal of enlightenment attained.

The mind must be completely reoriented from the worldly point of reference that produces only the cause to remain in the suffering state of cyclic existence, toward the transcendental, which culminates in enlightenment. In order to do this, the practitioner never defends his or her "self" in the face of even the greatest criticism, unfair treatment, or meanness. Instead, the true practitioner uses those opportunities to explore the nature of his or her suffering and to give up attachment to the worldly desire that binds that related concept to the mind. This is what is known as "giving the victory to other." In this way, the practitioner progresses toward the goal. Truly, there is nothing to give up and no one to give it up, except that which is completely dependent on the mind of the perceiver for its existence.

From beginning to end, this is how the path is generated in the mind of the practitioner. Even the final obstacles before enlightenment, the maras described earlier, are eliminated with the same basic tools: (1) the four point analysis, combined with (2) intense recollection of the three principal aspects of the path, while (3) investigating the meanings of the six perfections—generosity, patience, morality, joyous perseverance, concentration, and wisdom, all done within the extensive vows of ordination by which the most fortunate practitioner commits his or her life to be enlightened in that lifetime, only for others.

[Nothing at all is completed until the whole is accomplished. No practitioner is "almost" enlightened. Enlightenment is possible only after the attachment to the very last grasped-at thought is eliminated, replaced with insight into its true nature; not until the consciousness splits free from the physical support of the body. Not until all this is accomplished is it definite that the practitioner is going to be enlightened in his or her lifetime.]

It is important for the genuine practitioner to keep in mind that no matter how far along the path the individual travels, [if that path is not completed before the time of that individual's death, he or she will almost certainly assume another form within the suffering state of cyclic existence. If that should happen, then when will all the causes and conditions necessary for enlightenment (human being, intelligence, senses intact, time and opportunity to hear enlightened teachings and then to practice them) present themselves again? Time is so short, like the blink of an eye. Practice now, without distraction, while you can.

A common mistake made by novice practitioners is to think that if an individual is truly on the correct path to enlightenment, he or she will be well loved by those around. Unfortunately, it is the nature of the ignorant mind to be self-centered. It is the nature of such a mind to feel superior to those believed inferior, to feel competitive with those who appear to be superior, and to be critical of those approaching equality. That is how it is for those who relate every mere appearance of their minds back to the well-being and happiness of self. It is highly unlikely that an individual who withdraws from worldly involvements and enters a contemplative and, whether in the midst of a crowd or in solitude, solitary way of life is going to even be liked, let alone loved, by those around, even those purporting to be practitioners. Look at Shakyamuni Buddha. Certainly his own family disliked it when he chose to do something very far removed from their worldly interpretation of activities suitable for his life, and profitable. And later, when he left his fellow ascetics and sat alone under the bodhi tree where he eventually attained enlightenment, they reviled him.

[It is also a generally accepted misconception that if you are truly on the correct path to enlightenment, then you will not feel any suffering. The Buddhist path to enlightenment is about nothing other than the elimination of the ignorance that is the cause of all suffering. In order to deal with any appearance of the mind, you have to acknowledge it as a force to be dealt with. The path is one of feeling suffering (whether it takes the form of outright pathos or quiet sadness or embarrassment or frustration, to name a very few), of renouncing attachment first to the suffering, and then to its cause.[53] With renunciation comes a feeling of loss for the self, as well as some feeling of insecurity that can be removed only by continuing the process of the path by analyzing the true nature of the self that is suffering. However, with the suffering caused by progress along the path comes the most amazing sense of joy at the path, at the perfection of the teachings, at your good fortune to be on that path. And it is that joy that grows until, at the time of your enlightenment, it is known as the bliss that is inseparable from emptiness—an extraordinary level of being that engages every fiber of your being and is limitless.

The path to enlightenment is a solitary endeavor. It involves the work done by the individual practitioner, within his or her mind. The ultimate outcome is freedom from all suffering, but the process forces the individual to be sensitive to suffering in order to eliminate its cause. To think otherwise is to have completely misunderstood the point of the Buddhist path to enlightenment. The indication of a soft and loving heart is not displayed in tears or in public good works. Rather, such a heart of loving-kindness is truly expressed only through the practice of giving up one's life in order to achieve the goal and thereby be of ultimate and lasting benefit to others.

The root cause of all suffering is ignorance. It is ignorance that causes the mind's creations, or illusions, to appear to be real and the mind to then grasp at them. An illusion that is thus grasped at becomes a delusion. It is the volitional power of such delusions[54] that is imprinted on the consciousness at the moment the mind grasps at its own appearance. Those imprints are the seeds that will ripen when the necessary similar causes and conditions (the senses and their objects) come together. It is this volitional impulse that empowers the objects apprehended by the senses to

---

53. *Feeling suffering.* This in no way means that you will be in tears in public or morose to the point that those around would express concern. Such a practice is based in self-centered concern and only calls attention to the self of the practitioner. That sort of practice must be left behind since it only interferes with true practice by calling attention to self.

54. *Volitional power.* The spontaneous tendency or inclination of the mind to label the objects apprehended and compiled by the senses as good, bad, or indifferent as they are mistakenly believed to be able to affect the equally illusory self.

manifest as quality-filled appearances. Then, because the mind is unaware of its own action, these appearances are believed to exist substantially from their own side, and separate from the action of the mind of the perceiver.

With the removal of each instance of suffering, a commensurate level of insight is generated. This "path" to enlightenment culminates, finally, in the actual generation of the wisdom mind of enlightenment freed from the gross delusions. After an individual is enlightened, he or she eliminates the subtle delusions[55] remaining on the consciousness with the wisdom thus generated.

Teachings of the Buddhist path to enlightenment pertain only to the removal of the gross delusions that bind living beings to cyclic existence. In other words, they pertain only to the individual's liberation from belief in an inherently existent self. The individual who is enlightened and has attained the blissful state of lower nirvana, having eliminated the gross delusions that bound him or her to cyclic existence, will, without prompting or need of instruction, eliminate even the subtle delusions as they become apparent.[56]

It is absolutely impossible for you to be trapped within the network of your own delusions and to formulate any objective opinion separate from the deluded appearance of your own mind's action. For this reason, living beings are truly incapable of judging the level of mind of others. It is not until you have decided to stop "changing" the world around you, and concentrate only on your own mind, that the practice of the path to enlightenment can begin.

If an unenlightened individual hasn't generated the wisdom by

---

55. *Subtle delusions*. It is not until you have eliminated the gross delusions at the time of enlightenment that the subtle delusions become apparent to the mind. As the enlightened mind is inseparable from its meditation on emptiness, those delusions are dealt with and eliminated relatively quickly. Just as the ignorant mind cannot exist simultaneously with wisdom, neither can the wisdom mind exist simultaneously with even the most subtle forms of ignorance. It is only with the great clarity of mind born of wisdom that these subtle delusions can even be perceived. Once perceived, their imprints are burned off the consciousness with wisdom. When even the subtle delusions are eliminated, the omniscient state of a fully enlightened Buddha is attained.
56. *Enlightened mind*. An enlightened individual is freed from the gross delusions that bound him or her to the cycle of existence based in ignorance. The mind of such an individual does not in any way grasp at an inherently existent self, and so any action taken by such a mind is done only for "others" who seem to be suffering terribly. The enlightened level of mind is inseparable from the perfect virtue that does not, in any way, give harm to any living being. It takes approximately one and one-half to two years after achieving the state of lower nirvana for the mind to "settle down." After that time, the only motivation for such an individual will be to make the correct teachings of the path to enlightenment available to those still trapped in cyclic existence.

which he or she could come to know wisdom, then how will he or she find an enlightened teacher? By creating the cause similar to the effect. Generate the wish to know an enlightened being and think about the qualities of enlightenment. [By cultivating interest in the virtue based in wisdom, you will begin to see it. Having seen it, you will begin to practice it. Having practiced it, you will generate it.]

Chapter Six

PREPARING THE GROUND

Year after year, when the season was right and the sun just rising, he'd begin to transform the hard ground, stiff from the inactivity of winter, with shovel and spade. *Klup...klup...klup...klup...Slow and steady he worked, freeing the grateful earth with every stroke of his hoe. Klup...klup...klup...klup...Alone and intent on his task, cane hooked over one arm, he'd push the big-wheeled cultivator till the dark soil was soft, fluffy. Back and forth. Back and forth. His tuneless whistle blowing in and out with his breathing. The world quieted as he worked. Was it listening to his melody of life? Back and forth. Hour after hour. Only when the sun heated the day—till only an occasional noisy fly or nervous dragonfly moved furtively from shadow to shadow through lilac-scented air—would Pop walk slowly back to the house, mopping his brow, leaning heavily on his cane.*

He'd tap my welcoming shoulder as he passed through the opened door. As though we'd shared the hard day's work, that conspiratorial twinkle brightening the weathered blue of the eyes set so deep in his craggy face, he'd say, marking his words with meaning:

"Tomorrow, we'll plant the seed."

The Five Precepts

⌐*"T*o practice" means to become proficient or expert at some activity through repeated exercise or performance. A practitioner is one who makes a practice of repeating the activity appropriate and necessary to achieve mastery. It means becoming habituated to an activity. When an individual is finally enlightened, the practiced activity has been internalized and is inseparable from the action.

As was the case with Siddhartha Gautama, the quality of mind of the true practitioner of the Buddhist path to enlightenment does not include just a compelling wish to be enlightened in order to be of ultimate and lasting benefit to others. That thought must be tempered by an overwhelming and conscious thought to not give harm to any living being with any action of body, speech, or mind.[57] The thought to not give harm

---

57. *Body, speech, or mind.* Harm can be given through actions of the body, speech, or mind, alone or in combination. Harmful actions of the body or speech are easily understood by all living beings. Those of the mind, however, need a little explanation. Even though an angry thought toward another who is unaware of the thought has apparently not given harm to the "other," the perpetrator of such an action, in truth being inseparable from the mind that spawned both its self (the subject) and its object (other), did ignorantly give harm to another living being. The purpose of the practice of the path to enlightenment is to eliminate the duality of self and object/other through the cultivation of insight into how things truly exist. Through harmful thoughts, ignorance is perpetuated and harm done to the perpetrator. Why? Because the perpetrator, rather than creating the cause for release from cyclic existence, has created the cause to remain in that suffering state.

Besides that, however, every harmful action—whether it encounters a physical target or not—is like a pebble thrown into a quiet pool. The ripples caused by the disturbance, no matter how slight, do affect the environment of the pool, and generate a chain reaction of events that have far-reaching consequences, most of which cannot be seen by the casual observer.

must be accompanied by an investigation into the nature of the self and the objects/others that would cause harm. This is then followed by a disciplining or controlling of the inclination of the mind to grasp at its mere appearance, or it is not a practice on the path to enlightenment.

In order to not give harm to any living being, the practitioner should have committed, through a vow or promise from the heart, every action of body, speech, and mind to achieve that goal. There are five primary ways harm can be given by the ignorant self to others, and so, the sincere practitioner, with a thought only for others, vows to not commit these actions:

- Not to kill
- Not to steal
- Not to lie
- Not to engage in sexual misconduct
- Not to use intoxicants

These five precepts are guidelines for living within the wish "to not give harm to any living being." How they exist and how you will understand them and relate the practice to yourself is completely dependent on your mind. The Buddhist path to enlightenment is about nothing other than the generation of the virtuous conduct based in the wisdom of enlightenment that is freed of the delusions based in ignorance. Such a mind generation does not come like a snap of the fingers when you first think to be enlightened for others. It is the effect of its cause—the sincere wish to not give harm to any living being with any action of your body, speech, or mind. One or more of the vows can be taken at the time the student takes refuge in the teachings of the Buddhist path to enlightenment during a simple ceremony.

Not to kill. When you first consciously think "not to kill," most of you will immediately think, "But I don't kill." You will be referring to the grossest, most obvious form of killing that can come to the mind of a human being: the killing, or taking of the physical life, of another human being. Therefore, since you do not kill other human beings, you do not consider yourself to be a person who kills and, according to that level of mind, you practice "not killing."

However, after mulling over this "not killing" business with at first a little indignation and later just a quiet mind, you may find yourself walking down a garden pathway after a rain and there, sure to die in the sunshine, is a worm, stranded and unable to wriggle its way back into the cool dark earth. Perhaps, at first, with a little revulsion at the thought of actually touching that "creepy" thing, you bend down and, with a leaf, pick up the worm and put it in a shady spot to revive and continue doing what worms do. While completing that virtuous action, it occurs to you that saving the worm's life was a form of "not to kill."

A few days later you run into an out-of-sorts acquaintance. This acquaintance is someone who has often spoken rudely to you, and so, the acquaintance, although not an enemy, is not a friend. Sure enough, the acquaintance says something that you perceive to be typically mean and insensitive. Although, as is usually the case, you do not retaliate with similarly harsh words of judgment, in your mind quite a dialogue is going on. The words of that inner conversation, if they had been arrows, would have felled a mighty elephant. But let's say that, perhaps because of the gentleness resulting from helping the worm and thinking about virtue, you looked at the inner dialogue and realized that those unkind words spoken internally *were* a form of killing that did give harm to the other. Thinking about it over the minutes following the departure of the acquaintance, you realize that even an unexpressed thought to give harm to another living being can have the effect of a stone being thrown into a pond. Although it is not readily apparent, you understand that the environment of the pond can be changed as a result of the water's disturbance.

The point is that each and every action of the ignorant mind out of control is harmful not only to the object of the action but also to the perpetrator. It is only through the cultivation of virtue based in the thought for others that the wisdom mind of enlightenment can be accomplished. Ultimately, the virtuous mind of enlightenment does not and could not give harm to any living being with any action of the body, speech, or mind since the cause for giving such harm has been eliminated completely.

Not to steal. This means not to take anything at all that is not freely given to you. You generate insight into the meaning of this precept just as you did with the precept "not killing." You will come to know that the meaning of "not to steal" is similarly dependent on the mind of the perceiver. Initially, you may understand the precept to mean just not taking "things" belonging to others. It means much more than that: it also means to not steal the glory from a boastful person who is merely acting out his or her own particular brand of delusion; it means not getting involved in things that are someone else's concern; it means not depriving others of their happiness by failing to become enlightened in this lifetime.

How the precept exists is dependent on your own mind. How you generate more and more insight into any aspect of the practice of the path to enlightenment is dependent on the skillful use of the mind to investigate the meaning, true and interpretative, of every aspect of life appearing before the mind. Every appearance, after all, is nothing other than the mirror reflection of your own mind.

Not to lie. On a gross level, "not to lie" seems to mean simply not saying what you know is not the truth. Recall the previous example of the precept "not to kill," wherein you realized you could actually kill the "other" with your thoughts. What if you were to later recall the encounter and, in your mind, reestablish the harmful thought, claiming that the one harmed "deserved it" because he or she was "wrong" somehow? Then you would be lying in order to secure yourself because no living being "deserves" *any* harm. There are three aspects to such a lie: (1) the self of the individual doing the harm rises up as superior to the other; (2) the superiority of the perpetrator is based in the self-cherishing assumptions of ignorance; and (3) the self, by haphazardly shrugging off the dispute as settled and unimportant, lies again. This leaves innumerable imprints based in immorality[58] on the consciousness, thus continuing to create the cause to remain in cyclic existence by securing the well-being of self/me/mine at the expense of "other."

Not to engage in sexual misconduct. Again, how the precept is understood is dependent on the mind of the perceiver. Certainly, as with all practices on the path to enlightenment, to practice a more subtle, or deeper, level of meaning is not to forsake the grosser applications of the practice. The generation of the mind of wisdom, which is the effect of its cause—virtue based in the thought to not give harm to any living being—is a compounding of insights into the meaning of things and the implications of those meanings.

---

58. *Immorality.* Either (1) the thought to give harm to another living being or (2) the lack of thought to not give harm to any living being and its requisite action.

On a very gross level, "not to have sexual misconduct" would mean that the individuals making up a couple would not have sexual relations outside their avowed commitment to each other. That is pretty obvious. On another level, it might appear to mean certain acts are "good," while others are "bad," as they appear to constitute sexual misconduct. On the highest level of practice, the solitary meditator—the meditator alone— who has taken the vows to be enlightened in this lifetime uses desire as the path. Desire is the focus of the practitioner's concentration, and at this level of practice, "sexual misconduct" refers to the interruption of the visualized union[59] to relieve the appearance of physical suffering associated with desire, outside the visualization. This is because the meditator, while engaged in union with the visualized consort during the course of his or her meditation, must give up attachment to the appearances that are causing suffering and, at the same time, to the self that appears to be suffering. It is, after all, all an illusion. Clearly, there is nothing at all to grasp at. But because of the clarity of the visualization, as well as the mediator's skill at using visualization as a practice, it *seems* real. It is the opportunity for the highest level meditator to give up attachment to the strongest desires possible, which still bind him or her to the suffering state of cyclic existence. That it is a suffering state even in the midst of such excruciatingly delightful involvements is obvious to the self of the meditator who

---

59. *Visualized union.* During the highest level practice of the path to enlightenment, desire, because it fulfills the mind's wish for sensual pleasure, or happiness, is cultivated as a focus of the meditator's meditation (see chapter ten). The meditator is instructed to visualize a space or *mandala,* within which an enlightened being is also visualized. As the meditator becomes more skilled at generating and controlling the visualization, he or she visualizes him- or herself within the mandala and, eventually, in union with the visualized enlightened being. Because the visualization is as real as "reality," the senses do come in contact with their objects, thus causing the mind to *want* to concentrate, and the meditator has little trouble placing and holding the visualization. With practice and cultivation of the object of desire, the meditator becomes able to stay within the visualization for longer and longer periods of time, eventually able to remain without much effort within the meditation for ten to twenty hours at a stretch.

Other factors contribute to the meditator's ability to stay within the visualization. On a physical level, diet is extremely important. The mind, as it grows more and more subtle from generation of the highest level practice on the path to enlightenment, becomes more and more susceptible to the effects of various foods. Also, as long as food is being consumed, energy is being diverted from the mind. At the highest level practice, food consumption will be drastically limited. And obviously, the need to eat will interrupt the meditation, as will the need to relieve the body following digestion.

For the highest level practitioner, staying within the vows is of foremost importance. This goes hand in hand with meditation on the three principal aspects of the path. During tantric practice, the meditator will constantly have to meditate on the empty nature of the mere appearances of his or her own mind, as well as on the self involved in the visualization.

is controlling his or her responses with meditations on emptiness while engaged in the union. This is why the ordained practitioner takes vows of celibacy: in order to ensure the visualization that will lead to enlightenment can be entered into and cultivated.

Another form of sexual misconduct for the highest level practitioner would be to perceive the visualized partner as other than enlightened and freed from all delusions. As soon as the newly visualized sexual partner is seen in the worldly context, the practitioner then has, through the action of his or her own mind, brought the visualization to that worldly level of grasping (self for objects/others) and grasps at the visualized partner. The reason, ultimately, why this precept is so important is that, if the genuine practitioner approaching enlightenment cannot remained placed within the meditation by disciplining his or her mind according to the vows taken, then he or she will not be able to generate a level of concentration sufficient to cause the consciousness to split free from the physical support of the body.

Not to use intoxicants. If you hope to change your deluded mind, then the mind cannot be overwhelmed by the delusions created from the use of an intoxicant, whether it be a drug or an alcoholic beverage. That is pretty obvious. There is more to it than just that, however. There is a need to investigate the subject of addiction to any object/other that is strong enough to force you to deal with it on other than a "by choice" basis. For instance, if you have a lover you feel you cannot live without and so are constantly checking with him or her regarding his or her well-being in relation to yourself, then how can you expect to maintain a meditation that spans not just minutes or hours but weeks or even one or two years? Or if you smoke cigarettes, then at regular intervals your body will crave a cigarette and meditation will be interrupted.

The things that make you feel "complete" as a human being are all illusions. They are like intoxicants with the power to alter your feeling of well-being. You grow dependent on the "fix" and are stimulated over and over (usually by time, although it can be from memories) to seek out the source of your perceived wellness. There are many levels of insight into the meaning of "to not use intoxicants," and this is a difficult precept to practice. Whatever level of your awareness, however, the continued use of drugs or alcohol does not increase your ability to gain insight into the Buddhist path to enlightenment. Any insight believed to be gained while under the influence is quickly lost with the lessening of the effect of the drug, with the imprints on the consciousness *still* untouched.

During the practice that is the path to enlightenment, the practitioner reconditions the mind by burning the imprints off the consciousness with insight into the nature of how things truly exist. Once burned off, those particular seeds or imprints will not be able to empower a delusion. Eventually, as insight into the nature of the self and objects/others is cultivated, all of the gross imprints are burned off. When that occurs, the highest level practitioner even gives up attachment to his or her life in order to be of benefit to others and goes beyond, enlightened.

Chapter Seven

SOWING THE SEEDS

. . . *Next morning, with the first light, he was out there string-*
ing twine where the rows of seed would go and hoeing in the furrows.

"Here," he'd say, appraising the tiny seeds running through his fin-
gers before handing me the bag and motioning with his shoulder, "run
a row of these over there. Like this," he'd say, taking a handful of
the seed he was working with and dribbling it evenly, bing. . .
bing. . . bing. . . bing. . . .his black-nailed thumb familiar with the task.

Through the quiet morning our thoughts rose and fell with the
tuneless whistle that blew through his wrinkled ninety-some-year-old
lips with every breath.

In the cool evening when we checked our handiwork, I'd marvel at
his familiarity with other dimensions as he'd look up, beyond the lim-
its of the sky and superstitiously intone, "Right weather and this gar-
den'll do just fine. Just fine."

Everything that needed saying having been said, using my shoul-
der for support, we'd work our way back to the house, my happy foot-
prints close to his, marking our steady passage through the dampen-
ing grass. Inside, he'd hook his cane over the edge of the piano and,
with my aunt chording and everyone singing as they would—his eyes
closed and foot stomping, fiddle set into the crook of his arm and
shoulders swinging—he'd transport me with his surprising passion to
earlier times and other places where those he'd loved first still lived.

$\mathcal{T}$ he steps involved in planting a successful crop are like those required to achieve the path to enlightenment. First, just as the decision to plant the field has to be made before further action will be taken, so the decision to be enlightened in this lifetime must be made. Second, just as the hard-packed earth of the field has to be turned over, so do you have to "turn over a new leaf." This entails looking at things differently, making different kinds of choices for your life based on your decision, shrugging off what is old and tired and doesn't work anymore. Third, just as the earth has to be worked until it is soft enough to receive the seed, so too do you have to "soften" your heart and mind to the practice by actually doing the practice. That practice includes the five precepts—not to kill, steal, lie, have sexual misconduct, or use intoxicants. Those precepts protect you from not giving harm to any living being while cultivating the three principal aspects of the path—renunciation, bodhicitta, and wisdom. Fourth, just as the seeds that will yield the crop must be sown, so too must the seeds that will lead to enlightenment, the six perfections—generosity, patience, morality, joyous perseverance, concentration, and wisdom. Finally, just as the sun and water are needed to bring the crop to fruition in its season, it is only with regular practice and the guidance of a skilled teacher that enlightenment—the perfection of the six perfections—is achieved.

Many people in the world today who call themselves practitioners unfortunately believe that practicing the Buddhist path to enlightenment means doing rituals, chanting,[60] and paying homage to gods and demons separate from their own minds. Others focus on the mere words and, thus, avoid the practice, while engaging in endless dramatic and usually public debates over the nature of the truth. Although these approaches can be and are utilized in the correct practice of the Buddhist path to enlightenment, without the rest of the package they cannot create the cause for the generation of wisdom, or enlightenment.

[The practitioner who is truly on the path has committed his or her life to becoming enlightened for others and affirms that commitment with every breath, every step, and every action taken. It is only when the commitment and practice take over every moment of your life, waking or sleeping, that the cause for the elimination of the delusions that bind you to cyclic existence, and the generation of the wisdom mind of enlightenment, will have been created. Not a moment before.]As long as you are still bound to cyclic existence (wherein the self thinks objects/others are inherently good or bad, and so on), then you are still bound to cyclic existence. It *is* difficult to stay aware of everything necessary to achieve enlightenment all of the time. It is also nearly impossible to remain thoughtful and free from distracting involvements in worldly activities, no matter what level you're at when you're involved in worldly activities. It is for this reason that the sincere practitioner will find a need for solitude, whether in solitary retreat or "lost" within the crowd.

The practice you do tomorrow will be the effect of the cause you create today. The cause you created yesterday is the effect experienced today.

> *If you want to know the past, look at the present.*
> *If you want to know the future, look at the present.*

---

60. *Chanting.* Many students chant words in foreign languages they cannot and do not understand, believing there is something magical in the sounding out of the words that will cause them to become enlightened. Others believe a harmonic resonance is generated through chanting that gets them closer to the wisdom source they seek. This *is* unfortunate since wisdom is a level of mind attained only through the elimination of the delusions that grasp at self, and a power in objects/others greater than self, through intelligent analysis of the elements of the illusion.

The Six Perfections

GENEROSITY. GENEROSITY IS EVERY action of your body, speech, and mind that gives precedence to another living being. It is the "spirit" or "heart" of giving. It is a level of being that is not threatened by either your own loss or another's gain; it is a level of being that rejoices at another's "seeming" good fortune. It is the thought to save another's life before your own. It is the thought to alleviate another's suffering by taking responsibility to accomplish the monumental endeavor of becoming enlightened, only for others, by your empty (of inherent existence) self alone. It is the heart of the Buddhist path to enlightenment that culminates when you actually give up attachment to the mere appearance of life and self in order to achieve the goal and thereby go beyond.

For the worldly, generosity is "I am giving a penny to this beggar." That is the worldly way of practicing generosity. There is a "someone" to do something for another. But this is just another cause for you to remain within the dream, grasping at self and objects/others. In order to qualify as a correct practice of the path to enlightenment, the thought of giving must be based within the mantle of wisdom. So, when you practice generosity, do so with the thought, "This empty 'I' is doing the impossible task of 'giving' an empty penny to this empty beggar." Then, think about its meaning.

Some who read the example above may be quick to jump at this apparently subtle shift in perception, claiming it to be just semantics. Such a superficial judgment could not be more incorrect. It is only through the intelligent analysis of the true nature of every single appearance of your mind that you will eventually replace your previous ignorant perceptions with wisdom-based insight into the truth of their nature. Through this development, or generation of insight, into the true nature of things, the ignorant mind will complete the practice by giving up attachment to the delusions that form the basis upon which "self" is merely labeled.

The path to enlightenment is about mind generation. If you consider the meaning of generosity and practice it to the best of your ability with every action of your body, speech, and mind every single day, by the time you are enlightened your insight into the meaning of the mere appearances of the world will have eclipsed itself five or six times.

To practice means to grow by generating new insight into the meaning of things. It is done with best result during the difficult times—for instance, when someone is robbing you or when you're very poor or when things are difficult in your life and even more difficulty comes to your door. It is the practice done at those times that is based in the thought to not give harm—any harm, to any living being, not just those you consider to be friends—that is the practice of the path to enlightenment. It is this practice done at just such difficult times that will cause you to eliminate the delusions associated with the ignorance that grasps at self and objects/others. It is this practice that becomes the cause similar to the result: generation of the wisdom mind of enlightenment.

Patience. The second of the six perfections is patience. The practice of patience is also accomplished when things are difficult, not when they're easy. For instance, when you are tired, dirty, hungry, and there's one more intrusion that could tip the scale. Having generated the conscious thought to not give harm to any living being and to be enlightened in order to be of benefit to others, the practitioner considers the true nature of the self that is so tired, dirty, and hungry, as well as the thought of the true nature of whatever object appears to be imposing its "self" on him or her. The practice of patience is the generation of ever more sensitive levels of awareness, so that when the self feels intruded upon or harmed by others, you immediately think, "This is cyclic existence, and the mind that must ultimately be controlled is my own, not the others'." Thus, you bring the problem back to your own mind, where it belongs, and remain uninvolved with the intrusive or harmful objects/others by understanding that *how* they exist is dependent on the mind, and does not exist, in any way, "from the side of the object," or inherently.

The practitioner should never expect kindness and generosity from self-centered individuals who have not generated the conscious thought "to not give harm to any living being with any action of body, speech, or mind." By understanding that suffering is the nature of ignorance, you will no longer rail against the illusion of injustice. Suffering is the nature of the level of existence based in ignorance. To give up the cause of suffering, the intelligent practitioner will, therefore, give up attachment to the self that could be harmed as well as to the objects/others mistakenly believed to be able to do harm. To practice like this creates the cause of your enlightenment.

Morality. Third is morality. In the world today, morality is generally considered to be a restrictive/restricting concept. Nevertheless, morality is the underlying cause for any living being's enlightenment and is synonymous with ultimate freedom. Morality is the wish to not give any harm to any living being in any way. The very "thought to practice" morality forces the sincere practitioner to look within his or her own mind for the source of any and all problems since all problems, whether they appear to be your own or others', come from the ignorance that grasps at self and objects/others. In order to not give harm, the practitioner will slowly and steadily give up attachment to the delusions upon which self is merely posited, thereby creating the cause for the generation of the wisdom mind of enlightenment.

Only by giving up attachment to the illusion of self and objects/others as inherently existent will you get to this point: where there is neither any conditioned response of the mind to support the concept of an inherently existing self that could give harm, nor an object/other mistakenly believed to exist separate from the mind's own making that could precipitate the giving of harm. By constantly generating the sincere wish to not give harm to any living being, and practicing a modesty and humility that cause one to always seek the source of every problem within one's own continuum, rather than others', the practitioner step-by-step gives up attachment to the delusions that support the umbrella delusion of an inherently existing self, and progresses along the path to enlightenment.

Joyous Perseverance. The fourth of the six perfections is joyous perseverance. Paradoxically, joy is synonymous with this difficult and self-effacing path. Only the mind that is joyous at the possibility of attaining the goal of enlightenment and being of lasting benefit to others still trapped in the suffering state can and will achieve that goal. Only through the most loving and joyous perseverance will you not quit before the end and overcome every obstacle of your mind. This is accomplished by never losing sight of the goal—the beauty of the virtue and kindness of one who is enlightened—perceived in the guise of the enlightened teacher. Finally, through the practice of the path to enlightenment, the mind is freed from delusions that bind it to suffering, and a joy based in that freedom wells up in the mind of the practitioner. The mind of joy loves the freedom from which it grew and, therefore, perseveres in order to experience more joy.

Concentration. The fifth of the six perfections is concentration. As with all understanding, concentration—its purpose, its practice, and its point—changes as the delusions upon which self is merely labeled are steadily removed and the goal, the wisdom mind of enlightenment, draws closer. At first the practitioner must maintain a level of awareness of suffering, both one's own and others', in order to commit to a meditation on the nature of the self and object/other of the suffering. This is a form of concentration that carries right through to the end.

There are other concentrations, however, such as on a "truth," like "life is just a dream," within which all appearances of the world around are considered. Another kind of concentration is on the teachings. The practitioner never strays from his or her practice or considers any aspect of it to be unimportant or irrelevant. Should the practitioner find him- or herself considering a teaching to be unimportant or irrelevant or already "learned," then the practitioner would, because of the level of his or her concentration, investigate the cause for this sort of limiting thought. With concentration, the practitioner would again review the goal sought as well as the perfection of the teachings and, thereby, recondition his or her mind with the new insight gained from the analysis. This kind of concentration will cause the practitioner to eventually find the deepest understandings of the simple words that are nothing other than symbols representing the action of their own minds.

There are levels of concentration that are levels of insight gained by the practitioner as he or she creates the cause to generate the wisdom mind of enlightenment that is freed from delusion. For the practitioner actually involved in the practice and not in mindless posturing, the thought of "Where am I on the path or in relation to others?" will not occur. To be thinking such a thought is an indication that one is still operating on a very gross level and is not concentrating on the path but rather doting on the beauty of the self one loves so dearly. Once enlightened, the individual will recall general impressions/practices and feelings associated with the various levels of his or her practice. These are referred to as levels of concentration and relate to the highest practice on the path to enlightenment.

Wisdom. The sixth perfection is wisdom. With the elimination of attachment to each delusion that supports the merely labeled self, through analysis of the nature of his or her suffering, the practitioner creates the cause to generate the wisdom mind of enlightenment freed from delusion.

Until that level of mind is actually generated, and as long as the individual has delusions that cause him or her to grasp at the mere appearances of the mind as though they were real, the individual is still ignorant and trapped within the dream. But the sincere practitioner should not think he or she is accomplishing anything at all. The individual who is eliminating the delusions associated with the ignorance that grasps at self and objects/others as inherently existent is simultaneously generating insight into the wisdom understanding how things truly exist. It is an indication of the gross ignorance from which the individual is trying to escape to feel pride or superiority. Until the wisdom freed from delusion is finally achieved, one is not enlightened. Any discussion of the truth by the unenlightened will necessarily be filled with delusion.

When these six practices are perfected, one is enlightened. (1) Generosity—one finally gives one's very life in order to be of benefit to others; (2) Patience—one completely stills the angry mind of ignorance—the mind that rides the wind, in order to (3) not give harm to any living being with any action of one's body, speech, or mind (morality). With the (4) joyous perseverance that comes from deep within the heart that causes one to do the practice only for others, one does not give up, even when near the very end. Fearing one might quit too soon and never be of lasting benefit to others, one keeps going. (5) A concentration is entered into that cannot be interrupted because it is blissfully bound to the goal and the mind is single-pointedly directed toward the object of its desire. All of this leads finally to the actual generation of (6) wisdom, having eliminated the gross delusions that bind one to the mere appearances of one's own mind. This is wisdom that understands there is no subject (self) and no object (objects/others), except the appearance created by, and dependent on, the mind of the perceiver. With the generation of the wisdom mind of enlightenment, one finally and irreversibly goes beyond the limitation of the ignorant mind trapped in cyclic existence, to liberation from belief in an inherently existent self (having given up attachment to the delusions upon which it was merely labeled). At that very moment, the practitioner transcends cyclic existence, and wakens from the dream.

The only tool you have at your disposal to generate the wisdom mind of enlightenment is your ignorant mind. As all living beings are naturally desire-oriented, desire is used as the path. The practitioner, because of his or her desire, creates the cause similar to the result. By single-pointed concentration on the desired object—the enlightened being of the visualized union—the duality of self and objects/others is transcended and enlightenment attained. One grows to be the thing one loves.⎤

Karma: the law of cause and effect. How does it work? If you do not posit the wish to reach the goal, then you will not reach the goal. Not reaching the goal does not mean that there is no such goal to be reached. It simply means that you are not aware of the goal, had not thought to reach the goal, and therefore, did not create the cause necessary to reach the goal. The goal itself is empty of inherent existence, but generation of the wish to achieve the particular goal of enlightenment creates the cause to waken from the dream. Ultimately, whether or not you waken from the dream by generating the wisdom mind of enlightenment will be completely dependent on the force of your own wish to be enlightened and whether or not you take all action necessary and appropriate to achieve the desired effect, or result. In other words, the cause has to be created that is directly similar to the effect desired.

To make an extraordinary goal reachable, you must take extraordinary action, must first generate the wish to achieve the goal, and then, with constant longing and thoughts extolling the benefits or virtuous qualities of that goal, slowly and steadily do all the actions necessary to generate the qualities of that goal within the continuum of your mind:

• An individual who thinks, "Gee, it would be great to go on a trip," but does not take the necessary action appropriate to achieve the goal will not go on a trip.

• If the individual posits the wish to go on the trip but does only a portion of the appropriate actions necessary to achieve the goal, that individual will also not go on a trip.

• If the individual posits the wish, begins doing all the appropriate actions necessary to achieve the goal, but gets sidetracked by the actions and, thereby, loses sight of the goal, that individual also will not reach the goal.

• If the individual posits the correct wish but does inappropriate actions due to either ignorance or arrogant disregard for the correct course of action necessary, that individual also will not reach the goal.

• If the individual posits the wish, follows the appropriate course of action, but just before completion of the action, loses the motivation to achieve the goal, that individual also will fail to reach the goal.

• Needless to say, if the wish to go on the trip is never posited at all, then no appropriate actions will be taken and, thereby, the trip will not be taken.

But, if the wish is posited to reach the goal and all necessary actions appropriate to achieve that goal are taken—the individual follows through to the very end—then the desired effect will be attained.

To think that any extraordinary goal will be reached "as if by magic" is the ultimate in ignorance of the law of cause and effect, and complete relinquishment of your responsibility for the results of all your actions.

It is just like this with the path to enlightenment. The individual completely reconditions his or her consciousness to the truth, thereby giving up all gross attachment to self and objects/others, thus creating the cause to transcend the level of mind that is trapped within its own appearance.

For an unenlightened individual to even think that something is wrong, or unsatisfactory, with his or her current level of existence is something of a miracle. To follow through with that thought and begin to look for some way out of the general feeling of dissatisfaction is truly quite remarkable. To finally get to the correct path to enlightenment, having somehow escaped all the worldly scam artists, soothsayers, and fashionable trends, with humility and strength and a sincere thought to be of benefit to others, is nothing short of astounding, as it is so rare. To begin the practice of the path to enlightenment, however, and not to give up when obstacles arise is the sign of a great practitioner and a "noble" being.

Such practitioners are truly blessed and will rejoice in the beauty of the path that leads to truly selfless generosity. They will often be misunderstood by the worldly because they will no longer be perpetuating worldly concepts of right and wrong, good and bad. Instead, they will cultivate a practice according to the example of the enlightened being who went before them and whom they consider to be their teacher. Those fortunate practitioners will understand that the actions taken by that one who generated the wisdom mind of enlightenment were not manifested according to the trends of the world of his or her time, either, but according to the level of mind of that sincere practitioner. This is how it is to practice.

Whatever level you are at this particular time in your life, a sincere practice can be established according to that level. Whatever the level—since there will be some listening to wisdom-based teachings on the true nature of things as well as some thought of the practice that is done only for others—some imprints relating to the truth will be left on the consciousness. Those imprints will eventually create the cause for you to hear more teachings later that will bring you closer to the actual practice whereby delusions are eliminated and insight into the true nature of things is generated. From listening and thinking, you will come closer to the time when you will waken from the dream.

When read and thought about well, these simple words form the path that unfolds before you as you create the cause to reach its end: generation of the wisdom mind of enlightenment. The words will guide the sincere practitioner in reconfiguring his or her mind to be inseparable from the truth so that he or she might waken from the dream. Through the correct practice, the very fortunate few will recondition their consciousnesses to the true nature of how things really exist and thereby waken from the dream within which all suffering is experienced and every unenlightened being is presently stuck.

Although through the practice the practitioner will experience relief from the more gross forms of suffering, Buddhism is not about how to be happy in this life. Neither is Buddhism a very clever intellectual exercise, although it is often perceived that way and presented as a philosophical construct. Buddhism is also not a religion wherein belief in a power greater than the self is posited and promoted. Buddhism is the practice of the path to enlightenment as laid out by one who attained that goal before.

Generally, in the Buddhist world today, the rituals that were meant to be intelligent practices whereby the practitioner was forced to concentrate on the visualized "illusion" in order to understand the truth have become little more than the "magic" of the superstitious. An evident example of this is how Buddhism is being approached in the West. English-, French-, and Spanish-speaking people, for example, are being told to say words in foreign languages they are not fluent in, because this somehow connects them closer with "the source." For too many, a superstitious belief that is based in the grossest form of ignorance causes them

to believe that there is, therefore, some magic or power inherently existing within the "foreign" language itself that can cause them to be enlightened. [The truth is, the only "magic" to cause you to be enlightened in
words relating to the path comes from comprehension of their meaning
and your own ability to follow them to their logical conclusion.]

Students who have studied the teachings that originated with
Shakyamuni Buddha should keep in mind that when he taught in India,
Siddhartha Gautama (who became known as Shakyamuni Buddha) spoke
in the native dialect of the area he taught in. After he was first enlightened, for instance, the teachings from which all current Buddhist teachings spring were delivered in the Bihar state of India, where the native
dialect is Mogadha. That was the language he taught in because that was
the language that most of the people who came to listen to him could
understand. He taught for fifty years before he finally passed away, and it
was not until three years after his death that his disciples/students met for
the very first time to try to record his teachings. In the India of that time,
the formal language of the scholars was Sanskrit. Because the disciples
wished to make a formal record of the teachings as they recalled them,
those teachings were, therefore, recorded in Sanskrit. Later, scholars studied the Sanskrit teachings and, according to those scholars' insights into
the meaning of a practice they did not complete themselves, they enthusi-
astically carried the teachings, as they had understood them, to the different parts of the Far Eastern world. As the teachings were heard in the various places of the world, they were translated into the local languages:
Chinese, Japanese, Tibetan, Pali in Thailand, and so on. Only the opening
Sanskrit headings and shorthand mantra-type passages were retained within the myriad translations to indicate that the lineage of the teachings
descended from the Buddha.

Generations of scholars have taught generations of scholars.
Although the teachings can be read and understood to a limited degree by
anyone, the teachings are a practice, not a philosophy, and full and perfect
understanding of their meaning only comes with attainment of the goal,
having completed the practice that is a mind generation. Scholars have
turned the practice into theory. Every enlightened aspect of those teachings and how it relates to the whole has, thereby, been either lost or per-
verted to fit the conceptual network of the unenlightened scholars. In fact,
if queried, most scholars would admit that they do not truly believe they,
or anyone else for that matter, can be enlightened at all and certainly not

in their present lifetime,[61] creating the cause similar to the effect. This is the very subtle but extremely powerful impression left from the translations and commentaries of generations of unenlightened "teachers."

With the scholarly approach, which concentrates on theoretical philosophy rather than the practice of becoming enlightened, practices whereby the practitioner was meant to reinforce his or her insight into the true meaning of the illusion and thereby eliminate delusion based in ignorance have been turned into superstitious ritual that promote ignorant concepts of duality. In the rituals, the self pays homage to a power greater than the self[62] with no conscious thought of how the two truly exist, or understanding to use the ritual as a tool for the development of wisdom. If, perhaps, the intention to meditate on the path to enlightenment is there initially, it is often too quickly forgotten and not reinforced. Also, when the teachers are unenlightened and are working from a self-centered point of view, power is gained over devoted students by promoting self-

---

61. *To believe you can be enlightened at all,* let alone in this lifetime, requires the generation of a certain level of mind. As the motivation of the Buddhist path to enlightenment is to achieve the goal of enlightenment, until you can trust the words of the enlightened teachings/teacher that teach you just how to go about reaching that goal, you will stay very far from the actual practice.

A certain amount of self-confidence is necessary to set any goal. Then, the mind must be clear enough to be able to see the steps that must be followed in order to reach the goal. Finally, you must overcome the obstacles to completion of the path to achieve the goal by skillfully finding ways to either go around them or overcome them. It takes patience, with yourself and others, to achieve great goals. It takes perseverance, concentration, and aptitude. In the case of the Buddhist path to enlightenment, it takes the six perfections: generosity, patience, morality, joyous perseverance, concentration, and, finally, wisdom.

Also, unfortunately, many individuals are "self"-conscious and have been taught that it is arrogant to think one can do anything "great." Others coyly claim they "could not possibly." These are obstacles to practice.

Whether or not you think you can be enlightened is a private concern and motivation; to speak publicly about it would sidetrack you from the real practice. Still, it is important for you to repeat the wish to be enlightened for the benefit of others countless times every day in order to stay focused, and joyous.

62. *Power greater than the self.* The purpose of the Buddhist path to enlightenment is to eliminate the duality between the self and those objects/others that appear to have a power greater than that self capable of causing the self to be happy or suffer. Belief in a power greater than the self is the definition of religion. Buddhism *is not* a religion. Buddhism is the path out of the dualistically-oriented world of the ignorant mind, to the enlightened and omniscient state, at which time the individual understands perfectly the true nature of all things, without mistake.

When Buddhists set up altars for "worship" that include images of enlightened beings, it is not for the purpose of worshipping "gods" but for the purpose of meditating on the correct path to enlightenment followed by the enlightened beings. Every element of the Buddhist altar represents at least one aspect of the path to enlightenment that will be understood on many different levels, according to the level of mind of the practitioner.

centered superstition based in dualistically-oriented ignorance. It is in direct opposition to the purpose and practice of the Buddhist path to enlightenment to promote belief in a power greater than the self. Buddhism is neither a philosophy nor a religion. It is a practice that, when done correctly, is the cause for the practitioner to waken from the dream, freed from the dualistic delusions of self and objects/others of the dream.

To understand what happens when the teachings of an enlightened being are taught by non-practitioners, imagine that you want to make your living driving a tractor as a farmer. If you only go to the teacher who took instruction from the teacher who took instruction from the teacher, and so on, and this teacher has read all the books and can quote verse and paragraph but has never gotten on a tractor and made a living as a farmer, you will very likely not get correct information on how to "really" make a living as a farmer. Chances are, you'll get on the tractor for the first time and turn the key. There will be a deafening roar and surge of power that the teacher had not been able to prepare you for, you'll be scared to death to continue, or you'll think you've done something wrong. Your education was for educators, not for practitioners. However, if you'd gone to the farmer who made his living as a successful farmer, you could fairly expect to become a similarly successful farmer if you followed the practice he had done before you.

The unenlightened mind is tied to its dream state with uncountable conceptual ties that cause the individual to grasp at the dream as though the appearances existed from the side of the objects. To be unenlightened means to be unaware that every appearance is dependent on your mind for its existence and exists in no other way. The self of the dream also does not exist in any way other than as the mere appearance of the mind that has become lost in the conceptual network of the dream and believes its own appearance exists separate.

The Buddhist path to enlightenment is an introspective and solitary practice, and the teachings one follows must be those set out by someone who has already achieved the goal, by someone who is enlightened. Although you can look to the world around you for inspiration and insight into your own faults, you must always look only to the enlightened teachings/teacher for guidance, not to his or her fellow students. Why? If you don't believe your teacher is enlightened, then when the going gets tough and you run up against your own mind, fault will be found with the teacher and the teachings, and you will quit, settling back into your previous self-satisfied and self-serving state. Also, obviously, if you take instruction from a fellow student, then—because he or she has not completed the path, either, and so cannot speak of a correct practice followed that created the cause to achieve the goal—his or her interpretation of a level of practice not yet begun will be riddled with mistakes.

When one is enlightened, one is liberated, or freed from belief in an inherently existent self. "Self" is the umbrella concept that is supported by the gross delusions that are eliminated by the practice. By changing your perception of the reality of the dream through the generation of the insight that understands how anything truly exists, you give up attachment to the mere manifestations of the mind lost in the dreaming. In such a way, the mind comes to "know" the truth. Through the practice by which the student reconditions his or her response system or storehouse consciousness to give up attachment to the mere appearances of the mind by understanding the nature of the illusion, the student creates the cause similar to the result sought. Through this practice you free yourself from the prison of the conceptual network that is based in ignorance of the truth and is the cause of all suffering. Having given up attachment to the gross appearances of the dream by generating the wisdom understanding how those things truly exist, the sincere practitioner, compelled to complete the practice only for "others," rises from sleeping, wakened from the dream—enlightened.

Finally, to claim an interest in or to simply study texts does not qualify you as a sincere practitioner of anything. The act of controlling your own mind by meditating on the true nature of the mere appearance of self and objects/others, in conjunction with the giving up of attachment to those mere appearances in order to be of ultimate and lasting benefit to others, is the practice of the Buddhist path to enlightenment. Nothing else is. Not "sitting." Not ritual. Nothing else is the path to enlightenment.

If there is something you are interested in, you will pursue it according to the level of your interest. By generating loving thoughts to really help others in a lasting way, and with modesty acknowledging the need for a qualified teacher who has achieved the goal you wish to achieve and is therefore qualified to guide you, without error, to its end, you will begin to create the cause to know an enlightened being.

When you've generated some measure of conviction that you have found, or come in contact with, the very information needed to attain the goal of enlightenment and, thereby, truly be of benefit to others, you will know you have a priceless treasure. Never be careless with your treasure, or it will be lost. Such a treasure would never be found on the floor, in the rubbish, underneath the miscellaneous signs of the practitioner's daily life, carelessly pushed aside for other more important things, no matter how tired or poor or rushed the practitioner might be. The treasure would be high but where the eye constantly passes, out of the way of harm, well tended and thought about, the cause of one's joy. Treat the information given by an enlightened being, no matter what form that information might take—books, papers, thoughts, the signs of practice—as you would treat the most priceless treasure in the universe. Living a life according to the teachings means that every action of your daily life should be treated like a reflection of your understanding of those teachings. Lifestyle should be simple, chatter limited, you and your living quarters should be physically clean. When such actions are done with the constant thought of the meaning of the practice and a correlation of the gross activities of this life, to the highest level meaning of the teachings, then even the seemingly most mundane aspects of your life become the path.[63]

To practice means to stand quiet and alone, removed from the activities, thoughts, and considerations of those around who may or may not be trying to get out of the conceptual network that binds them to cyclic existence. Your treasure will exist dependent on and inseparable from your own mind for its existence, its value not inherently existent in the object.

Similarly, assume you are conditioned to believe in the conceptual network of the world and that world claims that to qualify as other than junk, all treasures must, for instance, have gold on them. Then, if you

---

63. *The practitioner,* for instance, when sweeping or dusting his or her living quarters should feel he or she is "sweeping" the obscurations, based in ignorance, from his or her mind. Similarly, when washing the body, the practitioner should think that all the obscurations based in ignorance are being eliminated with the dirt, leaving his or her mind clear of delusion. This is how the practitioner's life is turned into the path. Although it might appear to the observer that a room was cleaned or a body washed, in actuality, the practitioner who used those mundane activities as an opportunity to practice generates a mind intent on the path, and when the practice is cultivated, no matter what the activity, the mind of the practitioner will be inspired by the joy experienced from the activity, to enter even further into the practice that is the path.

Non-practitioners too easily claim such activities to be nothing other than "mere semantics." This is completely incorrect. The practitioner must create the cause similar to the effect desired. Until the mind has completely entered the path that is the practice and turned every activity of his or her life into the path, the individual will slip in and out of a very superficial level of practice that will be conducted only according to that individual's schedule of "practice" activities—as though practice was practice, and life is life.

come in contact with an appearance lacking gold, having already grasped at the worldly label "junk," it will not appear as a treasure. To free oneself from the conceptual network that is cyclic existence, you must change your conceptual network. It is a solitary practice, and the result is intangible. Cultivation of the status quo of the conceptual network of the unenlightened is not, on any level, the Buddhist path to enlightenment.

No worldly love for another/others compares with the mind that becomes inseparable from its object as a result of generating the wish that overwhelmed every other worldly consideration, including life and death in order to be only of ultimate and lasting benefit to others.

Chapter Eight

CULTIVATION OF THE FIELD

*Only in the field of the perfections
Is the fruit of one's labor unlimited.*

*A*lthough the path to enlightenment is a solitary practice, you will prosper in your practice and the teachings will flourish *only* in the context of a community interested in the same goal. Through the definition of the differing roles and levels of commitment, much confusion can be eliminated and you will be able to choose more easily the level or role that suits you.

Among practitioners, there are lay practitioners and ordained. While the lay practitioner may take certain vows pertaining to the practice based in virtue, the ordained practitioner takes all the vows pertaining to the practice based in virtue that bind every action of the individual's life to attainment of the goal of enlightenment in that lifetime. In order to begin a practice that will culminate in enlightenment, it is necessary for the layperson to give up the gross attachments to the mere appearances of his or her life and become ordained. But still, as a layperson, the practitioner can certainly have a very rich and rewarding practice according to the level of his or her commitment to the practice and, thereby, create a more compelling cause to be enlightened in another lifetime. Conversely, the ordained person must remain aware that the mere taking of spoken vows in no way creates the cause to be enlightened in that lifetime. Only when the level of commitment to those spoken vows seals their meaning inseparably within the heart and mind of the practitioner will he or she have generated sufficient cause to actually begin the practice and follow it to its end.

Whatever you do in this life, whether it involves a practice or not, by doing it to the best of your ability, you will progress toward the path. This is because as long as there is still something left to do, something you still want to accomplish in the world, something you need to be "happy," you will not be able to commit to the practice until that thing left undone is completed. For this reason, you should do those things quickly and very well. You will eventually—whether in this lifetime or the next or the next—become dissatisfied with whatever it was you were seeking, and will come closer to "knowing" suffering, your own or that of others. As you are reaching that point, or when that point is reached, the teachings can be listened to and thought about, and you can begin practicing.

It is necessary for both the lay and ordained community to practice the basics of Buddhism. This means to limit your critical involvements to your own ignorant mind, not others'. It means to not compare oneself with others, which would cause you to feel either superior or inferior to another who you are completely incapable of judging. Buddhism is about causing this mind, your mind, to be enlightened in this lifetime. It is not about perpetuating worldly thoughts like "So-and-so is not a good person or a good practitioner." It is about taking responsibility, finally, for your own mind in order to be of real benefit to others. It is about seeing the world around as a reflection of the level of mind, your own level of mind, trapped within its various illusions. Even if one took no vows at all but simply tried not to find fault with others, the world would be a better place to live. Whatever level of practice you are on, practice to the best of your ability. This creates the cause for the generation of another level of mind and a higher level of practice based in morality—the thought only for others.

Most important, keep in the back of your mind that until an individual is actually enlightened, he or she is no less ignorant, no less trapped in the level of mind based in ignorance, than any other unenlightened being. To judge one individual as "good" and another as "inferior" or "bad" is to cultivate the cause to continue in cyclic existence. Ultimately, every appearance of self-centered ignorance is the cause of suffering. Nothing more, nothing less.

A vow is a pledge or promise that causes the individual to act or behave in a particular way. To be ordained means to commit one's life to achieve the goal of enlightenment in order to be of benefit to others by keeping all actions of the body, speech, and mind within the field of the vows. To be ordained means to accept, as one's way of life, the actions or behaviors prescribed by the pledges made in order to achieve the goal of those vows. The vows set up guidelines that further create the cause to not give harm to any living being with any action of the body, speech, or mind.

Before an individual can see the need to make the pledge to consciously practice virtue, three things have to happen: (1) the individual will have already realized, whether vicariously or firsthand, that non-virtuous activity is harmful to others and virtuous activity does not give harm; (2) the individual must admit that he or she does not always practice virtue; and (3) he or she must have already established a wish to discontinue all harmful actions as well as an appreciation for the self-monitoring system the vow will trigger. Such a person will find that the pledge to practice only virtue will be inspiring as well as challenging. He or she will also experience a feeling of freedom rather than confinement within the parameters of virtuous activity.

By committing your life to the cultivation of virtue, its opposite, non-virtuous activity that harms both self and others (and is a very "tight" mind-set), is steadily eliminated. You experience a freedom of mind that did not exist previously. Because all actions of the mind create the cause directly similar to the effect, when you consciously commit your mind to deal with all appearances of that mind only from within the lovely field of virtue, you begin to consciously cultivate new insight into the meaning of virtue. You cultivate new insight into the meaning of the suffering of others caused by the non-virtuous actions of worldly minds completely dominated by the ignorant concept of self/me/mine. This cultivation of insight creates the cause for the generation of a new level of mind that in turn creates the cause for cultivation of a more profound level of insight, and so on. With the thought only for others, then the individual who has generated the three principal aspects of the path to enlightenment within his or her mind—(1) renunciation, (2) bodhicitta, and (3) emptiness—will have to, in order to keep his or her vow, give up attachment to the self that might give harm to the other. Such a practitioner, in order to keep even the most basic vow, will actually force him- or herself to give up attachment to the subject, to the action, and to the object, through the elimination of delusions and the generation of insight understanding that every appearance is created by and dependent upon the mind of the perceiver for its existence.

Let's very quickly review what was covered in the first chapters of this book in order to set the stage for its completion. The root cause for living beings to continue to cycle, or reincarnate, within a suffering level of existence is ignorance. Because of this ignorance of how things truly exist, the quality-filled dualistic appearance of self and objects/others is posited, believed to be real, and then grasped at. Because we believe the appearance exists separate from our mind, we grasp at it, which causes an imprint to be left, like a seed to ripen later on the field of the consciousness. The mind based in ignorance thus perpetuates its own deluded level of existence.

What needs to be done, then, in order to transcend that deluded level of existence, the nature of which is inseparable from suffering? The practitioner must eliminate the ignorance from which every delusion springs. The delusions are like weeds choking a large and unproductive field. The transcendental virtue of enlightenment is cultivated by actually burning the delusions off the consciousness with fiery insight into how those delusions truly exist. Non-virtuous activity is always the result of a "self" giving harm to object/other, mistakenly believing both to be inherently existent. With the removal of the delusions that form the basis for the concept "self," every cause for non-virtuous activity is also eliminated.

In order to create the cause to cultivate the insight necessary to eliminate those delusions, every action of your body, speech, and mind must be based in morality: *the wish not to give harm to any living being.* Through the practice, an ever deepening level of awareness of and insight into the nature of self-centered actions evolves. Morality and the virtuous actions it spawns are only possible within the framework of the three principal aspects of the path: (1) renunciation of the mere appearances of the mind; (2) an overwhelmingly compelling wish to be enlightened in order to be of lasting benefit to others; and (3) emptiness, if not actual insight, then at least an intellectual understanding of the true nature of things. This virtuous level of mind is of a transcendental rather than worldly nature because it creates the cause to eliminate the delusions that bind the practitioner to the suffering state of cyclic existence. This virtuous level of mind is the field of practice within which all other practices must be done. The practices within this level of mind create the cause for the unification of the dualistically-oriented mind and elimination of its root cause, ignorance.

Until every aspect of the Buddhist path to enlightenment has been generated, achievement of the goal is not possible. Therefore, the intelligent practitioner will begin consciously cultivating as many practices on the path to enlightenment as he or she is able, as quickly as possible. The practice should be similar to the way in which a smart manufacturer would build a vehicle. That manufacturer would have the many parts and pieces that make up the finished car produced simultaneously and then gathered at the time of assembly. If the manufacturer waited for each individual piece to be manufactured before production of the next was begun, the vehicle would never be assembled.

You must approach your practice in similar fashion. You should work on every appearance of your mind as it relates to the path to enlightenment. Having done so, store those many insights in an organized way in your mind. As your practice progresses, you will acquire this bit of information, then that. Your mind will store that data and use it to analyze new situations, eliminate delusions, and gather insights into the true nature of things, including virtue, correct practice, and emptiness. Over and over, day in and day out, it will become clear to you how efficient and reliable your mind is becoming. By the time you are ready to do highest level meditation, it will be as easily accessible as a well-organized computer database.

At first, though, while the delusions are being eliminated, there will be no feeling of a pattern, nor possibly even an awareness that such an efficient organizational process is taking place within the mind. It will not be until very far along the path, and close to the time of final meditation, that the practitioner will become aware of how the mind has become an unbelievably trustworthy, efficient, and virtuous processing machine. Finally, when the practitioner sits down and enters the final meditation, wherein the practices done every day for years are finally put to use, the mind—which by then will have eliminated most of the gross delusions upon which self was believed to exist separate from its own action—begins to access all those files/insights in unbelievable combination and at breathtaking speed. Through this highest level meditation, one eliminates the delusions still binding the practitioner to the suffering level of existence based in ignorance.

Every individual who becomes enlightened will have similar experiences and realizations. By following the instructions and gleaning insight into the insights shared by an enlightened being, through listening or reading and then contemplation, the practitioner will find the path clearly marked and, therefore, easier to follow, and also less threatening to the self.

The Buddhist path to enlightenment is a mind generation that leads to the direct realization of the empty nature of the self and the objects/ others appearing to the mind of the perceiver. "Mind generation" means a *total* involvement of the mind, not a partial involvement and not a compartmentalized one. The mind of the genuine practitioner is "oneness" with, or inseparable from, its object: the wish to be enlightened for others. Every action of the mind, every awareness of new insight, should be encouraged to develop as a whole.

On the other hand, when very unaware people practice "not giving harm to any living being," it will be practiced from within the mental framework of a self grasping at objects/others as good, bad, or unimportant. For this reason, certain living beings will be chosen as worthy of consideration for the individual's largesse, and others as not. Having grasped at the entire process based in ignorance of how things truly exist, the individual perpetuates the self-centered view of the perceived world, which ultimately gives harm to all living beings since the mind will change and with it the criteria for good, bad, or unimportant. Such living beings are certainly doing the very best they can. They seek to practice virtue, but every appearance of the mind's creation is judged according to how the perceiver is conditioned to believe it relates to "self/me/mine." Thus, actions of such individuals are unintentionally self-centered and self-serving.

For instance, take the "enemy." One person has an enemy; every bit of that individual's self finds every bit of that "enemy" distasteful. To another person, however, that "enemy" is a father or mother, son or daughter, loved one, friend. How does either "enemy" or "friend" truly exist? Dependent on the mind of the perceiver due to his or her conditioning. That conditioned response that is believed in is the basis upon which self is labeled.[64] The person grasps at "enemy" and tries to get rid of that threat to self while the other person grasps at "friend" and tries to secure what is mistakenly believed to be the cause of happiness. Both individuals are equally deluded and non-virtuous. However, to the worldly observer, the one perceiving the "enemy" might be thought to be non-virtuous

---

64. *Friend or enemy?* Can't you remember at least once in your life a "best" friend who became your "worst" enemy, or vice versa? Many have. What did the appearances depend upon for their existence? Your own mind. Neither friend nor enemy existed as more than the mere appearance of your mind due to conditioning although it appeared that each existed independent, from the side of the object.

while the other perceiving "friend," virtuous. Living beings who mistakenly grasp at self and objects/others as real from the side of the object, or inherently existent, set up the causes for all suffering of self and others.⎤

Those practitioners, whether on a lay level or ordained, who have grown weary of the meanness of this life must take up pledges, or vows, that set up the boundaries within which no action of the body, speech, or mind will be allowed to give harm to any other living being. By setting up such boundaries, the necessary action will be taken and, as the delusions are eliminated, so will the insights be generated. The practitioner must keep in mind that it is not the times of relative ease that he or she is preparing for. Rather, it is the difficult times, when there is some problem occurring within the mind that one prepares for, for instance, when there is an appearance of "enemy"[65] or "unkindness" directed at the practitioner. It is those mere appearances of "problems" that, when handled within the field of morality and the three principal aspects of the path, create the cause for enlightenment and the possibility of contributing to the solution rather than the ongoing problem.

The path to enlightenment, as well as every aspect of the practice, is inseparable from a developmental mind generation. It is the nature of practice to cause the mind to develop new levels of awareness associated with the practice. Practitioners must understand that, until enlightened, all practices will indeed be imperfect because they will be done according to the level of mind that is still based in ignorance of the true nature of things. The ignorant mind is deluded. Those delusions obscure clarity of mind. But don't despair; time drills holes in stone.

• • •

---

65. *The practitioner should cultivate another understanding* of the labels "friend," "enemy," and "stranger." If the practitioner, in truth, really wants the opportunity to practice by eliminating the cause of every appearance of suffering, then, isn't the "enemy," who causes so much unhappiness in the mind of the practitioner, actually the cause for the practitioner's eventual enlightenment? Isn't it true, in fact, that if the motivation of the practitioner is to be enlightened in order to be of benefit to others, then isn't the "enemy," who causes the practitioner to have so many opportunities to generate the path, the practitioner's "best" friend? Think about this. This is exactly how adverse circumstances are turned into the path. The "easy" times, the "acceptable" circumstances, are not the ones that cause the practitioner to do the hard work that is the path. In fact, this is why the work is "hard."

Is there then, really, either a "friend" or an "enemy" existing inherently? Isn't it obvious that how the "friend" or "enemy" *truly* exists is completely dependent on the mind of the perceiver?

IF YOU ARE INVOLVED IN THE genuine practice of virtue, then tomorrow, having gained new insight into its meaning today, you will practice on a higher, more insightful level. This is how practice works, and this is why the practice *must* be done. The point of stating this is to help you understand that you are not perfect and that, as long as *you* are doing the very best you can with the thought to not give harm to any living being uppermost in your minds, then you can give up attachment to the perception of personal failure—which is not only a very self-centered view but also the ignorant mind's way of obstructing your progress.

Speaking of personal failure: As soon as you make a pledge or take a vow—which makes you very conscious of a non-virtuous action you don't want to commit—you'll notice yourself committing the action. Many people panic, thinking that in a mere five minutes, for instance, the vow has been broken. But this just is not the case. Be aware that for any vow or pledge to be broken completely, four things have to happen (1) the wish has to be generated to do the harmful action; (2) the object of the action must be identified and the decision made to do the harmful action; (3) the action must be completed and the harm done, whether by one's own hand or through the commissioning of another; and (4) having completed the harmful action, the individual then rejoices. These four actions of the mind of the individual involved must be "realized" for the vow or pledge to be completely broken. Obviously, when an individual has completed such action, he or she is far outside the realm of morality and the wisdom-based teachings and has, through the thoroughness of the involvement with the giving of harm to another, left very powerful imprints on the consciousness to give harm the next time the appearance of a cause arises.

If you realize that you have broken a vow and have given harm to another through complacency or casual lack of awareness, the purity of the vow can be reestablished. The following four actions, called the four opponent powers should be taken. (1) The power of regret. You deeply regret the thought to give harm and the actions made to fulfill the thought. (2) The power of reliance, by which you reassert your wish and pledge to the enlightened teacher/teachings to keep the vow. (3) The power of the opponent force. Think of all you hope to accomplish on the path to enlightenment, and why. Consider that nothing at all will be accomplished by a mind that could give harm to another. (4) The power of the promise. Vow to never commit that particular action again, and to police your mind more carefully. Commit to always put others before self.

No matter how many sincere pledges you've made or vows you've taken, staying focused within the parameters of the practice is nearly impossible even for the "best" mind on its "best" day. The mind that has to deal with worldly activities—making decisions, going here and there, being involved on that level of "things"—will bounce around in its attempt to try to handle the brushfires of life. It is not possible for a person involved with worldly activities to practice on the level required for the period of time required in order to achieve the goal in this lifetime. No matter how great the personal wish to achieve the goal, it is simply impossible. In the world today, there are many teachers, lay and ordained, who are themselves unenlightened because they have no personal insight into the correct practice of the path to enlightenment. Often they tell the lay students that laypeople, still involved with worldly concerns and activities, can be enlightened. Often they feel they might lose their lay students if they were to state the facts correctly, as taught by enlightened beings.

If you are still attached to the mere appearances of your mind based in self and still grasp at "good, bad or indifferent" as it is believed to affect "self, me, and mine," then you cannot transcend those delusions that bind you to the level of mind called the suffering state of cyclic existence. Most of the teachers today, whether from the West or the East, are themselves unenlightened. Such teachers have become far removed from the correct teachings of an enlightened being. Even ordained teachers in the 20th century are encouraging ordained students from the West to live and work as laypeople. This switch in role assignment by those far removed from the correct teachings of the path to enlightenment laid out by an enlightened teacher is encouraged in order to support not only the ordained individual's mixed lifestyle but also the lifestyles of the teachers and, generally, the Asian monastic system. It is commonly insinuated by all involved that such worldly practices are "beneficial" for students and others. The focus of such unenlightened teachers has been moved away from *correct* practice, which is the control of the mind in order to eliminate the cause of suffering and be enlightened and, thereby, be of ultimate and lasting benefit to others. The focus instead has moved toward a practice by which the unenlightened teacher manipulates the appearances of his or her current level of existence in order to, temporarily, change the appearance of suffering on the worldly level. Going back to the example of the computer again: The true practitioner, seeing a problem, eliminates its root cause by changing the program. The misguided practitioner, seeing a problem, merely changes the appearance on the screen either through manipulation of the screen or by inputting different information in order to change what is appearing on the screen. In the second case, the root cause of the problem is not eliminated and the program is not corrected. The problem will soon resurface.

Most people in this world who have a thought to help end the suffering of others feel that the greatest good is done through service-oriented activities. Whatever the service, it is done with the thought to alleviate one form of deprivation or another. When the resources of the service are exhausted or calamity elsewhere calls out more urgently, those who were helped still struggle to overcome the deprivation felt, always with the wish to secure happiness and freedom from suffering for self/me/mine.

But the root cause of all suffering is, ultimately, the ignorance that binds living beings to the suffering state of cyclic existence. Until that ignorance is completely eliminated through the generation of wisdom understanding how things truly exist, the suffering will never end. Actually, because of the way the consciousness is conditioned to respond to suffering with the thought to save self, the longer an individual remains on that level struggling to secure self/me/mine, the more non-virtuous the individual will become. Very primal levels of thinking based in fear for self/me/mine become imprinted on the consciousness. These imprinted consciousnesses take rebirth in a downward spiral that becomes more and more exclusively self-centered, with lessening concern "to not give harm to any living being," or morality. Eventually, the focus of the living being caught in this spiral becomes so limited and self-cherishing that even the offspring do not figure in the equation of securing happiness and freedom from suffering for self/me/mine. At that time, every activity is only for me, me, me.

The practice of the path to enlightenment is so difficult. It is done only for others. It is only by becoming enlightened in order to be of benefit to others that any individual is capable of leading any other living being out of suffering. When an individual has a direct realization of emptiness and is liberated from belief in an inherently existent self, it is only done for others. The courageous individual "threw him- or herself over the wall," so to speak and, like a great athlete, did the hard work of attaining the goal of enlightenment. The kind of person that accomplishes this most noble goal is the kind of person who is not willing to suffer a little bit over a very long period of time. Such a person prefers to "suffer a lot" now, in order to get through the pain. There is an old saying that would certainly apply to the true practitioner of the Buddhist path to enlightenment, "Cowards die many times before their deaths, valiant ones but once." [Only a person who has renounced attachment to suffering will get beyond it. Only a person with highest level of motivation to be of benefit to others will be able to follow this path to its end.]

Each of us must certainly practice all manner of kindness toward others in our lives as opportunity presents itself. Still, the greater view—focusing on the elimination of the root cause of all suffering, which is ignorance—*must be* maintained and cultivated. For the practitioner, an incessant meditation must be done on the nature of cyclic existence, spurred on by every instance of suffering encountered. From such worthwhile activities the practitioner will find inspiration to "go beyond" in order to lead those who are suffering "out" of the cycle of existence that binds them to suffer.

The Buddhist path to enlightenment is not for everyone, there should be no doubt of that. But the teachings of the Buddhist path to enlightenment, based in morality born of wisdom, are the most precious treasure and can be studied by everyone. Cultivation of such wealth causes all to prosper. The genuine practitioner who has entered the path will have come to understand, through experience and observation,[66] that even if every starving person is fed today, tomorrow they'll once again be hungry. The futility of worldly actions will become more and more clear as associated delusions are eliminated through careful analysis. It is only through the practice of the Buddhist path to enlightenment that suffering will, once and for all, be completely eliminated.

So, here we are. We've talked about how the mind works, virtue, renunciation, bodhicitta and emptiness, vows. So many things. Now I would like to talk about a very touchy subject—perhaps even more touchy than discussions on *tantra* or death. That is the relationship of the lay community to the ordained one as well as the ordained community in its own right.

The ordained community—Western and Eastern alike—needs the emotional as well as the financial support of the lay practitioners. The

---

66. *Experience and observation.* It is not necessary to experience every single thing personally in order to know it is unsatisfactory. By observing the world around you, you will be able to infer all that is necessary in order to begin a serious practice and to give up attachment to the belief that happiness can be attained in some other, worldly way.

ordained community, in turn, creates the cause to receive the support of the lay community by living as ordained people are instructed by both the example of the enlightened beings who practiced before them and the pledges made when the vows of ordination were taken. Although it is *very* difficult not to, the lay community should not be concerned with or attempt to judge the quality of practice of the individuals ordained.

The ordained community should be joyous to have the time and place to practice. With every prayer, those practitioners should recall the kindness of the lay community that has, through its virtuous practice of generosity, helped create the conditions needed for them to practice to become enlightened in that lifetime. For the laity, then, and for all others, each member of the ordained community must practice tirelessly to discipline the mind in order to attain the goal.

The lay community, in turn, should feel great happiness to know that it is creating the cause for its own enlightenment through the practice of generosity. It also should be thankful that the perfect teachings of the perfect teacher will survive because of the practices of the ordained community they are helping until the lay community itself is ready to give up its worldly attachments in order to become enlightened.

The practice is hard work and very difficult. The reward is not tangible. Not even a single one of your unenlightened compatriots will ever be able to see what is happening in your own mind. Even just listening to your words, those others will not be able to determine where you are on the path, or even if you are on the path at all. They themselves have not generated a level of insight sufficiently freed from delusions to be able to determine that. You, then, must forgo the acclaim of your peers because acclaim simply is not going to happen. In fact, since you will not be cultivating worldly "friendships" or interests, you may actually be perceived by those others as failing or as selfish or having no compassion for the others' never-ending worldly woes based in ignorance. Acclaim will go, more often than not, to the ones who "please" others well and interact with them as peers dealing with their worldly woes, from a mind still completely obscured to the truth.

The path to enlightenment is not about maintaining your current level of mind or actions or interests. You are most fortunate to have so many opportunities to remotivate your mind to achieve the goal for the "others" who are suffering so much and are still completely lost within the dream. A true demeanor of mental and physical modesty, one that does not seek to exert its ignorant self in any way, is the correct mental state for the practice.

It is time to seek inspiration within your mind to do this practice in order to be of benefit to others. If you can find that inspiration, there is a chance that you might also reach the goal in this lifetime. Needless to say, if you don't believe you can be enlightened, then you certainly will not be enlightened. The cause similar to the effect; a self-fulfilling prophecy.

When Siddhartha Gautama was enlightened, the misconceptions of the practitioners of his day were quite similar to those occurring with great regularity now. Far too often the ordained community is urged to serve the lay community. Elsewhere, the most misguided ordained practitioners, like petulant spoiled children masquerading in robes, are allowed to act out their self-centered delusions at the expense of less-aggressive individuals around them. Too often these "spoiled" ones are major benefactors of their teachers. That such behavior is tolerated, let alone encouraged, is an indication of just how far away from the correct path to enlightenment too many calling themselves practitioners today have wandered. Such misguided behavior and practice are clear signs of the degeneration of the teachings of Shakyamuni Buddha.

This book is a set of guidelines for the correct practice of the Buddhist path to enlightenment. If you wish to be enlightened, then you must follow the instructions of one who has done it before you. You must walk in his or her footsteps. There is no other way to achieve the goal or to follow this difficult path—a path that the mind constantly finds reasons to run away from.

This is not a scholarly commentary on an ancient practice. It is the path followed by an individual who appears to be no different from yourself but who attained the goal. The instructions given in this book are the very same ones that you, when you are enlightened, will relate to those few with the karma to listen. It is these instructions that will guide them out of the labyrinthine network of their minds based in ignorance of its true nature.

Just as it is for you now, it will be very confusing and difficult for them to decide whether or not you truly know. When you are finally enlightened, all you will be able to do is present the information to them and work with them as long as they are able to follow. Possibly no one who listens to you in the lifetime of your enlightenment will follow the teaching to its conclusion. With time, though, lifetimes of it, the information of the teaching will be disseminated, eventually reaching many listeners.

At some point, some individual will generate a level of mind sufficient to begin the practice. That individual, like the enlightened beings before, will fill in the blanks left by the imprecise teachings of the unenlightened interpreters of your teachings, and become enlightened, having attained a state of perfect virtue. It is a slow process in the linearly posited concept of time of this world of illusion. In fact, beyond this level of existence, this level of existence does not exist at all, nor does time.

When you become ordained, you take the vows that are a commitment of every action of conscious life to the practice of becoming enlightened in this lifetime. You also give up the worldly life of the lay and all that that entails: clothing, lifestyle, interests. Taking such vows and giving up gross worldly attachments does not mean you do not respect or love the "others" from whom you have separated. In actuality, you love them even more than yourself. The ordained individual is accepting responsibility, based on the incredible love for others he or she feels, to take on the suffering of all others,[67] even to the point of giving up his or her life, in order to be of ultimate and lasting benefit to those others.

The mere taking of vows, of listening to words and intellectually saying "yes" does not denote ordination. As with all things on the Buddhist path to enlightenment, there has to be a commitment from the heart to achieve this most noble of goals in order to end the suffering of others once and for all. The path is a mind generation that is achieved

---

67. "... _to take on the suffering of others._" There is a practice, visualized as are all the Buddhist practices, whereby the genuine practitioner imagines the incredible suffering of every living being in "all the universes"—beyond even the scope of conscious knowing. In this practice, the practitioner imagines that all the suffering being experienced by all others is entering his or her body. At the same time, the practitioner visualizes that every cause he or she has created to be enlightened in this lifetime is going out to those "others." It takes so many qualities, so much "merit," to be enlightened, and you, the practitioner, are going to create all the merit needed by all others by yourself because "they" need help so badly. This exchange of self for others, although merely visualized, is a very powerful practice for the individual who truly recognizes the suffering of others, and the end of all suffering, and who experiences the exchange.

This particular practice is a particularly excellent one for practitioners who are not feeling well, or are unhappy. By visualizing that he or she has taken on the suffering of others, the ill feeling or unhappiness will be known as the suffering of others, taken upon the individual in order to help them. Such an individual can actually turn perceived misfortune into the cause of generating the loving heart of giving that is the basis for practice and, thereby, turn a "negative" into the cause for enlightenment. In such ways, the skillful practitioner will maintain an uninterrupted practice, no matter what the circumstances.

based on your constant recommitment, or reengagement, of your mind with its purpose, and a conscious thought to keep every vow perfectly in order to achieve that goal. In this way, the six perfections are generated and achieved.

Many people, whether they call themselves Buddhist or not, have taken vows and, when the going get rough, have broken those vows, putting blame on "objects/others" for their failure. For the genuine practitioner, vows are taken from the heart. When the going gets rough, as it certainly does on this path, then you are more able to give up attachment to the self and the mere appearance of objects/others that appears as an obstacle to "happiness." Because of the vow, which you treasure more dearly even than your own life, you eventually will get beyond the obstacle and, coincidentally, generate the next level of mind. That is what the vows are for and how the pledge works. It is only within the vows that the practice will be completed.

Among both Western and Eastern lay and ordained communities in this degenerate time of Shakyamuni Buddha's teachings, vows are given up all too frequently. These unfortunate individuals create the cause, by the action of their own minds, that leaves imprints for similar actions in the future to continue within the ignorance of cyclic existence. Sometimes vows are given up out of laziness; an individual just isn't willing to fulfill the commitment to do a practice every day as he or she had pledged. The first time the individual makes the choice *not* to fulfill his or her pledge to the enlightened teacher/teachings is the most difficult. The second time is easier; and all too soon it becomes the habit, and its opposite the exception. When an unenlightened student cannot see enlightened qualities in the teacher or the teachings of the Buddhist path to enlightenment, then the student will pick and choose what bits and pieces of the teaching are worthwhile and correct and discard everything else. Usually those things discarded are the ones that "offend" his or her sense of self, the very obstacles that are removed by the practice of the path. For this reason, too, many students decide to forsake the daily practice committed to previously at the feet (with a devoted mind seeking enlightenment) of the master (the enlightened being).

It is only natural as well that laypeople feel competitive with the ordained community they see before them. Unable to give up their attachments to the worldly life and yet somehow able to see how wonderful the teachings are, those individuals with their critical eye to others' imperfections will find endless fault with the individual members of the ordained community and assert their own superiority over those lowly individuals.

Of course, individuals in the ordained community are often led by their unenlightened teachers into "service" jobs to the lay community. Their original inspiration to be ordained is channeled into worldly activities promoted as "selfless acts of those who will be enlightened." Look to the activities of the Buddha for confirmation that such activities are *not* the activities that lead an individual to enlightenment. If they were, then Siddhartha Gautama would have remained in the palace of his father and tried to help the suffering "others" of this world with even grander service-oriented activities than you could begin to hope to do, since he certainly had unbelievable resources of wealth and influence at his disposal. But he did not make that his practice. He left that level of activity behind and, although he was ridiculed for it, he meditated in a solitary fashion, removed from the concerns of the world while he practiced and created the cause to transcend the level of mind attached to its own appearance. Thereby, he achieved the effect: liberation from belief in an inherently existing self, having eliminated the delusions upon which self is merely labeled by doing the practice only for others.

Chapter Nine

DEATH:
THE ONLY REALITY OF LIFE

The only thing we know for sure of life is that it will surely end in death,
and yet we weave our tangled webs of captivating intrigue
and spin endless streams of futile fantasy to bind our happiness to life.

Stuck upon the sticky gossamer—the unimportant work of one obsessed—
Too quickly the heavy hand of ignorance from out of nowhere
destroys the whole with morbid certainty.

*D*eath is the only reality of life. Yet, in the face of this singular reality, we ignore and turn our backs on it, put it out of our minds and prefer instead to immerse our every waking moment in the pursuit of happiness. If we could deal with the thought of our impending death, we would prepare for it and would not waste time on meaningless activities. If we would only deal with the reality of our situation, we would forgo most of the activities of our lives in order to prepare for the time that will surely come, sooner or later.

What do we know about death? (1) We know that every living being's "life" will end in death. (2) We know that death will occur, whether suddenly, by accident, or slowly, by sickness or, finally, as the natural end of "life." This last cause of death sounds more pacific than the others. In reality, because it is associated with old age, sickness, and the degeneration of the physical support of the body, it is no more pleasant than the other forms death takes. (3) We know that we cannot choose the time of death. (4) We know that at the time of death, all of the objects/others cherished and nurtured in this life will have to be left behind. (5) Although some individuals live to be more than 100 years old, it is a pretty fair bet that by the end of the next 100 years, every living being living today—including babies, parents, strangers, creatures—will all be dead. Start counting. (6) We know there is no way for any living being to escape death.

Death is inseparable from the suffering state of cyclic existence. The individual trapped within the dualistically-oriented appearance of self and objects/others grasps for the mere appearance of "life" in order to maintain the happiness of self. Having so grasped, believing that the self is inherently existent and that there is something to be lost through "death," the individual experiences incredible suffering when the causes of happiness are not secured.

Some of you reading this may think that the solution to the suffering experienced at the thought of death, or by death itself, could be eliminated by developing some cavalier view of death, or some conceptual system within which the self would feel comfortable or would experience a lessening of the suffering associated with death. And certainly, the mind can be conditioned to do any single thing a determined person wishes in order to create or maintain the self's unthreatened/happy status. But why not finally free your mind once and for all from the very cycle within which death follows every life spent in a futile pursuit of lasting happiness?

Reincarnation means "to take, once again, a physical form or body that is apprehended as substantial by the senses." It is a seemingly beginningless and endless cycle of death and rebirth, death and rebirth. If you can understand how the minds of living beings dread even to hear about death, let alone experience it, then you might understand the endless round of suffering experienced by the "selves" of each rebirth when forced to separate from the things believed to be the causes of happiness. Time after time the consciousness is implanted on another "living"[68] form. Over and over. The round will never end until decisive action is taken to end it.

What constitutes a living being, also known as a sentient being, is the ability to sense objects. The ability to sense objects indicates there must be a processing mechanism to handle that information—a mind. This mind then takes the sensed objects (causes and conditions), triggers imprints left on the consciousness from previous similar causes and conditions, and labels those qualities "good," "bad," or "unimportant" on the object, which then appears to relate to self accordingly, just as labeled. Such beings are trapped by the conditioned action of their own minds (karma) to sensory stimuli within the cycle of existence known to be of a suffering nature.

---

68. *Living.* If there is "living," then there must be "dying." It is not until you are freed from grasping at the mere appearances of this "life," which is inseparable from death, that you will transcend that two-dimensional level of existence and attain a level of mind freed from the limitations based in ignorance that grasps at self and objects/others, and is the cause of all suffering.

Plants are not sentient beings. They respond to environmental stimulation in a nondifferentiating photosynthetic process. They have no central nervous system, which would indicate a brain and mind function.

Serious students must remember that at the time of death, the consciousness splits free from the physical support of the body and enters a formless state. All the consciousnesses of every living being (all the millions of ants, the birds, the incredible number of creatures, along with the relatively few humans) that has passed away and not yet taken rebirth are in this formless state. The consciousness trapped in delusion is not able to *choose* a rebirth. Because human rebirths, by virtue of their relatively small number, are so rare, human beings in this life are unlikely to take rebirth as a human in the next one. Even when a human rebirth is obtained, physical or mental problems can interfere with the individual's ability to practice the path.

Life is short. Not to begin to practice now, while you are healthy, intelligent, and with the time and opportunity to do the practice, is to cheat yourself of a rare opportunity. When the time for taking the next form comes, there is no choice and no one to do the choosing. Human rebirth will be taken again only when the exact causes and conditions come together.

This is why it is so important for human beings, in this very short lifetime, to stop procrastinating (thinking to do it "later") and commit their lives, this life, to follow this noble path to its end. Only then will any individual be able to know for sure that the suffering state of cyclic existence is, once and for all, finished. Only by accomplishing the goal will he or she be able to utilize life in a way that will be of ultimate and lasting benefit to others who are still trapped within the conceptual network of their own minds.

When rebirth does take place, the consciousness is simply implanted on an available egg at the moment of its fertilization. It immediately begins to respond to sensory stimulation. To respond to sensory stimulation means that qualities are perceived in the objects apprehended (even by developing fetuses) as good, bad, or indifferent, which relate directly back to the self of that being. As the sense apparatus of the fetus develops, so does the mind's ability to apprehend objects and cultivate the "self" those objects relate back to. By the time the fully developed embryo is born, there is a "self" that is actively seeking a happiness freed from suffering in the objects apprehended around.

Human beings rarely consider "creatures"—or other-than-human formed beings—to have feelings of self. But if you think about it, you will know that all creatures seek the happiness of self/me/mine in the same basic ways: "good" food, "good" shelter, physical security through the elimination of threats, and the defense of boundaries that offset what is then believed to be their own/their home.

Parents with children will recall how each developing fetus responded differently to different sensory stimulation such as sound, foods, temperature, and so on while still within the womb. When the children were finally born, each had a definite personality that was unique. The differences perceived in the newborn children are not learned behaviors from conditioning in this life. They were the visible impressions of activated imprints left on the consciousness from previous lifetimes' conditioning.

Although children are conditioned in a socially acceptable way—which means within a generally acceptable set of guidelines necessary for the ongoing happiness of family culture—still, each child develops as an individual. This is due to the imprints from endless lifetimes of "selves" securing "happiness." Because the world is believed to exist only in the way perceived by each individual, every individual truly believes that every single action of his or her body, speech, and mind is correct and the cause of happiness and freedom from suffering.

So the world is a self-centered level of existence within which all activities will necessarily be believed to be beneficial by some, and harmful by others. There is no "real" common meeting ground within a self-centered level of mind that is constantly changing. In a mind where self, whether associated with one single individual or a collective, is mistakenly believed to exist separate from objects/others, the dualistically-established two can never meet as one. And so, leaders of the world seek resolution to self-centered problems from self-centered viewpoints. At best, only an appearance of harm kept temporarily at bay can occur. Actually, there is no "best" at all since every action of the dualistically-oriented mind can only result in suffering when the criteria for happiness are not met or as the mind is reconditioned by its own action. Then, when the object/other that was previously believed to be the cause of happiness is again encountered, it will be perceived to be the cause of suffering. Even if the feeling of suffering remains uncompounded by associated memories stimulated by the change in appearance, the self will suffer from the feeling of loss of the cause of happiness. This level of existence based in delusion must be transcended before the suffering can end.

How should an intelligent[69] individual go about it? Such an individual must wake up every morning with the thought, "This is the last twenty-four hours[70] of my life. What am I going to do?" This is an excellent meditation for every reader and, if it is done correctly, is quite revealing.

The practice. To remind yourself of your intention to do this meditation, leave a large note beside your bed as a reminder—immediately upon waking—of the practice. Then, still before rising, repeat to yourself, "I have only twenty-four hours left to live, I have only twenty-four hours to live." Now, begin your day. What will you do?

With only twenty-four hours left before death, will you worry about whether or not this piece of clothing or that one is better? Will you style your hair carefully before the mirror? Will you apply the cologne? Will you go to work? Will you go to the grocery store to stock up on sale items? Will you call your friend to gossip about last night's goings-on? Will you read the morning newspaper or watch the news? Will you hear the neighbor's dog barking in the distance and hate it for disturbing your morning? Will you make plans for tomorrow's activities, so you won't be bored, or

---

69. *To practice the Buddhist path to enlightenment*, the being must be of a human form, intelligent, and sensitive:
• Only the qualities and conditions of the human form and its relation to the environment create the cause for an individual to have not only an analytical mind capable of investigating the qualities of virtuous and non-virtuous activity and intuition that would spark it to action but also a position of "stature" or responsibility among the living beings of this world sufficient to see the suffering of those around. For instance, a dog cannot be enlightened. All such creatures can do is to hear unintelligible sounds of teachings that, because the meaning of those sounds in no way generates any insight, cannot become the cause of the being's eventual enlightenment.
• The human being must be intelligent. Although the Buddhist path to enlightenment is a practice and not an intellectual exercise for the effete who do not have energy for practice, it takes an extraordinarily skillful mind—one that can use itself like a tool, a skill developed through practice—to establish the goal and follow the path to its end.
• If the individual has blocked the pain the self feels from apprehending injustice, unfairness, meanness, the suffering of others, then that individual will not be able to motivate sufficiently to create the cause to end the suffering of self by eliminating the delusions upon which self is merely labeled. It is very unfortunate but completely understandable why in today's world people are encouraged to circumvent or numb the mind to its "painful" awareness of various forms of suffering in cyclic existence with clever rationales or techniques of reconditioning.
70. *"This is the last twenty-four hours of my life..."* Since the inevitability of death is the only reality of this life, one of these twenty four-hours must be the last. With this reality in mind at all times, the individual will create the cause not to waste his or her very precious human rebirth on the meaningless activities of this life that occupy those bound to the delusions believing there to be either a happiness or a suffering, inherently existing in "life," to grasp at.

left out or unproductive? Will you worry what so-and-so thinks of you? Will you lounge around all morning in your pajamas, procrastinating and wasting time?

You should keep a piece of paper handy to jot down notes on what you find yourself doing and not doing. You will quickly become aware that almost everything that you usually do would not be done if you believed the time left to you was so very short. As it is.

This is a very worthwhile practice for all human beings. At best, it will cause you to take the difficult steps to begin the practice, leaving the worldly things behind once and for all in order to achieve the goal before time runs out. At worst, you will feel uncomfortable at your own paralysis when confronted by your imminent death. This is how you must practice. If you only want to be happy, relaxed, and comfortable all the time, the path to enlightenment is not for you. If there is no cognition of the imminence of your death, then you will not feel "panicked" by the thought of missing the opportunity to complete the path before death and will not hurry along it quickly, without faltering in the face of obstacles or admiring the ground covered or the beauty of the self doing the practice.

A good visualization for any practitioner is this: Visualize yourself as a racehorse. You are standing at the starting gate with blinders on. There is much confusion around you as the other horses nervously wait to commit themselves to the race. The bell sounds and, your heart pounding, you're off and out of the starting gate. Blinders hide the other contestants from your view. It wouldn't matter anyway, really, because your goal is the end of the track and you're doing the very best you can. So you're running, running, running; your legs and mind are involved only in the goal. It feels good to run. You feel strong when you run. The sun shines on your back, the load seems light. Halfway around the track your enthusiasm begins to lag as fatigue set in. The white fencing enclosing the lusciously green grass of the inner pasture comes to your attention. "How lovely that grass would taste. How nice it would be to walk in." Spurred on by your more compelling wish to reach that goal, you bring your attention back and, revitalized, proceed. The sounds of your hooves tap a pleasing tune for your ears. "Where are the others, anyway?" You cannot hear them any longer. It does not matter. On and on you go. One stride after another, you are hurtling down the track, like a locomotive that never quits. Forget the others in this race. Forget fatigue. Forget pleasure. Reach the goal.

Blinders blocking distractions from view, eyes fixed only on the goal, on you go.

This is how it is to practice. Visualization is a way to set up a parallel reality within which the self of that visualization can get beyond the obstructions of its "alternate reality" without dealing with them head on.

The ignorant mind that grasps at self and objects/others as inherently existent is like a superior army under the leadership of a powerful general. In comparison, you, the practitioner, with just a bit of insight into the practice, are like an inferior ragtag bunch of undisciplined conscripts culled from among the dregs of society against their will, led by one who, although wearing the insignia of a general, has no skill or experience commensurate with the title. How could the second general ever hope to overcome the power of the first? By not engaging his or her inferior forces in battle at all.

How can a war be won if no battle is waged? Simple. The second general, whom the first will perceive as very foolish for even thinking to overcome such might, will locate his or her troops in direct view of the superior force. That ragtag army will go about its daily business, causing a spectacle of sorts with various kinds of nonsensical foolishness, thus engaging the attention of the superior army. In the meantime, small numbers of the inferior troops will go around the superior army, come up from behind the unsuspecting troops, and steadily eliminate them, one by one. At the same time, the inferior army very skillfully engages the superior forces with its humorous, self-effacing antics at the front. Amused and convinced there is no threat (the cause), there is no thought to resist (its effect). The inferior army never falters in its efforts, nor gives in to the hardships of the enterprise. As the troops become more and more aware of the wisdom-based skill of their general, they gladly begin to follow direction quickly and easily, without any fuss. Eventually, the superior force will become aware of its losses and, should it try to rise up against the other, will find itself rising up against a well-trained and disciplined, unified force of superior number led by a general of such caliber that war was won without ever engaging in a single battle.

The reason for not attacking your problem (the ignorance that grasps at self and objects/others as real and separate from the mind of the perceiver) head on, is threefold: (1) the wise general will seek a solution that will not destroy the very ones he or she wishes to protect; (2) the wise general will want the resources of the country left intact so that life can continue with a minimum of disturbance when the war is finally over; (3) the wise general, when the war is won, will want the enemy sufficiently demoralized so that it will not rise up again in the near future to threaten to cause more harm.

This is how the genuine practitioner must deal with his or her ignorance that grasps at self and objects/others as real. First of all, never "hate" yourself. To hate is to bind the mind to its object. Love is like the opening of the hand to let the other go. There is an old saying: "If it is truly your horse, if you let it go, it will return to you."

Guilt must also be ended if you wish to practice this path. "Guilt" is the action of an ignorant mind that grasps at self and object/other as inherently existent. The only effect created by guilt is that you will have dropped right back into the middle of the non-objective "self"-centered view that you are supposedly wishing to transcend. Just give it up. It is a very ignorant and unproductive practice.

Pride is the badge, similar to the waving of a red flag, that indicates the self is viewing its own mind-made image with narcissistic fondness. At best, it is like a bag of jewels exposed to the view of thieves who will soon find a way to rob you of them.

Jealousy is a greedy grasping mind that has no thought of generosity for the apparent good fortune of another. Sloth is a careless, imprecise mind that cannot even pull itself together enough to define the self it seeks to gratify. Such a mind lacks even the vigor necessary to utilize its own ignorant concepts as they relate to self. Such a mind cannot be marshaled for any purpose on the path to enlightenment.

Competitiveness indicates a lack of wisdom: It is the way of the inferior to seek to cause harm to the one perceived to be superior; it is the way of the one of comparable ability to seek to cause the other to appear to be inferior; and it is the way of the one who considers him- or herself to be superior to treat all others as inferior. When an individual has generated the wisdom mind of enlightenment and is liberated from belief in an inherently existent self, having eliminated the delusions upon which self is merely labeled, that individual never gives harm to any living being at all.

How should a practitioner "sit" and why? A genuine practitioner will practice, whether sitting or standing, alone or in a crowd. The best way to practice is the way that is least obvious to others. So, if you are sitting in a public park, for instance, a highest level meditation could be going on, but no one would be aware of it if you sat with your legs either

146

straight down in front or crossed at the knee, hands in meditative posture, hidden from view. In the world today where privacy is difficult to find, it is important not to flaunt your practice. Not only because it would be an arrogant thing to do but because it would focus the attention of those around you, possibly disrupting your practice and probably making you self-conscious, and thus undermine the purpose of the practice. It is good to always try to keep your practice to yourself.

The Seven Point Posture

IF YOU HAVE THE PLACE and the wish to sit in the seven point posture, you should by all means do so. The posture itself is symbolic of various aspects of the path as well as the seven impure "grounds"[71] or levels of mind generation that must be achieved before one is enlightened. It is good for you to sit in this posture because it helps maintain your body on a solid foundation from which, during the time of the final meditation on the path to enlightenment, even if heartily jostled by someone intending to disturb your meditation, you will not fall over or be forced to break off the meditation in order to organize the body again.

Ideally, you should be able to sit in the full lotus position but if you cannot, this is not a problem. If you attempt it every day, eventually the posture will become easier and you will be able to maintain it for longer periods of time. It really doesn't matter if you cannot sit in the full lotus during your practice. If a practitioner actually can begin the final meditation before enlightenment, then as the mind gets less deluded and more supple, so will the body. There is nothing really to worry about at all in this regard.

---

71. *Grounds.* There are ten grounds (bhumis) or levels of mind generation on the Buddhist path to enlightenment. The first seven relate to what is referred to as the "impure" grounds. These are the seven levels of mind generation that precede attainment of the state of lower nirvana. When, for the first time, the practitioner has a direct realization of the emptiness of the self and is enlightened, having eliminated the gross delusions upon which self was merely labeled, the eighth ground has been reached. The eighth through tenth bhumis refer to the "pure" grounds, or realizations, of the mind that is now based in wisdom. All of the grounds are levels of knowing or understanding along the path to the omniscient state. The grounds are simply symbols that accord either with some insight or perception of the appearances of the mind generated or, more often, with a level of joy that correlates to a level of insight experienced by the practitioner on the path.

Sitting on a firm support[72] that raises the back approximately four inches off the floor, you should try to maintain the seven following attitudes of the body:

1. The legs should be in the lotus position, with the left ankle on the right thigh, the right ankle on the left. The position locks the whole body on a stable base.

2. The back should be straight since the visualizations that will be meditated upon will eventually be placed within visualized chakras and channels that run, straight and unobstructed, just in front of the spine. (A discussion of the channels follows in chapter ten.)

3. The shoulders should be straight and the arms slightly away from the body. This allows the body to insulate itself so that it will grow neither too warm nor too cold. The hands should be held in the lap comfortably, the left hand cradling the right. The two thumbs should meet to signify the unification of the mind (the subject) with its appearance (its object). The left symbolizes wisdom/female, the right symbolizes method or skillful means/male.

4. The head should rest comfortably at the top of the spine, bent slightly forward as though you were about to gaze at the floor.

5. So long as you do not have a tendency to fall asleep, the eyes should be closed. The eye sense power is so strong that if the eyes are left open, the mind will be filled with causes for distraction. With the eyes closed, you will find that the other senses relax as well. Needless to say, practice is not a time to sleep. If you find yourself falling asleep, then the practice should be discontinued and you should immerse yourself in the teachings so that real interest born of understanding might be generated.

6. The mouth should be relaxed, jaw slightly closed.

---

72. *Sitting.* If you must have a pillow or cushion always handy in order to sit and practice, then you will be deprived of many opportunities to practice. If you are able to "settle" for whatever is available, for instance, a rock or a brick or some other material, then one more "thing" associated with a concept to secure "happiness" for self can be eliminated. It is good to keep your needs to the very bare essentials.

7. The tip of the tongue should touch the top of the palate just behind the tops of the upper teeth. This will stop the mouth from producing saliva.

You will find this posture very comfortable after some practice, although at first it may be very difficult to maintain for any length of time. If it is too difficult, just don't do it. It is not that important. When the time is right and it finally is important, you will have little trouble with it. As is the case with each and every aspect of the practice that is the Buddhist path to enlightenment, this posture is meant to be practiced, through meditation on the meaning of the symbols, on many different levels, in many different ways. The highest level practitioner will cultivate a deep and enriching concentration into the meaning of the practice of the path as a whole by drawing correlations between its different aspects. For instance, you should investigate the correlation between the number of offering bowls on the Buddhist altar (seven) and this posture. You should also attempt to draw correlations between the meanings of the symbols of the seven point posture as well as your body/mind association within that posture, to the seven limb practice, and so on. As every concept is a symbol of the action of the mind, and as the mind that is oneness with the path to enlightenment is cultivating symbols of the practice of that path as tools for progress in the generation of insight into its meanings, the symbols do relate to each other. By disciplining the mind to enter a meditation on the myriad levels of insight into the symbols being used in practice, the highest level practitioner trains the mind to hold a difficult concentration, and cultivate deeper insight, based in practice. Ultimately, it will be the ability of your mind to hold and view simultaneously uncountable impressions and insights and meditations that will cause you to achieve enlightenment. The genuine practitioner should remember that the symbols are not the practice; they are merely the tools of it.

It is important to develop a habit of practice, whether that habit involves just a prayer[73] to bless one's food and drink offered every time the individual takes a sip of water or a meal, or fifteen minutes of prayer each morning. When your habit is to practice the path to enlightenment, and

---

73. *Blessing the food.* "May this be the cause for my life to be long enough and healthy enough to complete the path to enlightenment before my death. May this food be taken as a contributing cause to the fulfillment of this purpose, which is done only for others."

concerns of this world no longer engage your mind at all, then you are well upon the path leading to the goal.

There is one more thing you should be aware of that might help with meditation. Everything consumed by your body affects the environment of the mind. Some foods have the effect of exciting the mind, others of dulling it, and so on. If you truly wish to set up the best environment for the disciplining of the mind, you should eliminate from your diet certain foods called the "black foods,"[74] because they interfere with the elimination of delusions. A vegetarian diet helps keep the mind from getting dull when you're meditating. The practice of vegetarianism also helps in the practice of morality by not giving harm to any living being. The fact that most human beings in this world—Buddhist and non-Buddhist, teacher and student, ordained and lay alike—eat meat is no reason to believe that eating the flesh of creatures is, therefore, acceptable or has anything to do with virtue. The fact that so many human beings eat meat is nothing more than an indication that most human beings have not yet established a "conscious" thought to not give harm to any single living being with any action of the individual's body, speech, or mind. Because that "conscious" thought or wish has not gained enough importance to override the habit of eating meat, most human beings have not begun to take the action necessary to turn the mental exercise into his or her life.

Beware. Living beings create the cause exactly similar to the effect. Through the process of reincarnation within the suffering state of cyclic existence, it will not be long before the tables are turned and the consumer becomes the consumed. It stands to reason that the creatures being eaten, in other lives and lifetimes, were known to the one eating them and, one could assume, not casually. It is unfortunate that non-vegetarians, usually several steps removed from the cruelty of the killing process, feel themselves to be "innocent" of the harm given to supply them with their worldly needs. Also, unfortunately, many believe modern techniques of killing are quick and painless and justify the habit of eating meat with that rationale. That such a rationale can be formulated at all is an indication of the individual's conditioning that causes him or her "to give harm." Always when harm is given, it is to secure happiness for self. All practi-

---

74. *The black foods.* These foods are all meat or flesh of creatures (whether animal, fowl, or fish), which affect the mind on a very gross level, as well as garlic, onions, radishes, and other very hot or spicy foods, which tend to cause the mind to scatter or wander.

tioners should be aware of the guidelines for food consumption. During retreats, try to follow a strict vegetarian diet that excludes the black foods and consumes only one meal before noon each day. Ordained practitioners should try to follow vegetarian guidelines and eliminate the black foods all the time. When an ordained practitioner wants to do more rigorous practice, the single-meal-a-day schedule should be instituted and followed. When eating only one meal a day, a warm beverage with honey in it can be drunk if necessary. Always, common sense should prevail.

For other than the highest level practitioner, practices including dietary restrictions are done simply to eliminate the incredible amount of time and attention the normal person pays to food consumption. This attention takes away from the practice and interferes with the individual's success. Also, when the body is involved with the digestion of food, energy that would otherwise be available for meditation is diverted for digestion, causing the practitioner to be less concentrated and more easily distracted. Even the least bit of food in the system interferes with the practice. It is a good idea to limit food consumption to one meal a day.

Obviously, if you have a chemical imbalance in your body that necessitates a special diet, your first responsibility is to maintain the health of the body. The same applies to drugs prescribed to control or regulate some condition. Do not discontinue medications in favor of the practice. You must understand that a healthy body is absolutely necessary for completion of the path, and your health must be maintained. To maintain "health" does not mean you have to be obsessed with it or go to any length to promote its appearance (such as lifting weights, taking supplementary vitamins to reduce aging, and this and that, and so on). The fewer crutches or "needs" you have to have in order to be comfortable or happy, the more likely it is that you will be able to complete the path. Remember: "To end suffering, abandon desire."

Laypeople, of course, should always do the best they can within the family setting. Since they have not yet renounced attachment to that way of life, it is only natural for them to act in ways that would not be appropriate for the ordained. However, individuals considering themselves to be Buddhists, at the very least, should not eat the flesh of other sentient beings. Alternatives should be investigated and, through practice, made to be the habit. Children learn what is taught by the parents in the family setting. Therefore, parents should consider preceding each meal with a prayer of thanks and, when the child is of an age to understand, should make a point of explaining that flesh is not eaten by family members because they do not wish to give harm to any living being. It is a lovely thought based in kindness that will set a mental tone for the other actions in the child's life and development.

This book is for all who are interested in the Buddhist path to enlightenment and is not intended specifically for the lay or the ordained, the beginner or the advanced, one "breed" of Buddhist practitioner over another. There is a correct path to enlightenment that was followed by an enlightened being. When that path is turned into a reason to think one's path to enlightenment is more accurate or more correct than another's, the path being fought over is of a very worldly level, and for that practitioner the goal of enlightenment will not be attained.

In the old days, when oceans and mountains divided the world into distinct geographic areas, the teachings of the path carried by scholars to those areas necessarily developed according to the level of mind of the scholar and the cultural "look" of that area. However, every form of practice evolved from the teachings of one enlightened being and the different "forms," although geographically and culturally separated, should be the same. The fact that one group of practitioners thinks the wisdom teachings are not part of the path taught by Siddhartha Gautama or that there is no tantric path, and another claims there is no need to utilize visualization on the path, while another thinks women cannot be enlightened, is no reflection on the enlightened teachings of the path to enlightenment. Those mistaken concepts and attitudes are a reflection of the misguided understanding of the ignorant practitioner. Those concepts and attitudes amount to the limited view of the teachings picked up by unenlightened and non-practicing scholars who carried the teachings to the various areas of the world. In the 20th—almost 21st century—when we can be on the other side of the world within hours, the barriers separating the world and its practitioners exist *only* in the self-centered minds of such misguided practitioners.

The information related in this book concerns the correct and complete Buddhist path to enlightenment. The path to be followed is not different for practitioners of the East or West, North or South. The practice is not different for different nationalities or age groups. The practice for men is the same as that for women. It is the same for people living in mansions and those living impoverished on the street. There is only one very precise path to enlightenment taught by an enlightened being. To think there is another path, or a "variation on the theme," is to follow ignorance. Following ignorance creates the cause that is exactly similar to its effect— more ignorance.

Although the complete path to enlightenment based in wisdom is presented here, each reader will find more or less value in the information presented, dependent on your level of mind. For all Buddhists, it is important to understand exactly what constitutes the lifestyle of the ordained and the lay, and how the two relate to each other in the practice that is the path to enlightenment. Whether lay or ordained, every individual who has the good fortune to understand the value of the wisdom teachings of enlightenment can do some practice that will create the cause to be enlightened someday. For the ordained, who have given up gross attachment to worldly life, the path, if practiced perfectly, will lead to enlightenment in the lifetime of the practice. For the lay, it will happen in another lifetime, when a perfect human rebirth has been once again acquired.

The basis for all Buddhist practice is morality, and through the practice, each individual is urged to give up attachment to the self-cherishing self in order to practice loving-kindness to others. It is most important that both the lay and ordained fulfill their chosen roles by being of benefit each to the other, as they are able.

Neither the lay nor the ordained community can exist without the other. The ordained community will fulfill the highest level of meaning of the practice, while the lay community will provide the support necessary to make that happen. When the ordained community forgets its role and ceases fulfilling its obligation to devote every action of the body, speech, and mind to becoming enlightened in this lifetime, then the teachings will degenerate and their meaning will be lost. The lay community, in turn, must live the life chosen to the best of its ability, at least within the boundaries of the five precepts. For the lay practitioner to compare him- or herself to the ordained and vie for recognition of a level of practice he or she has not yet been able to commit to is only a sign of that practitioner's lack of the most basic understanding of the path.

There is a point, just before an individual takes ordination, where the mind really wants to be ordained but really cannot give up the lay life. It is a struggle to leave the known for the unknown. It is so difficult to leave the beautiful faces of your family, friends, and loved ones behind. That point is a jumping-off place, and until the individual finds a sufficiently greater number of reasons to become ordained than to remain lay, the struggle will go on. At some point, however, one side of the mental debate will establish itself over the other, and the individual will choose. It may actually take one or more years after ordination for the individual to settle into the new role. All ordained individuals are helped by the lay community that understands their need for separation, as well as the nobility of the goal they have staked their life on attaining.

Visualization

LET'S RETURN TO OUR DISCUSSION on the various physically and mentally oriented aspects of practice by investigating visualization and its role in the practice. Most people believe they're no good at "it" and feel terrible about that because it is an integral part of the Buddhist path to enlightenment. They are wrong. Let me show you why.

When I say the word "box," what happens? The mind creates a vague impression of the object called "box." As the word "box" usually indicates "square," it may vaguely appear to be a "square" box. At the least, the mind will have created an object with 90-degree, or "square," corners. The impression of the box created by the mind, if investigated, will appear against "nothingness," which would be, generally, a dark background—probably a light box against a dark background, as opposed to a dark box against a light background.

If I add information to the symbol "box," by saying, "The box is white and the top opens," the previously vague impression will suddenly sharpen up into a white box with sides that enclose some space and with a top that can open. Possibly you'll see the box with opened top, on a diagonal that would reveal the interior space. Now, if I say, "The box is small enough to just hold a velvet box with a ring in it from the jeweler," you would suddenly see the box as small, although it may fill the screen of your mind, and the top of the velvet box might be seen just below the upper edge of the sides of the box. The color of the velvet box in your visualization, since color has not yet been specified, would depend completely on imprints of previous contacts of your senses with similar objects. As boxes and jewelers and rings are generally perceived as "good" things (non-threatening and associated with happiness of self), the experience of the visualization will feel similarly good, because you are conditioned to know that particular combination of objects by the senses. If I ask you to remove the velvet box from the white one, open it, and describe the ring to me, you will have some impression of the ring inside. "It's a lovely yellow gold wedding band," for instance.

Visualization is very easy. You just watch your mind as information is fed into its processing system. The mere mention of any word will trigger an appearance. Some words will take longer to process than others because more variables will be involved. For instance, the word "box" was a fairly simple and straightforward object for the mind to generate. If I had said, "square box," it would have been even easier because more specific information was fed in. Those words would have triggered the senses to generate an imprint left on the consciousness by similar causes and conditions to qualify the object, and then it would appear.

Probably due to the mind's natural tendency to find a straight line more soothing than a jagged line, and 90-degree angles quite stable, the mind would have felt "comfortable" with the object thus generated. The 90-degree angle is less threatening than a 30-degree angle, for instance, which "feels" restrictive, or a 140-degree angle, which "feels" about to fall over. The ignorant mind, even though it just created the appearance through its own conditioned response to sensory stimulation, is immediately affected by the appearance. "What" is affected is called "self." The thing that does the affecting is what is termed "object/other." There is no "self" except as the "thing" that relates to the object/other that is, ignorantly, believed to exist separate from the mind's creation. Although this idea has been explored before in this book within different contexts, it is important for you to keep trying to bring that understanding "closer" to your modus operandi, so to speak, in order to begin to give up attachment to the delusions.

As is the case with all visualizations utilized on the path, this visualization relating to the box is intended to show, firsthand, how the mind is made to feel comfortable or uncomfortable by a change in the appearance generated by its own action due to sensory stimulation generated by simple words that generated a qualified appearance, or "symbol" of the mind's own action. The "self," uncomfortable in relation to its perceived object, the acute or obtuse angle, felt a need or inclination to get away from that appearance that generated its suffering. When introduced to the 90-degree right angle, the self felt "balanced" in relation to its object and was, therefore, comfortable, or happy.

It is all nothing more than an illusion, and the mind generating the appearance is the magician. Those who grasp at self, however, are like the audience fooled into believing the illusion is real because they are ignorant of how the trick is done.

Every single object appearing—as well as the self apprehending every single object—is created and dependent on the mind of the perceiver for its existence. Every single object appearing exists as nothing other than a mere visualization generated as a conditioned response to sensory stimulation. Nothing at all comes from the side of any object.

Although your best friend may appear to be standing before you, and you believe the friend to be your friend because of qualities within that individual, that friend may also be another's enemy, someone's daughter or son, or someone else's lover. The qualities do not exist in the object; they are dependent on one's own mind. There actually is no basis for "friend" from the side of the object because the criteria for that particular label are completely dependent upon your mind for their creation and continuation. If you define "friend" as someone who speaks kindly of others, likes the same things you like, and is of a similar age and culture, then if you look at each aspect you used to define the basis for the label "friend," you will find every one of those aspects to be empty of inherent existence as well. For instance, "one who speaks kindly of others" is a quality that actually exists completely dependent on the mind of the perceiver due to his or her conditioning. What is "kind speaking" to one is harsh to another. Some individuals actually believe that speaking of others at all, whether kindly or not, is a form of gossip and therefore "bad." Each of your criteria for "friend" is empty of inherent existence or, in other words, dependent on the mind of the perceiver for its creation and continuation.

So you say then that "to speak kindly of others" means not to say anything about another that might cause someone to dislike the person you are talking about. To you, that definition could also mean that whenever "friend" speaks of others at all, she prefaces her words with a smile and laugh that, to your mind, indicates a lightness to the critical words that follow.

It will not matter what object/other you investigate. Every level of your investigation will leave you empty-handed in your search for something "inherently existent" about that object. That is why visualization is an integral part of the Buddhist path to enlightenment. The purpose is very simple. On the Buddhist path to enlightenment the practitioner is given very detailed instructions on the appearance of an environment, or mandala, and of an enlightened being who exists within that mandala. A mandala is the world created through your visualization. It is a "perfect" world since it is clearly understood to be empty of inherent existence, created by and dependent on the mind of the perceiver. The main object of your attention is the enlightened being visualized within the mandala. Mandalas are often depicted as flat two-dimensional, four-sided, symmetrical spaces. Actually, the practitioner, when using such aids in meditation, is meant to visualize the "flat" in a three-dimensional way, thus allowing the practitioner to "enter" the mandala with his or her mind. The symbolism of the visualized mandala can also be meditated on through the use of a physical, hand-held mandala, composed of a base plate and four graduated rings, topped with an ornament representing the heart chakra, at which place the final meditations on the path to enlightenment are completed. The practitioner recites a poemlike meditation, every element of which represents the various levels of mind generated on the path to enlightenment. Like all meditational aids, the mandala is intended to involve your total "being" (body, speech, and mind) in the virtuous practice that, if the meaning is investigated well, will eventually unlock the doors of understanding.

Once the visualization is established, you begin to memorize a myriad of details, down to an almost ridiculous level, qualifying that mandala. In your mind, while reviewing the details, the world is created. As you grow more familiar with the details, you will be instructed by your teacher in the qualities of specific details. "The lovely sound of running water can be heard," or "The stone floor of lapis lazuli is soft beneath the enlightened being's feet, and indents slightly, like foam might, when walked upon." In your visualization, while you watch, you can see the cool, blue floor sink slightly with each footstep. Before long, from daily practice, you become as familiar with the world of the visualization as with your own world that is believed to exist inherently.

The enlightened being is placed within the visualized scenario so that you can consider the qualities of enlightenment and, by the action of generating devotion to those qualities as well as the appearance of that enlightened being, generate a level of mind that can "know" those qualities. The more qualities perceived in the "holy" object, the more those qualities have been generated in the mind of the perceiver—the cause directly similar to the effect.

With practice, you will be generating the visualization at will, whether during teachings, at times set aside specifically for practice, or while carrying out the various activities of your life. You will get very comfortable with the visualization and, rather than viewing the mandala from the "outside," will actually enter into it. When you begin to visualize complete mandalas, at first that "reality" will be very large and "beyond" your body. You should attempt to hold the visualization with interest (by generating familiarity with the visualization through practice and devotion to the qualities of the teacher perceived within). After some time, try to decrease the size of the visualization before you without losing detail or focus. It takes great skill to do this; most of that skill relates directly to your ability to relax as soon as the mind is perceived to be "uptight." By practicing keeping the mind loose, the mind will become loose. When the mind becomes comfortable with the reduced size, reduce it again. By this time, you (whose overriding interest lies in the path to enlightenment and the qualities of the enlightened mind rather than in the gross appearances of the world around) will naturally want to "get closer" to what is being visualized as something separate from him or yourself. Follow the natural inclination of the mind that has entered the path then, with a constant contemplation of the true nature of that which is being visualized as well as the "self" that feels to be separate. You will skillfully ease your mind into allowing the self to exist on the same level as the visualization.

Why does it take skill? Because the mind is constantly grabbing at the objects of its attention, sifting and sorting those mere appearances as they are mistakenly believed to be able to affect "self" and is thereby grabbing at self, as though it were "real," too. Also, the "self" does not want to know it does not exist inherently. The skill comes in your ability to relax the mind's natural tendency to grab, spasmodically, at its own appearances.

At this point of the path, you will have eliminated some of the gross delusions associated with the ignorance that binds living beings to the suffering state, and will have generated enough insight into the nature of those delusions to be able to begin to use that insight like a tool for the practice. Until that level of mind is attained, this level of practice will elude you. The practice of the path to enlightenment is truly a nuts and bolts, step-by-step mind generation. There are no graceful leaps based on sex, race, social standing, or alma mater. One practitioner is no less obscured to wisdom than the next. Every practitioner must, through his or her own effort in this lifetime, generate the path within the conceptual network of his or her mind.

Eventually, you should begin visualizing the system of channels and chakras. As are all appearances of the mind, this visualization is not inherently existent.

There are three channels running side by side from the bridge of the nose up just below the bone of the skull to the crown of the skull and curving at that point downward, running just in front of the spine (toward the "back" of the body), squarely in the center of the body. The channels end about four finger widths below the navel. These channels are very soft and supple, the nature of light. They are smooth and unobstructed inside. The side channels are approximately the diameter of a wooden pencil, hollow inside. The one on your right is bright red, and the one on your left is white. The upper openings of these two channels are at the top of the nostrils. Between the two side channels is the central channel. It is slightly larger than the side channels. It is a deep blue outside and a dark slick oily red inside. The central channel is closed at the top but has an opening below. The two side channels curve out slightly near the bottom of the central channel and curve back into the central channel's opening, blocking it. There are four places along the central channel—at the crown, the throat, the heart, and the navel—where the side channels wrap around the central channel. These places are called chakras. At all but the heart chakra, the side channels, traveling along the sides of the central channel, wrap around the central channel once, leave a small space, wrap around again (which puts them back in their original alignment of the red channel on the practitioner's right, the white on the left), continuing along the way. The point between the wrappings, the chakra, is where the main arteries branch out, beginning the constantly branching arterial network through which the energies/winds are carried to all parts of the body. At the heart chakra, the side channels wrap around the central channel three times above and three below before realigning and continuing on to the navel.

When you visualize the channels and chakras, picture yourself, whatever direction you might actually be facing, to be sitting in the east, facing west. Visualize the arteries emitting from the chakras as they relate to the cardinal points of a compass. You are in the east, directly across from you is the west, to your left is the south, to your right the north. At each of the chakras (which are really very tiny), the arterial system begins in the four directions but immediately branches out.

At the crown, from each of the four directions, each artery immediately branches into two, which branch into four, for a total of thirty-two arteries following the curve of the skull through the head and downward.

From the four directions at the throat chakra, the arteries immediately branch into two, which branch again into two, for a total of sixteen arteries at the throat chakra. These arteries branch upward like an upside-down umbrella, and thus, between the crown and throat chakras, the upper body is accessed by the arterial system.

The heart chakra, located toward the backside of the body, is not associated with your actual heart but rather with the center of the chest area, located toward the backside of the body. The arteries emitting from the four main directions immediately split into two, for a total of eight arteries at the heart chakra. Those arteries branch downward.

At the navel chakra, each artery in the four main directions immediately branches into four, each of which immediately branches into four more, for a total of sixty-four arteries at the navel chakra. These arteries branch upward.

Thus, the entire body is filled with a system of arteries that feed energy/wind to it.

By combining this visualization with the visualization of the mandala, you will cause the side channels constricting the central channel to relax, thus allowing the winds or energies of the body to enter freely into the central channel. As a result of this highest level meditation, the meditator creates the cause to begin the death absorptions, thus causing the consciousness to split free from the physical support of the body and attain enlightenment.

When you become versed in the basics of the system of channels and chakras, you should begin incorporating this visualization in your practice.

The Nine Round Breathing Meditation

VISUALIZE YOUR BODY TO BE like a balloon with nothing obstructing the central space bounded by the skin. Within this open and unobstructed space are the channels and chakras. The arteries carry the winds/energies freely throughout the body. The "foul" wind/energy that has been trapped within the side and central channels for some time must be removed.

While blocking the right nostril, inhale through the left and visualize that as you inhale, the wind enters the left channel and passes down to the bottom of the central channel, where it enters the central channel and fills it. When the passage is comfortably full, block the left nostril while visualizing the wind passing from the central channel into the right, after which it is exhaled from the right nostril. Do this three times.

Then, while blocking the left nostril, inhale through the right and visualize that as you inhale, the wind enters the right channel and passes down to the bottom of the central channel, where it enters the central channel and fills it. When the passage is comfortably full, block the right nostril while visualizing the wind passing from the central channel into the left, after which it is exhaled from the left nostril. Do this three times.

Finally, inhale through both nostrils simultaneously, visualizing that the wind passes down the side channels, entering the central channel, and with the exhalation through the nostrils, the central channel is cleared of the "foul" air and filled with fresh. Do this three times.

The Nine Round Breathing Meditation is very relaxing. Your ability to relax and the visualization associated with this technique become essential skills that will contribute to your success later on the path.

With attainment of the goal of enlightenment, you are liberated from belief in an inherently existent self, but in order to begin to get there at all, you must have some very conscious and very strong feelings of suffering relating to self as well as others. An individual in the world today who is confused about "self," who is emotionally grappling to define "self," is not capable of giving up attachment to "self" or the delusions that support it. An individual in the world today who has never set a difficult goal, established a plan to accomplish that goal, and then accomplished the goal will not have sufficient insight into how to accomplish goals or enough skill to be able to generate the goal of enlightenment and then to see, clearly, the steps that must be taken to accomplish that goal. An individual in the world today who has not felt disgust at his or her indulgent self-serving and self-cherishing attitudes and practices will not have generated a level of mind capable of understanding that there might be a need to transcend that level of existence. An individual in the world today who has not felt suffering in his or her heart will not understand the need to eliminate its cause completely. Only someone who has seen the grossness of their own faults and been disgusted by them will be motivated to give up those faults.

Unfortunately, on this level of existence people become very self-conscious and uncomfortable at the sight or knowledge of what they perceive to be their shortcomings. People generally cannot deal with the fact that they are not "perfect." This is unfortunate because this "feeling"—that there is something "wrong" with thinking there is something "wrong"—actually creates the cause for the individual to not take action to change those shortcomings. And what are those shortcomings except the very concepts that bind the individual to the suffering state of cyclic existence? Just as the path out of that level of mind is multileveled, so is the ignorance that binds the being to it.

You develop your skill of visualization with every tool available to you. In the case of physical skills that can be utilized in the path, it is essential that you learn to be able to relax on cue. The moment the mind gets "uptight" must be the cue for the body to relax. Relaxing the body (releasing tension in the neck and shoulders, for example) is a secondary but immediately effective approach to calming the mind. When the body is relaxed, the mind is relaxed, and vice versa. When an approach to relax the body fails, try another, this time on the mind. The ability to find a way to accomplish what you need to accomplish when you need to accomplish it takes skill. It is a method practitioners develop to control the mind. It is accomplished by maintaining awareness of the body and mind's tendencies and using those inclinations to generate new levels of ability to control the mind. In the process, the practitioner's skill level increases.

With an understanding of the skills necessary for meditation, let us return to our mandala visualization. Once you are able to enter into the visualization that is, generally, of a size similar or slightly smaller than the size of the "real" world, you should consciously begin to decrease the size of the visualization. Even though it is nothing more than an appearance of the mind, the visualization "seems" big from its own side, or inherently. It is of a size that is "comfortable" to the mind of the perceiver. Decreasing the size of the mandala, or the world being visualized, should begin with intense "looking" at the visualization. While looking, think about its true nature and how the self, mistakenly grasped at as inherently existing in relation to its object, has established the size of that mandala arbitrarily based on previous conditioning. For instance, the mind of the perceiver sets up the visualization to be the size of the known world and in "correct" proportion to the "self" of the perceiver.

Decrease the size of the mandala by relaxing the mind. Play with it. By now you are comfortable "within" the full-sized mandala. While remaining "outside" the visualized mandala, make the decision to place the reduced mandala at your approximate eye level. The visualization, if it was "real," would "float" before you. Imagine it to be of a size that could easily fit within the two outstretched arms, the whole being easy to view without the need to turn or reposition the head. Then, with the parameters roughly established, "see" the mandala where you have placed it. Get used to this. If approached easily, you will be able to generate the visualization. If you cannot "relax," nothing will happen. Learn to relax. Take deep breaths. Certainly, precede this practice with the Nine Round Breathing Meditation, and any time the mind gets "grabby," do the Nine Round Breathing Meditation again. Shrug the shoulders when they're "tight." Whenever there is a problem in maintaining the visualization, check to see what the mind is grabbing at and why, and relax the mind, relax the body. When the mind starts to grab, analyze the true nature of the appearance being grabbed at, and the self that relates to it. Keep at it; it will come.

This part of the practice of the path is what is called the generation stage of the path to enlightenment. It is not until the generation stage of practice is fully functional and operative like a well-oiled machine that the completion stage of practice, which is the meditation that can lead to enlightenment, will begin. You should develop every part of the practice, from contemplation of suffering to its cause, to the goal, to the path to that goal, all the time, until enlightenment. The more faith you develop as a result of your practice, the more joy you will feel in having the incredible opportunity to practice the path, and the more rapidly the various elements of the practice will begin to develop. If you allow yourself to be lazy, then by that very attitude, you will have created the cause *not* to achieve the goal.

"This is the last-twenty four hours of my life; what am I going to do?" This meditation should become not just a daily morning contemplation. It should flow like a tragic aria running like a lovely but dangerous river through every single action of your life. The very real possibility of dying before becoming enlightened will cause you to settle down, relax, work quickly (as there is no time to spare), stay organized, and not give up, even for a moment. Knowledge of your imminent death causes you to give up attachment to all the meaningless and "silly" things of life. In this way, the life becomes the path. As when manufacturing a vehicle, the many parts should be developed separately but simultaneously, in an organized and efficient manner, and brought together at the end.

Once you have generated the ability to maintain the reduced mandala, you should enter into the mandala, and grow comfortable functioning and interacting within it. The more you interact with the qualities of the enlightened being, the more real he or she becomes. Those qualities will become more and more apparent, and your heart will fill with joy and purpose at the feet of such virtue. It is because of your interest in what is being visualized and because of the beautiful attributes of the visualization that the "self" will be able to enter into the mandala, and there remain. When the "self" enters into the mandala, then who is left to maintain its smallness? Your mind, creating the visualization, must maintain the smallest awareness of the "whole." It is almost as though an unsubstantial, almost ethereal, alter ego was viewing the scene: the seated practitioner viewing the mandala within which he or she is sitting before an enlightened being and interacting with that being.

Through practice, just the right amount of focus in the right place will be maintained to "hold" it all together comfortably. If the mind "grabs," you will not be able to maintain the visualization. If the mind is "lazy," the visualization will simply fall apart. A balance is eventually struck through practice.

When you feel fairly comfortable within the reduced mandala, you should make the decision to reduce the mandala again, this time to, say, the size of a beautiful pearl, and place it before you either at eye level or slightly below eye level. With the skill developed through initial visualization and first reduction, you will, with more practice, develop the skill necessary to be able to reduce the size further, and maintain it. Again, when comfortable with holding the pearl-sized visualization, you should enter into the mandala while maintaining awareness of the whole.

When you are comfortable with this, then the mandala should be further reduced to the size of a mustard seed. The whole visualization, previously life-sized, is now—down to the smallest detail, vibrant color, smell, and so on—comfortably situated in front of and slightly below your eye level. Again, when you are comfortable, enter the visualization. Relax the mind, relax the body. Just let it be and observe the whole while, within the mandala, you do your prayers and practices at the feet of the enlightened being. A balance will eventually be struck—between awareness and no awareness—within which the visualization can be maintained. In this way, you live within the sensually pleasing visualization you have consciously developed.

At some point, when you are playfully entering the mandala at will, saying your prayers and studying the completion stage practices for more and more hours every day, you will arise from that "world"—which you now feel closer to and more interested in than the "real" world—and, for the first time, begin to actually understand that how everything truly exists is, indeed, dependent on the mind of the perceiver. This is just a beginning, but it is a definite point along the path that is reached only as a result of the practice of contemplation of the mandala.

Once you are able to reduce the size of the mandala to a mustard seed and enter it, then with the skills thus developed, the mandala should be placed in the center of the heart chakra. Before attempting to do this, you must begin with the visualization of the body as hollow and of the nature of light. Visualize and become aware of the channels and chakras, and of the extensive arterial network that carries the winds or energies throughout the body. This should be followed by the Nine Round Breathing Meditation to clear the mind and "settle down." Then you should call up the visualization of the mustard-seed-sized mandala. Then your mind should enter into the central channel and, like a light illuminating whatever is before it, travel the length of the central channel, shining out the opening at the top of the nostrils, looking at the branching chakras, being aware of the smooth and unobstructed nature of the channels, traveling down below the navel. Place your mind like a light at the heart chakra and stay there for some time. The inside walls of the central channel are a slick, deep, oily red. You should see the walls of the chakra that color, and the four main arteries branching off into the four directions should be clear. The mind should travel the very short distance down each of those main arteries to where they branch into two and follow each of those branches to where they quickly branch again into three, and so on. After each side trip, return to the center of the chakra. You do not have to consciously keep track of every detail simultaneously, but you investigate any detail of the visualization since the mind is "there," and you should be able to see whatever is there. This is no different than entering a room and, quickly glancing around, taking inventory of the surroundings. Afterward, you are familiar with the room and its contents. Afterward, you know your way around.

You should not try to be "something else." You must use your good mind, as it is, to generate the path. Discomfort experienced during practice usually results from the "self" feeling unsure of what merely seems to be new territory, and trying to establish "new" relationships arbitrarily. Comfort is experienced when the mind relaxes, gives up attachment to delusions that "this is this and that is that," and quietly accepts what is appearing as it is, very clearly, nothing more than the mere appearance of the mind and, therefore, nothing at all existing from the side of the object to be "worried" about.

Very calmly, place your attention at the center of the heart chakra and create the mustard-seed-sized visualization there. You should see the chamber of the heart chakra around the mandala. The mandala, down to the smallest detail, brightest color, loveliest smell, is comfortably right there. At first you should look at the whole from a "bigger" viewpoint. Eventually, very calmly and very relaxed, you will be able to enter into the mandala at the heart chakra (from here forward referred to as "the heart") and develop simultaneous awareness of the extensive arterial network while doing practices within the mandala, at the feet of the enlightened being. Do you see what is happening? A level of awareness maintains the whole visualization: the practitioner, within whose gross physical body there is a system of visualized channels and chakras; at the heart chakra is the mustard-seed-sized mandala within which the practitioner (with a visualized system of channels and chakras as well) sits at the feet of the enlightened being, doing various practices involving further visualizations.

There should be nothing "uptight" about your mind while doing this visualization. If there is, then you will simply not be able to do it. At this point, the mind of the practitioner is beginning to be what is called "supple." Whatever the practitioner wants the mind to do, it will do. The practitioner, having fun with the focus of his or her interest, will "play" with the visualization, trying to maintain one or two more similar levels of visualization simultaneously, and so on. At first, as it is with all things, it is tricky to maintain the correct balance within the mind to maintain such an extensive visualization without grabbing or laxity, by which it would be lost. With practice, however, the mind enters into countless types and combinations of visualization, not just for play—although it feels "fun"—but in order to investigate the various components of the visualization and develop ever deepening levels of insight into the meaning of those visualizations and their relationship to the mind that is the path. It is fascinating work for someone who has generated that level of mind, and although it is a very difficult practice, you will not be bored or feel unchallenged by your contemplations.

It is not until after this level of mind generation, when the mandala can be placed, maintained, and entered into on a multileveled format, that the completion stage can begin. When the completion stage does begin, the mind is like a most incredible computer. With all the files organized and filled with the data necessary to accomplish the goal, the processing unit begins to access that information at breakneck speed, with brilliant daring and no regard for preexisting concepts, to formulate nothing less than the mind of enlightenment, freed from delusion.

It is through this parallel construction of "reality" that the practitioner creates the cause to give up attachment to the illusion, and wakens from the dream.

The more you practice, the more qualities of the practice will become apparent, and the more quickly you will generate the path. When you have developed a daily habit of practice to the point where the enlightened teacher remains before the student at all times without effort, then you will have the strength necessary to complete the path. The practitioner who will be enlightened in this lifetime will always, even during sleep, be working to cultivate insights into things. He or she will have no time or thought for talking, for eating much, or for sleeping. Devotion to the enlightened teacher and his or her teachings becomes the practice; there is no other at all.

This individual will feel great joy and elation, almost an ecstasy, to be so near an enlightened being who is perceived to be virtuous and noble beyond measure. Such a practitioner rises fresh after just a few hours of sleep, smiling at the sight of the teacher in his or her mind. While practicing, that enlightened being's "presence" will be like a conscience that will cause the practitioner to work without tiring, completing everything needing completion. And when that practitioner grows too weary to continue, then he or she will continue anyway, revived, knowing that deep within the heart, the enlightened being's energy has "kicked in." The path to enlightenment is generated based on perfect devotion to the enlightened teacher. It is the cause similar to its effect.

The process of maintaining the complete visualization at the heart chakra as described above is what is known as "meditation" as it relates to the Buddhist path to enlightenment. Anything else, although of equal value to the progress of the practitioner along the path, should be thought of as intense contemplation. You should be very careful to never think of yourself, with pride, as a "meditator." Just thinking such a thing indicates that you are very far removed from that point. Be careful to always watch the mind that seeks to secure happiness for self.

To meditate means to be able to generate various visualizations, become fluent in them to the point that you function fully within the visualization, while maintaining awareness of that which is visualized.

In conjunction with your ongoing contemplation of the three principal aspects of the path, you will be able to place the mandala at the heart chakra and generate the intense concentration necessary to transcend cyclic existence by using desire as the path. By maintaining a relaxed state through the use of the Nine Point Breathing Meditation, you will learn to control the winds/energies of the body upon which the mind rides. Through practice, you finally cause those winds/energies to enter and subside at the heart chakra. This is the signal of the initiation of the death process and the twenty-five absorptions associated with that process. The whole process culminates with the collapse of the physical body's power to support the consciousness and the freeing of the consciousness from the gross body that existed dependent upon karma and delusions based in ignorance. At this point, the Dharmakaya is attained and from this point "gone beyond"; the mind rises, enlightened, in the Sambhogakaya.[75]

---

75. *The source.* When one is enlightened, one has not "created" anything new. One has simply eliminated the delusions that support the concept self (the secondary conceptual network that supports the primary one) and generated the wisdom understanding how things truly exist. The "source" from which the wisdom mind then springs is called various names, including the Dharmakaya, or truth body, of the Buddha. It is a state of existence beyond mind.

If the reader can remember the meaning of "Form is emptiness, emptiness is form. Form is not other than emptiness, emptiness is not other than form," then he or she will know that "beyond mind" indicates a lack of appearance, as the mind has been transcended. It is the state of perfect peace. From this source then, the enlightened mind, now based in wisdom rather than delusion, begins to act, only now the senses are in direct contact with their objects with no conceptual barriers to block or limit sensation. This state of mind is what is referred to as the very blissful state of lower nirvana. It is also referred to as the Sambhogakaya, the rainbow body, and the unification of the mind of clear light with the illusory body. Because the practitioner created the cause to be of benefit to others, the wind upon which the mind rides eventually becomes more and more active and, therefore, the appearance generated by the mind less and less subtle until, at the very moment the senses can apprehend this level of existence, the consciousness is once again installed on the physical support of the meditator's body. This level of existence is what is referred to as the Nirmanakaya, or the emanation body of the Buddha. At this point, the body and senses will appear on the level of cyclic existence, but the mind will have been freed

Although it certainly accomplishes the purpose, visualization is not utilized just to create a parallel universe in order to come closer to understanding the nature of illusion. By teaching the fully expanded mind (that is engaged in the visualization of the mandala) to concentrate[76] within a more and more specific point and combining that pinpoint focus with desire, you actually cause all the energies of the body to enter into that point and subside. This is how, with greatest skill that combines every single aspect of the enlightened teachings of the Buddhist path to enlightenment, you cause the death absorptions to begin.

If enough of the delusions[77] have been eliminated before the individual's death, the skillful practitioner will be able to control the death process, enter into a meditative state and thereby become enlightened. (1) In the case of accidental death, because of the sudden trauma and its immediate effect on the mind, a meditative state will not be able to be prepared for and entered. (2) In the case of natural death, due to the degeneration of the physical body and the "shutting down" of the mental functions controlling that body, it is highly unlikely that enough clarity of

---

of the gross delusions that had previously bound it to the suffering state of cyclic existence. With the wisdom generated at enlightenment then, the subtle delusions become apparent and are eliminated, and the omniscient state of fully enlightened Buddhahood is attained.

Because the practitioner, through his or her practice, returns to "the source," people often jump to the conclusion that, therefore, all living beings are already enlightened. This is obviously an absolutely incorrect assumption. Until "the source" is reached, having eliminated the delusions obscuring it completely from view, the being is ignorant.

76. *Concentration,* for most people, involves limiting the investigated data involved to one or two specific things that are then thought about with great concentration. In the case of the practitioner, the mind is purposely filled with gross data of a "real" as well as symbolic nature, which the developing meditator then thinks about intensely. The concentration is, on the whole, upon the parts as they relate to one another and to the path and on the nature of everything appearing and, ultimately, on the object of desire. This fully expanded mandala is then reduced to a smaller and smaller size.

"Concentration" on the Buddhist path to enlightenment is like a lens focused on dry tinder in the sun. As long as the lens is not focused, the tinder will not smoke and then burn. The elements are there—a huge sun with incredible power to burn, the object to be ignited, and the lens to use as the focus between the two. As soon as the lens is focused to precisely refract the full force of the sun on a small point in the tinder, the tinder begins to smoke and quickly bursts into flame. The more unfocused, the larger the reflected spot of light and the more dilute is the effect of the sun's great power. The more focused, the smaller the spot and the more powerful is the effect.

It is like this with the meditator. Concentration does not refer to limiting the tinder; it refers to focusing the mind on a more and more precise point.

77. The *"maras"* that appeared to interrupt Siddhartha Gautama just before his enlightenment arose during this final part of the practice of the path to enlightenment and represent the fears generated by the "shutting down" of the physical body and the imminent demise of the gross appearance of the mind that, to the meditator, is merely labeled "myself."

mind can be sustained to complete a meditation, even if the dying person could enter it once the degenerate state of has begun.

For the ignorant being, once death has occurred, the consciousness splits free from the physical support of the body and enters a formless state from which it takes rebirth, because of ignorance, according to the availability of forms. And as we've already discussed, when one considers how few human births occur compared with the vast numbers of insect, fish, bird, mammal, amphibian, and reptile births, the thoughtful practitioner will understand that the chance of getting a "perfect" human rebirth are very slim. It is for this reason that enlightenment must be sought in this lifetime.

If the meditator calmly deals with every appearance and with the self reacting to those appearances by using the three principal aspects of the path, then he or she will reach the point where the last decision is made: to give up the mere appearance of one's life in order to be of benefit to others. If, at the very last moment before the consciousness absorbs, the practitioner thinks to save his or her "self," then the meditation will not be completed and enlightenment will not be attained in that lifetime. At the time of enlightenment, when the mind arises from the Dharmakaya, it is in union with its appearance. This is what is called the direct realization of emptiness, and is what is also known as "liberation from belief in an inherently existent self." Immediately after that decision is made, the consciousness actually does split free from the physical support of the body and "goes beyond." It is a wonderful and blissful experience based in a transcendental love for others.

Needless to say, if the requisite insights and skills have not been developed, you cannot possibly accomplish the goal. For those who may have thought visualization was an unimportant activity, perhaps it is now clear how visualization is a vital and integral part of the path to enlightenment. It should also be clear that the path to enlightenment incorporates every single element of the practice and that no element is "less important" than another.

Because of the inevitability of death, and because of its important place in the practice that is the Buddhist path to enlightenment, no Buddhist practice is complete, even on the most basic level, without a meditation on the death process. Even non-Buddhists would benefit from practicing, beforehand, the death process that will definitely be experienced all too soon. Why? Because at the least the dying person, through familiarity, will not be surprised by the various experiences that are surely going to occur. Fear can be alleviated to some degree, and an aware observer might skillfully help a dying person "pass away."

Because the only reality of life is death, the very finest practitioner will become skilled, through daily practice, in the death process. When the generation stage of practice is completed and the completion stage begins, the death absorptions meditation comes into play. (We will look at this in chapter ten.) Such a practitioner will review over and over again in the mind the words of the death process as related by an enlightened being who has gone through the experience and now teaches it as part of the Buddhist path to enlightenment. The practitioner will be able to utilize the meditation on the death process, practiced just as it was taught, to alleviate the fears that arise to the mind at that time, and to actually "pace" the mind through death, so that it does not become overwhelmed by the practice. By this point of the practice, the practitioner's mind is like the finest precision mechanism made of the most indestructible materials. The mind cannot get to this point if it is not ready to handle it. So, all practitioners should review the death process often. Please, have no fear that the death process might inadvertently be initiated through normal meditation. That would be impossible since it takes application of the highest levels of skill and concentration, which must then be sustained well into the process. The truth is, neither the sheer force of your will to achieve this nor "luck" will let you in. It takes abilities of a type that people still operating on a level of will or luck haven't even begun to imagine. But it's good to prepare for what must certainly come—our deaths—so no harm will come from being aware of what happens at that time.

To reiterate just the barest essentials necessary for any practitioner to get to the point of being able to enter the death absorption: you must have almost complete renunciation to the mere appearances of your mind, the most compelling wish to be enlightened only for others, and highest level insight into the nature of things by having eliminated most of the gross delusions upon which self is merely based. Aside from these three principal aspects of the path, you must be living within the vows of ordination, as well as be following the most strict dietary regime. These skeletal essentials for highest level practice are mentioned here only to reassure the timid that it is impossible, if the commensurate level of mind has not been generated, to enter any level of meditation and certainly not the highest.

This has nothing at all to do with talking about the path or with ritualistic incantations but, rather, with mind generation. It is only through practice of the path to enlightenment that the death process can be utilized by the most skillful practitioner in order to "go beyond" after the visualization is in place and the winds/energies begin to enter the central channel.

Chapter Ten

TANTRA:
THE UNIFICATION OF THE MIND WITH ITS OBJECT

To not give harm to any living being,
To practice only perfect virtue,
To subdue one's own mind,
This is the teaching of the Buddha.

*T*antra is the final practice of the Buddhist path to enlightenment that uses desire as the path. Without this practice, the path cannot be completed. One is finally enlightened and "goes beyond" when one gives up attachment to every mere appearance of this life, including the "life" associated with "self." This occurs when the consciousness splits free from the physical support of the body at the time of death.

If the meditator must go through the death process in order to cause the consciousness to split free from the physical support of the body, then one question must arise. Why shouldn't we just wait for death to come naturally and prepare to be enlightened at that time? Why cause it to happen through the force of one's meditation? The reason is that we cannot be sure that we will be able to control our minds at the time of death. If the body is already weakened by age or disease, the mind may not be sharp and focused; that's logical. Also, the time of our deaths is not definite. If death results from an accident or trauma to the body, it is unlikely that anyone will be in the excellent mental shape needed to control the death process. The practitioner must thus find a way to cause the death process to begin in the healthy body associated with the very sharp and clear mind of the practitioner.

The Death Absorptions

WHY SHOULD THE DAILY PRACTICE of the genuine practitioner include a meditation on the death absorptions? It takes great familiarity with the teaching of what happens at the time of death—as taught by one who experienced it and has returned to tell about it in the teachings of the path to enlightenment—for the practitioner to learn to relax within that particular frame of reference and to handle objectively the appearances that threaten "self" as they arise at that time.

In all there are twenty-five absorptions at the time of death. "Absorption" means the loss of the ability of some element contributing to the physical ability of the body to support consciousness. What are absorbed basically are the five aggregates, the four elements, the six sense faculties, the five objects, and the five wisdoms.

1–5. **Five aggregates**. An aggregate, loosely translated, is considered a "whole" as it relates to its parts. The five are the aggregates of (1) form, (2) feeling, (3) recognition, (4) compositional factors, and (5) consciousness.

6–9. **Four elements**. These include: (6) the earth element, (7) the water element, (8) the fire element, and (9) the wind element.

10–15. **Six sense powers**. These are the sense powers of: (10) the eye, (11) the ear, (12) of the nose, (13) the tongue, (14) the body, and (15) the mind.

16–20. **Five objects**. These are the objects of the senses which are empty of inherent existence: (16) form, (17) sound, (18) smell, (19) taste, and (20) tactile sensation.

21–25. **Five wisdoms**. The practitioner has not generated the wisdom of enlightenment, until enlightenment. But at the highest level of practice, by the end of the mind generation just preceding the dissolutions of death, the practitioner will have realized the meaning of these five ways in which the mind "knows." This level of knowing, then, is a contributing cause to the commencement of the dissolution, or absorptions, and represents the absorption of even, finally, the mind generated to that point of the absorption. They are (21) mirrorlike wisdom, (22) the wisdom of equality, (23) the wisdom of discernment, (24) the wisdom of completion, and (25) the wisdom of *dharmadhatu*.

There are five kinds of visions or perceptions associated with the twenty-five absorptions that appear to the dying person. These visions are caused by a lessening of the power of the five elements making up the physical body to support the consciousness. Briefly, they are (1) the vision like a mirage, (2) the smokelike vision, (3) the vision like sparks, (4) the vision like a lamp, (5) the white vision.

1. The vision like a mirage. This vision is associated with the dissolution of the earth element at the time of death, which, in conjunction with the degeneration of the body at the time of death, is losing its power to support the consciousness. When this occurs, the dying person will see things around him or her, but those things will appear "like a mirage," shimmering and unsteady. This element is related to the eye sense power, which is losing its ability to apprehend its object. The dying person feels a heaviness in his or her chest and tries to rise against the oppression.

2. The smokelike vision. The dissolution of the water element is associated with this vision, and although the dying person can see things around, the individual seems to be wrapped in a smoke that interferes with vision. The ear sense power now loses its ability to apprehend objects, and even the inner hum of the ear drum is gone. The dying person can no longer discriminate between things—which are good, which are bad, and so on. The person's mouth will become very dry.

3. The vision like sparks, or fireflies. This is the point just before the loss of consciousness. If you've ever almost fainted and suddenly revived, you'll recall there were sparks on a pitch-black background appearing to your mind. This is no different. This is the point at which the dissolution of the fire element occurs. At this time, all digestive processes that might generate heat in the body cease functioning. This is when the nose sense power can no longer apprehend its object. The dying person is near losing consciousness; the body is weak, unresponsive, and nearly incapable of supporting the consciousness and no longer "knows" objects.

4. The vision like a lamp. To the mind of the dying person, there is an appearance of a whitish glow. The ability to sense tastes is finished, and the wind element has been absorbed. There is no conscious mind operating after the dissolution of the wind element.

5. **The white vision**. As there is no one left to see nor any sense to apprehend an object, this vision is actually the separation of the consciousness from the physical support of the body.

This is not the same thing as the "great white light" seen by individuals who have had a near-death experience. Those accounts differ greatly in that those individuals had a vision of a great light that they longed to be near. The truth is, these individuals, although declared clinically dead, were simply experiencing a type or level of astral projection. They were not entrapped in the death process, which is very frightening to the dying self, and which leads not to the light but simply to another rebirth that wasn't chosen.

Although you may not be aware of it, there are five occasions during which all living beings enter into the death absorptions. Only during one of those occasions, however, does the process of losing consciousness actually result in death. They are:

1. When you faint
2. When you sneeze
3. While falling asleep
4. During sexual orgasm
5. At the time of death

During these five occurrences, although you are rarely aware of it, the absorption of the consciousness does occur. The result, however (as the cause is not similar to the effect), is not death. Perhaps you can recall a time you fainted or were aware, just before falling asleep, of deep blackness and sparks flashing in front of your mind's eye. This actually is the third vision related with the absorption of the senses before one loses consciousness. When you sneeze, obviously the sneeze is over almost before it began, and you are not consciously aware of the change in your consciousness.

While the first three events listed above are occurring, you are overcome by the loss of consciousness in a way that cannot be controlled, or consciously worked with, to some more meaningful conclusion. At those times you are really under the power of the event itself—the faint, the sneeze, or falling asleep—and cannot change the course of the event substantially.

The only time you can possibly hope to gain control of a situation whereby the consciousness splits free from the physical support of the body is during sexual orgasm. However, because of one's total immersion in the sensations that occur during that relatively brief period of time, it is near- ly impossible to maintain the necessary objectivity to practice on the level necessary to obtain the goal.

In a previous analogy, the mind of the practitioner was compared to a computer processor. In that analogy, the insights gained from practice are filed away by the mind. Those files of insights are accessed in various combinations to formulate new insights, all of which are then filed away. Finally, near the end of the path to enlightenment, and with the com- mencement of the actual utilization of the final practices, the mind begins to use its familiarity with its materials at a high level. Like a powerful machine functioning at peak capacity and level, this is the most intense processing of sensory-based information.

The computer—the extraordinarily skillful mind of the genuine practitioner—has been assembled and programmed to fulfill the monu- mental task of enlightenment, to bring it all together at this point. So how exactly is it that sexual orgasm can possibly create the cause similar to the effect desired?

Every living being is desire-oriented. The mind is a processing cen- ter for information generated by the senses coming in contact with their objects. When the causes and conditions come together, an imprint left on the consciousness from previous similar causes and conditions ripens, empowering the object to appear in a certain way. Whatever the appear- ance—good, bad, or indifferent—that appearance is grasped at as "real." The grasping causes a new imprint to be left on the consciousness to "know" similar causes and conditions, in the same incorrect way.

Because this is how the mind works, it is only natural to use its natural inclinations to generate the goal. This is done in two ways: (1) by creating the opportunity, through meditation, for the mind to give up attachment to those engaging objects/others as well as the self, mistaken- ly believed to be separate from that mind (2) and by creating the necessary level of single-pointed concentration on an object sufficient to cause the energies of the body to gather and begin to subside, thus triggering the death process.

Hence, the practitioner sets up a visualization, or mandala, which is known to be empty of inherent existence or completely dependent on the mind of the perceiver for its existence. The practitioner actually visualizes an enlightened being in the mandala and then learns, through the practice, to continually decrease the size of that visualized mandala. Eventually, the practitioner enters the mandala during practice, and at that point the sole purpose of the gross body of the practitioner is simply to maintain some slight awareness of the mandala visualized with the mind of the practitioner within it, interacting with that environment. Through the practice, you will learn that by relaxing the mind's natural reaction to grab anxiously at "the unknown" and by simply relaxing the conceptual network of the mind's orientation, you will be able to reduce the mandala to the size of a mustard seed while your mind is comfortably within. The tendency of the mind to grab or to be too tight to feel comfortable in the juxtaposition of "realities" is lessened in three ways:

1. By actually physically relaxing the body, the mind will also calm and open or relax as well. The Nine Round Breathing Meditation should be done whenever the mind feels tight and cannot stay placed.

2. The center of the chest area "opens" as you generate the thought from the heart to be enlightened in order to be of benefit to others. This opening of the heart, although also merely an appearance of the mind, opens the mind's constricted and limited conceptual network that interferes with change. Without the thought to be of benefit to others deep within your very core, you cannot possibly begin the practice of the path, let alone finish it. Only softening rigid mental boundaries caused by love for others allows you to proceed.

3. Always, the meditation on the nature of objects/others as well as the self believed to be in relation to those objects/others will remove the delusions that cause the mind to be "tight" and not malleable.

In tantric practice, the practitioner cultivates a visualization of the appearance of an enlightened being (who is therefore not subject to worldly delusions) with whom, *in the visualization,* the practitioner joins in the most intimate sexual union for the express purpose of triggering death absorptions at the moment of orgasm. The practitioner constantly meditates on the three principal aspects of the path. The practitioner maintains awareness that, although the senses are apprehending their objects and relating the ensuing appearances directly to self, nevertheless the objects/others thus appearing are nothing more than mere illusions. With the constant reaffirmation that every appearance of each and every object of the practitioner's desire is nothing more than a mere visualization created by his or her mind, the mind of the practitioner continues disciplining its own inclination by reviewing, over and over again, that therefore, there is nothing at all coming from the side of the object to grasp at.

It is so brilliant. You create a parallel existence to the one you currently grasp at and call "the world." You do every practice within this very detailed and quality-filled world that is generated by your mind due to its conditioned response to the visualized self and objects/others of the illusion. Practice as many hours of the day as possible, entering into the various visualizations, analyzing their nature, feeling inspired by the beauty of the virtuous qualities of enlightenment you perceive in the teacher/teachings.

Eventually, you will be spending more time within the visualization than without. Only one thing can come from that uninterrupted level of practice. Eventually, what was known to be reality will have been supplanted by the world known to have been created by the very mind of the practitioner. From creating and maintaining, over and over again, what was at first merely an illusion, the "known" illusion attains a substantial reality, enough to become the "world" within which you actually operate. Eventually, the mind begins to know the illusion to be no less real than "reality." At some point, the reality of both appearances will be so similar in origin and inseparable in your own mind that you will stop grasping at the mere appearances of your mind and, for the very first time, become objective to the illusion. And you will feel much like you felt when you were instructed to watch yourself reading in the in the first pages of the introduction to this book.

With this level of insight into the true nature of things, the highest level of practice that is the end of the path that leads to the goal—known as the tantric path—is begun. It is still on an intellectual level and has not been directly realized (without conceptual barriers) by the mind apprehending its dualistically-oriented appearance.

To be able to get to the point of entering into such a visualization, you must have been practicing many hours every day for some time. It isn't possible to "suddenly" be able to begin this level of practice without having established a foundation for it before. The path to enlightenment is a cumulative mind generation, and every individual element of the practice places an important role in the final meditation that leads to enlightenment. Students and practitioners should not despair if success does not come easily. They must learn to not attach to such delusions. Through practice, the path is generated.

Of course, to qualify as a practitioner who could possibly utilize these precious teachings, the novice practitioner must take vows commensurate with the practice committed to and then keep them. If the vows to do a daily practice are carelessly put aside for "more important" worldly activities or because the practitioner later claims to have thought the practice to be unimportant since he or she did not really believe in the goal to be attained, then that individual will have created the cause to not keep vows in the future and will have by his or her own action created the cause to not achieve the goal of enlightenment in order to be of benefit to others.

The practitioner eventually learns to place the tiny mandala at the center of the heart chakra. The practitioner then enters the mandala and learns by being there, to be comfortable in what to the worldly mind must sound like very constricted quarters but which is, in actuality, limitless space. Through familiarity born of the practice, and with ever more clarity of mind generated by the elimination of the delusions associated with self in order to maintain and cultivate the practice, the practitioner prepares for the final stages of the path to enlightenment.

The mind of the practitioner will enter into union with the beloved enlightened being in the mandala. By maintaining his or her vows, which force the practitioner to practice on an other than "worldly" level, and not giving in to appearances created by his or her mind, the practitioner constantly seeks the cause for enlightenment freed from the delusions of ignorance. This inclination of the mind of the practitioner, who by now has eliminated many delusions from the consciousness, is like a rolling ball: it picks up speed and power in its very movement. The practitioner by now realizes that the enlightened teacher and his or her good fortune to be able to "see" those qualities of enlightenment in the teacher are the most incredibly precious treasure any living being could ever hope to have. Among treasures, it is equal to all other treasures combined multiplied beyond measure. For this reason, the practitioner always is most careful not to be even the least bit careless (or worldly) with his or her treasure.

Desire is used as the path in conjunction with the visualization of the mandala. This is because the practitioner's mind, naturally seeking those objects of the senses that "feel good," will be able to maintain profound interest in the object of his or her desire deep within the multi-leveled visualization. This interest allows the mind to stay placed and focused. Such a highest level practitioner will discipline his or her mind to never grasp at the mere appearances of the mind as a worldly person might (for instance, the object of one's desire) because (1) he or she knows that treating an enlightened being in a worldly way creates the cause to lose the enlightened being; (2) enough insight has been generated by now for the practitioner to know that even though "it feels" like his or her senses are in contact with their objects in the visualization, it is indeed nothing other than the mere appearance of the mind of the practitioner, as is the self experiencing the illusion; and (3) such an extraordinary practitioner will have renounced attachment to many of the gross appearances of his or her mind as well as to the self relating to those objects/others. By this point, such a practitioner cannot maintain attachments to what is known intellectually to be of an illusory nature. He or she is compelled, by the self-disciplining action of his or her own mind, to "give up" attachment to those appearances, even though that giving up must be done even on a second-by-second basis, due to the individual's extreme attachment.

The way the Buddhist path to enlightenment is presented by the unenlightened philosophers, religious leaders, and translators (who have attained a mighty status among the Buddhist teaching establishment today) often indicates or implies that another person, separate from the practitioner, is utilized in the tantric practice. Because of this gross error in the interpretation and understanding of the Buddhist path to enlightenment, laypeople "practice" the path with a partner, mistakenly believing this to be the way to achieve enlightenment.

In these very degenerate times of Shakyamuni Buddha's teachings, the ordained community is being governed by leaders lacking the clarity of mind generated from fruitful practice. Far too often these leaders, who themselves were instructed by similarly unenlightened and/or misinformed teachers, broach the subject of the "union" of the tantric path with the lack of clarity and insight based in ignorance. Much like children might discuss "the forbidden" among themselves in hushed voices, the meanings insinuated by innuendo, so do these poor teachers deal with the more intimate details of tantra. Those details of the tantric teachings are dealt with either in a titillating way (as though there was something "more" that is very worldly in content) or in a very general way that does not establish exact guidelines for the practice. The student is left to "fill in the gaps" of that which the teachers were unable to explain.

The tantric practices, where desire is used as the path, must be done by the individual practitioner *alone.* There is no other way.

The assumption of the need for an external sexual partner has, clearly, been cultivated by teachers who did not have the experience gained through practice necessary to know differently. This mistaken assumption helped to establish women as the mere sexual partners of the male practitioners of an age where women were traditionally bound to marriage, children, and the cultivation of crops. The role of women[78] in the historical perspective of the Buddhist path to enlightenment has been rarely more than as a consort, wife, or mother, to fulfill this "need" by the male.

It has been a common practice for hundreds of years to instruct students to say prayers that, in their next life, they not be reborn a woman.[79] The disadvantages, historically, have been too oppressive to overcome.[80] Even among the Western ordained men at this time, there is an insidious perpetuation of the myth of the superiority of the male to the female within the Buddhist community, even though, if asked, such an assertion

---

78. *Women* historically, whether of the Eastern or Western parts of this world, until very recently, were married as soon as they were of childbearing age and bore children until their deaths. It was the woman's lot in life to care for the home, for the children, for the husband, for the plowing and planting and harvesting of the fields. Only the men might have the time or access to expendable money that might allow them to hear teachings and practice the Buddhist path to enlightenment. Therefore, historically, the Buddhist teachings are male-oriented and dominated.

79. *In the case of Tibetan Buddhism,* it is actually recorded as being one of the practices that makes up the "Lamrim," or "graduated path to enlightenment." When asked, teachers aware of Western women's assertion of equality quickly claim it is "just an old prayer" but continue the practice and, in private, affirm its "correctness." Of course, this creates the cause similar to the effect. Since the cause is based in ignorance, the effect will be also.

80. Historically, it has been nearly impossible for a woman alone to hope to practice the Buddhist path to enlightenment. First, there was always the problem of extricating herself from the family's wish to marry her to a worthy suitor. Second, if she did not marry, then the woman was forced to abstain from all sexual relations (whether engaged in by personal wish or by force) that might cause the birth of a child, since the birth of a child would end any opportunity to practice. Even if a woman could escape marriage and pregnancy, it was nearly impossible for her to have an opportunity to hear the teachings of the path to enlightenment, since women were excluded from monasteries where the path was commonly taught to the lay and ordained men. Even women who had been ordained and entered a nunnery were kept separated from the monastic activities of their male counterparts. They were excluded from the studies, the mentorship, the time and materials with which to practice. The ordained female practitioners were forced to remain, for the most part, uneducated. They were treated as the lowest of the low, as little more than slaves to their "more worthy" male counterparts.

would be quickly denied and a few "examples" brought forward to attest to the opposite. Suffice it to say that if an external partner is used in practice, you will never transcend grasping at the mere appearances of your mind. It would be impossible.

Meditation Upon the Union in Tantra

So, THE STAGE IS SET for the final pieces of the practice of the path to enlightenment to be brought together and played. There are seven points you should become familiar with ahead of time that will help you control the mind within a meditation that will lead to enlightenment when you reach this point. While so very many things are occurring almost simultaneously at the time of death:

1. First, you, the meditator, visualize yourself joined in sexual union with an enlightened[81] being within a mandala. While visualizing the system of channels and chakras, place this mandala in the exact center of your heart chakra (we'll call this level of the visualization "A"). Second, at the precise juncture of the four main arteries emanating from the heart chakra of yourself visualized at the heart chakra of the gross level (A), again place another complete mandala with yourself in sexual union with the enlightened being ("B"). Third, again, at the center of the heart chakra of yourself visualized in level B, which is at the center of yourself in the heart chakra visualized in level A, place another complete mandala with yourself joined in sexual union with the enlightened being ("C"). Finally, at the precise center of the juncture of the four main arteries emanating from this last heart chakra, while maintaining awareness of the whole with all its levels, visualize a symbol[82] representing the complete path to enlightenment ("D").

---

81. *Awareness of the empty nature* of the appearance must be maintained in order to complete the meditation and thereby attain the enlightened state.

82. *This symbol can take various forms,* traditionally representative of the word "Om," which symbolizes the perfect body, speech, and mind of the Buddha, or "Hung," which symbolizes the complete tantric path to enlightenment. Whatever the symbol, it is intended to be used to cause the mind of the gross level practitioner to be totally involved within the visualization—leaving only the most subtle awareness "outside" to maintain the whole—and thinking intensely about the myriad aspects of the path, according to the new levels of mind being generated, more and more quickly, from actualization of this highest level practice.

To summarize, you sit in the meditation posture and visualize a series of meditations within meditations, placing your mind at the heart chakra of yourself in each level of visualization. At the heart chakra of the visualization of yourself, a symbol is placed and, within that symbol, you place your mind. The whole time, you maintain awareness of every level of the meditation, engaging in sexual union with the visualized enlightened being.[83] In order to *not* give into the sensations of the sexual act, you meditate on the emptiness of the object of your desire as well as the self doing the desiring. You also try to keep the mind steadily concentrated in the symbol. While all this is going on, you are also visualizing the entire system of channels and chakras—that they are free of obstructions and the wind is flowing freely through them. By maintaining concentration for a very extended period of time on the symbol in this way, you will cause the winds to actually begin to enter the central channel. The purpose of all practices on the path to enlightenment is to cultivate the extraordinary skill necessary to accomplish this meditation.[84]

2. While maintaining this many-leveled visualization, you must constantly review the three principal aspects of the path: renunciation, bodhicitta, and emptiness. In order to maintain the visualization that, due to the level of involvement of your mind with its visualized object, is as "real" as "real," the visualized practitioner in union must be constantly renouncing attachment to the appearance of the objects/others of his or her desire by meditation on the empty nature of those mere appearances. The practitioner's compelling wish to reach[85] enlightenment in order to be of true

---

83. *Enlightened being.* (1) One who has attained enlightenment and is freed, at least, from the gross delusions that bound him or her to the suffering state of cyclic existence. (2) One qualified to teach the Buddhist path to enlightenment, having accomplished the goal.

84. *This meditation* is the only "true" level of investigation of the appearance of the mind qualified to be called "meditation," since the purpose of meditation is to transform the mind through the insight gained from the practice. Until this level work is reached, however, it is best for the genuine practitioner to simply consider his or her practice in terms of contemplation, or intense analysis. Otherwise, by thinking oneself to be either this or that, the careless practitioner will actually create the cause to remain in cyclic existence.

85. *"Compelling wish."* In the case of the path to enlightenment, the wish to be of benefit to others that surpasses or, through the clarity of the practitioner's purpose, transcends any thought of securing happiness for self. *"... reach."* It is not until this point of practice that it occurs to the practitioner that attainment of the goal of enlightenment "might," finally, be at hand. This cognition is like the sun breaking through clouds on a rainy spring day. The entire practice includes frequent thoughts of your imminent death. Now, when enlightenment appears to be a definite possibility in this lifetime, the practitioner begins to hurry as much as possible the practice that will lead to enlightenment, for fear that death might come before enlightenment.

and lasting benefit to others generates the power to give up attachment to the self-cherishing mind that would grasp at the object/other of its desire.

3. Such an accomplished practitioner by now will have discovered that when his or her mind gets too "tight," the practice immediately disintegrates and the focus is lost. Such a practitioner will have learned to use various techniques—whether the Nine Round Breathing Meditation or a simple shrug of the shoulders or the taking of a few deep breaths—to immediately relax the tightness of the mind. This skill in controlling the body to control the mind becomes of utmost importance at this point when all elements of the visualization must be maintained simultaneously. If, during the final weeks of meditation, the mind is allowed to become or remain "tight," the practitioner will quickly tire of the fruitless effort, unable to get beyond the most gross level of what becomes a blissfully subtle meditation.

4. As though the three points enumerated above were not enough, you must also maintain and occasionally review the complex system of channels and chakras connecting even the extremities of the body to the heart chakras of not only the gross practitioner but also those visualized within mandalas (A, B, and C) identified above.

5. While maintaining the whole, you must also, through techniques of relaxation perfected from previous practice, be attempting to loosen the constrictions of the central channel by the two side channels that wrap around it at the site of the chakras. This is done by "calming" the mind and controlling it, not allowing it to follow the object/other of its desire.

6. When the winds begin to enter the central channel and the death absorptions actually begin,[86] the meditator will have to maintain a care-

---

86. *Death absorption.* Although the practice of the Buddhist path to enlightenment ends with the commencement of the death absorptions, the series of events that lead directly to that point begin with this final meditation. The practitioner establishes, brings together, and develops all of the elements of the meditation, with the necessary concentration and wisdom to "go beyond" during the time of the final meditation. This is what is referred to as the completion stage of highest tantric practice. During this time the practitioner will fast, and because of the prolonged fasting, the body's basic digestive function will "shut down," and the meditator will be able to stay within the meditation for many hours on end. Because of the fasting and the subtle level of mind being cultivated through this highest level of practice, the senses will become extraordinarily acute. Eventually, the meditator will be able to ingest only water with a little honey.

ful eye on the self that grasps at its own appearance as the body loses its power to support the consciousness. In order to reach this point, this wonderful meditator will have developed the very skillful means of dealing with the "enemy," the self, like the great general talked about earlier in this book.

7. Ultimately, having renounced attachment to every mere appearance of the mind, with a tidal wave of love for others, the meditator gives up attachment to "life," aware that it too, is a mere illusion and what is referred to as "life" by the ignorant is just a form of "death" that is inseparable from the suffering state of cyclic existence.

• • •

THE THOUGHTFUL PERSON MUST PREPARE for death if for no other reason than it is the only reality of this life. If you can control your mind at the time of death, perhaps you can create the cause for rebirth as a human— giving you the opportunity to practice the path to enlightenment again. The real reason every practitioner of the Buddhist path to enlightenment should prepare for his or her death is that it is an integral part of highest level meditation.

When you go through the death absorption every day, you should sit quietly, and begin by saying the words, "Now I'm dying. Now I'm really dying." You should enter into the meditation until you are actually simulating the experience to the best of your ability. Then you say the words of every step of the death absorptions described earlier. ("The first vision is the vision like a mirage. The earth element is losing its power to support the consciousness and the eye sense power is losing its ability to apprehend its object. There is a heavy feeling in my chest, and when I try to sit up, it is as though something was pushing me back.") Visualize and feel each element of the absorption. Imagine how you might feel panicked, or trapped or frightened, and meditate on the empty nature of the mere appearance of the mind as well as the self feeling the panic.

Be aware that while these absorptions are going on and these visions are occurring, the mind of the dying person is also involved in a three-dimensional movie in which the "self" of the dying person is experiencing death as the reality of the moment. One moment, the mind of the dying person will play like a movie in which he or she is running to greet a loved one, the next moment he or she is thrown into a frightening situation. The dying person's mind is thrown this way and that by the jarring changes in imagery. It is like a fun house of mirrors: around every corner, with every glance, the mind, oneness with its object, is jolted at the "switched" reality, and the self is unnerved. The death process, however, is far quicker and more involving than a fun house. As the physical support of the consciousness loses its power to support the consciousness, these dreamlike, totally enthralling visions come to play in the mind of the dying person. One moment the dying person will be lucidly talking, the next moment he or she will be completely involved in the scenario of the mind. All the time, the dissolutions continue.

You must prepare for these totally engaging appearances of the mind at the time of death. You must practice not to get involved but to remain as an observer, by meditating on the nature of every appearance of the mind and also of the nature of the self relating to every one of those appearances. This is the correct practice for highest enlightenment. At the time of enlightenment, an individual will also be inseparable from a meditation on the three principal aspects of the path: renunciation bodhicitta, and emptiness. Only in this way will the practitioner be able to survive the tantric meditation and then get through the confusion of the dissolution to attain the goal. On page 177, we discussed the first five visions associated with the death absorptions. Here we will discuss three more: (6) the red vision, (7) the black vision, and (8) the clear light.

These three visions are commonly believed to be visions that appear to the mind of the dying person. In actuality, these visions refer to levels of mind generated by the enlightened being *after* the consciousness has split free from the physical support of the body and has risen in the enlightened state.

Immediately before the consciousness splits free, the meditator consciously gives up his or her life in order to be enlightened for others. This is when the six perfections are perfected and when the practice, which is done only for others, is completed. It is accomplished only by one who has accomplished the cause similar to the effect. At the highest level of practice, it is important for the meditator to generate insights based on his or her own experience and not from the words of another.[87]

The black vision refers to the Dharmakaya, or the level of mind "gone beyond." This means simply that the mind ceases to work at all. There is, therefore, no appearance generated, no activity whatsoever. It is the point from which the mind will eventually arise freed from the final gross delusions that bound it to its previous suffering state.

Finally, when the mind begins operating again, it is a very subtle mind (not bound to the physical body of the suffering level of existence) and it is inseparable from its beautiful appearance. This is what is called the Sambhogakaya, or illusory body, also known as the rainbow body. The senses are in direct contact with their objects, with no conceptual network blocking perception. This is what is known as unification of the mind of clear light with the illusory body, which is the same as the unification of bliss and emptiness. The pictures you've seen of radiant beings sitting within rainbows and emitting light from their every pore are the very static artists' renderings of the experience of one who is enlightened. To this level of very subtle mind based in wisdom, there is no appearance of the suffering state of cyclic existence. There is only the appearance of the mind apprehending its objects, inseparable from an overwhelming feeling of bliss.

Even though enlightened, after some time the wind upon which the mind rides becomes more and more active, causing a more and more gross level of appearance to be generated. At the very moment the senses can apprehend the level of cyclic existence, the consciousness is once again implanted on the healthy body of the meditator. At that moment, the consciousness is again joined to the body. The body, which would have been declared clinically dead if checked, begins functioning again. This happens for two reasons: (1) the practitioner generated the overwhelming wish to

---

87. *At the highest level of practice*, many details are never shared with the unenlightened. Otherwise, as so often is seen to happen today, a self-serving "practitioner" can, simply by memorizing the details of the enlightened being's practice, claim him- or herself to be similarly enlightened. The individual, although he or she may parrot the words of the enlightened teacher, will make many mistakes that will be readily apparent to the enlightened one whose teachings were the object of the theft. For this reason, some aspects of the final stages of the path that could only be known by the one who achieved the goal have been and should always be left out. Finally, it is only at the time of enlightenment—when the gross delusions have been replaced with the wisdom understanding how things truly exist—that the meditator has a direct realization of the empty nature of the self.

be of benefit to others and (2) although the gross delusions have been eliminated, the subtle delusions still remain. The meditator must return to this
level of existence in order to remove them.

However, what has changed is the mind of the meditator. Now it is
a very subtle, very beautiful, and virtuous mind freed of the gross delusions upon which self was merely labeled. Although once again relating to
the mere appearance of the gross body with its senses, the practitioner's
mind stays in an extremely subtle state for well over one year. It is not
actually until two years or more have passed that the consciousness is
settled back into this "worldly" level of existence. While the mind of the
meditator is in that most subtle state, he or she will outwardly appear to
be at least a "little" crazy to people, perhaps very crazy. This is because the
boundaries by which living beings define every action of their lives have
been transcended and no longer apply to the enlightened being's frame of
reference. To that being, the truth is so "clear," so obvious, that everything
is like a great riddle unfolding. During the years following enlightenment,
the enlightened being has such insight into the meaning of things that he
or she is really "not of this world" during that period.

Eventually, with the wisdom gained at the time of enlightenment,
the practitioner, whose mind is inseparable from the truth, eliminates
every subtle delusion apprehended as quickly as possible. After some years,
four or five, even the subtle delusions are eliminated, and that meditator
is omniscient:[88] he or she understands perfectly the true nature of all
things as they really are.

> To not give harm to any living being.(1)
> To practice only perfect virtue.(2)
> To subdue one's own mind.(3)
> This is the teaching of the Buddha.(4)

In the four-line teaching above, each line represents a different level
of practice, the four together constituting the complete path to the fully
enlightened state. Line one refers to the practice of the generation of the

---

88. *Meditator is omniscient.* Usually this level of mind is believed to be of an encyclopedic nature
relating to awareness of, and retention of, socially conditioned information generated by the
complex network of the ignorant mind grasping at self. In fact, on the highest level, this term
applies to the wisdom level of mind freed from all delusions associated with the ignorance that
grasps at self and objects/others as "real," or inherently existent, that understands perfectly the
true nature of all things as they really exist.

mind not based in the wisdom of enlightenment on the impure grounds. Line two refers to the practice of an enlightened being who, by giving up the gross delusions associated with self, is therefore said to be on the "pure grounds," and who has perfected morality. Line three refers to elimination of the final delusions (the subtle ones) on the path to enlightenment by utilizing the skills and wisdom generated at the time of that individual's achievement of the enlightened state of lower nirvana. And line four reiterates that these are the complete instructions of the path to enlightenment with nothing missing, as related by one who followed it to its conclusion.

The world is made up of living beings, all of whom are trapped within the same basic level of existence due to ignorance of its true nature. Each of these living beings, however, because of karma—the conditioned response of their minds to sensory stimulation—"sees" that world differently from others. According to what is known, each individual makes choices, always with the thought to secure a happiness freed from suffering for self/me/mine. Only individuals who have reached the point of understanding the suffering nature of cyclic existence will look for an alternative way of "being." Of those, only a fortunate few, through experience in this and other lifetimes, will arrive at the door to this path ready to listen. Then, of those fortunate few, the truly blessed[89] will commit their lives to complete the path in this lifetime, and do it.

---

89. *The truly blessed.* Those possessing all of the qualities necessary to follow the path to its end.

Dedication of the Merits

At the end of any practice, throughout the day, or whenever there is joy in the heart, the practitioner should dedicate the merits, or new insights generated on the path to enlightenment, to others. Dedication of the merits is a way of "giving away" the very thing the individual needs for his or her own enlightenment, so that others might be enlightened first. Generosity is the first of the six perfections practiced, and it is the last. It is within the perfecting of generosity that the other perfections are practiced. It begins with giving a coin to a beggar and ends with giving one's very life in order to be of ultimate benefit to others. The heart of the practitioner who will be enlightened in this lifetime is a heart of giving:

Visualize the infinite space around you filled with all the living beings. You can't see each one but you know the space is filled with beings trapped within their suffering. Then think. It takes so much merit, or mind generation, for any living being to be enlightened. Visualize the merit you've generated from reading this book going out to all the living beings filling the space around you. Imagine the merit is multiplied so that all will have a share of it. Imagine you keep none at all for yourself even though so much merit is needed for your own enlightenment. Then say this simple prayer:

"May this empty I create all the empty merit needed by all the empty other sentient beings equaling the empty infinite space by my empty self alone. This empty I takes empty responsibility to create the empty merit needed, by my empty self, alone."

In this way, by giving it all away in order to help the others who are suffering so much and not keeping even a little for yourself, you create the cause to be enlightened.

About the Author

DETONG CHOYIN is an American-born Buddhist nun ordained by the 14th Dalai Lama, Tenzin Gyatso, in Bodh Gaya, India. At the time of her ordination, he gave her the name ChoYin—which refers to attainment of the enlightened state.

She first met the Dalai Lama at his "palace" in Dharamsala, India, during a meeting in which she asked him what she should do next and, among other things, he urged her to travel to Tibet as soon as possible. Leaving the very next day to begin her journey, she met the lama who would become her primary teacher—Lama Thubten Zopa Rinpoche—at the Jokhang Temple in Lhasa, where he was performing a Lama Choepa, or "Guru Puja." Soon afterward and still a laywoman, she took refuge in the Buddhist teachings; Zopa Rinpoche gave her the name Detong—the unification of bliss and emptiness.

Well respected for her years of intense solitary study and practice in Asia, Europe, and the South Pacific, ChoYin taught in India and Europe before returning to the United States, where she now resides and teaches.

Along with some of her students, ChoYin founded *The Foundation of Peace is the Wish Not to Give Harm to Any Living Being.* She also produced and hosted a year-long series of television shows on public television as well as six videotapes under the title "The Buddhist Path to Enlightenment."

Although well schooled in texts from the unbroken lineage of Tibetan Buddhism that can be traced back to Siddhartha Gautama, ChoYin teaches with the special added insights gained from her personal practice in this and other lifetimes.